Overcoming Barriers to Entrepreneurship in the United States

Overcoming Barriers to Entrepreneurship in the United States

EDITED BY DIANA FURCHTGOTT-ROTH

LEXINGTON BOOKS

A Division of
ROWMAN & LITTLEFIELD PUBLISHERS, INC.
Lanham • Boulder • New York • Toronto • Plymouth, UK

LEXINGTON BOOKS

A division of Rowman & Littlefield Publishers, Inc.
A wholly owned subsidiary of The Rowman & Littlefield Publishing Group, Inc.
4501 Forbes Boulevard, Suite 200
Lanham, MD 20706

Estover Road
Plymouth PL6 7PY
United Kingdom

British Library Cataloguing in Publication Information Available

Library of Congress Cataloging-in-Publication Data

Overcoming barriers to entrepreneurship in the United States / edited by Diana
Furchtgott-Roth.
    p. cm.
Includes index.
ISBN-13: 978-0-7391-2110-8 (cloth : alk. paper)
ISBN-10: 0-7391-2110-3 (cloth : alk. paper)
ISBN-13: 978-0-7391-2111-5 (pbk. : alk. paper)
ISBN-10: 0-7391-2111-1 (pbk. : alk. paper)
   1. Entrepreneurship—United States. 2. New business enterprises—United States. I.
Furchtgott-Roth, Diana.
   HB615.O922 2008
   338'.040973—dc22   2007046972

Printed in the United States of America

♾™ The paper used in this publication meets the minimum requirements of American
National Standard for Information Sciences—Permanence of Paper for Printed Library
Materials, ANSI/NISO Z39.48-1992.

Contents

List of Figures

List of Tables

Acknowledgments

Although many students of public policy and economics learn about corporations and their role in American life, few learn about entrepreneurs. This book provides material for those who want to learn about entrepreneurs. They supply innovation to the U.S. economy, and deserve equal treatment with corporations. We are grateful to the Kauffman Foundation for funding the grant that made this work possible.

I wish to thank the following contributors, who wrote the chapters for this book which made this project a success: Junfu Zhang, Erik Hurst, Annamaria Lusardi, Donald J. Bruce, Tami Gurley-Calvez, Robert W. Fairlie, Christopher M. Woodruff, William E. Even, David A. Macpherson, and Eric Meltzer.

I would like to acknowledge the valuable assistance of Anne Himmelfarb for her professional editing and comments; Xiuyue Zhu for her reviews, editing, and, together with Andrew Brown and Brian Casey, for preparing a summary of the studies' findings; David Kalita and Yana Morgulis for providing suggestions; and Ryan Tang for various help and support.

The chapter "Do Household Savings Encourage Entrepreneurship?" is drawn in part from the 2004 article "Liquidity Constraints, Household Wealth, and Entrepreneurship" (*Journal of Political Economy*, 2004, vol. 112, no. 2) © 2004 by the

University of Chicago. Permission has been granted by the journal to reproduce the portions of the chapter that reference the original article.

In particular, I wish to thank Kenneth R. Weinstein, CEO of the Hudson Institute. Without his generous support and encouragement, the project would not have been made possible.

Diana Furchtgott-Roth
Senior Fellow
Directory, Center for Employment Policy
Hudson Institute
December 2007

1

What Are the Barriers for Entrepreneurs?

Diana Furchtgott-Roth

Why should we care about entrepreneurs? What difference does it make if an economy is populated by a few large, regulated firms, or by a base of entrepreneurial activity that rises and falls on its own merits? Why does the composition of firms in the economy matter, as long as there are enough income and jobs for all?

The answer is that entrepreneurs produce new ideas, some of which, if allowed to develop, lead to greater wealth and economic growth. Other ideas are doomed from the start. The beauty of our economic system is that it separates the productive ideas from the unproductive and allows the former to flourish. This can be contrasted with more regulated economies, where innovation is in the hands of a central governmental body. In that case the government becomes the judge of the productive ideas—which means that some good ideas may perish, and some poor ideas may reach the market, doomed to fail after the government has spent millions—or even billions—of taxpayers' dollars. The European Galileo global positioning system is one such example of a failed government-directed enterprise.

In the United States, entrepreneurs are major drivers of the economy. The dynamism and innovation that entrepreneurs provide have been instrumental to American growth over the past century. The entrepreneurial spirit in our economy is one of the most important factors distinguishing it from other industrial economies. Entrepreneurship results in higher productivity and GDP, and additional job creation. Hence, it is vital to examine whether entrepreneurs face unnecessary burdens and whether these burdens could be eased or removed through policy changes.

Much empirical evidence documents that entrepreneurs have played a crucial role in stimulating economic growth and improving economic performance. Hence, many countries have designed programs and institutions to encourage business ownership. In the United States, the Small Business Administration (SBA), established in 1953, aims to monitor and promote business ownership.

In this book renowned academics evaluate barriers to entrepreneurship and suggest how to overcome them. The volume ends with the experiences of Eric Meltzer, managing director of Curtis Financial Group, who analyzes his experiences as an entrepreneur.

The ease of access to venture capital may regulate which entrepreneurs can successfully enter into the market. Many state and local governments seek to encourage business growth, attempting to duplicate the incredible economic success of Silicon Valley and its venture capital market. Where business owners have no access to the resources of venture capital markets, policymakers concern themselves with whether entrepreneurs are able to access the funds from traditional financial institutions or from their own wealth.

If the budget constraints faced by entrepreneurs severely limit the possibility of starting a business, it may be necessary for policy initiatives to ease the path to entrepreneurship, which could include improving access to wealth and capital, or could take the form of tax breaks to small-business owners to encourage business creation. There are also concerns that race or ethnic background may factor into barriers to entry; if likely, these obstacles would have to be dealt with.

Potential entrepreneurs often face excess labor costs, such as fringe benefits in the form of employer contributions for pensions, health care, and other employee costs mandated by government. If such benefit programs are to be widely adopted, policymakers will need to consider how to encourage both business owners and employees to take advantage of them.

This book presents six aspects of entrepreneurship in order to explore their significance and economic effects on the creation, growth, and development of U.S. small businesses.

ACCESS TO VENTURE CAPITAL

Policymakers have devoted a great deal of energy and resources toward replicating the rapid growth and success of numerous Silicon Valley start-ups during the last half of the twentieth century, despite the fact that no government policy or direct intervention spurred Silicon Valley's growth. These policymakers, however, recognized the two key components of this rapid growth: business creation and easy access to a large venture capital (VC) industry.

Chapter 2, "Easier Access to Venture Capital in Silicon Valley: Some Empirical Evidence," by Junfu Zhang, discusses how the VC industry has supported the growth of Silicon Valley, so that states considering supporting VC through direct and pension investment in VC, investment in technology companies, and tax credits can understand the mechanisms by which VC supports growth.

Previous literature has explored the history of Silicon Valley, observing many VC firms entering and exiting the market, as well as firm merging and entrepreneur networking, which create a unique landscape for investment. This landscape supports primarily local investment, and Silicon Valley companies benefit the most from it.

Anecdotal evidence showed that venture capitalists in Silicon Valley were likely to have engineering or technology backgrounds, as they could help venture capitalists in making sound investment decisions. Venture capitalists in the region also frequently help entrepreneurs develop their ideas into viable businesses, contributing more than financial support to the projects. Some conclude that the lack of involvement of venture capitalists at this level led to the collapse of the recent Internet bubble.

Zhang investigates whether the qualities of Silicon Valley—most prominently the access to VC in the region—create more successful companies. Using data from VentureOne's records during the period 1992 to 2001, he tracks the size, founding date, and financing stage of technology firms, as well as the age of firms, growth, and status until entering into an Initial Public Offering (IPO), bankruptcy, or a merger and acquisition. Zhang compares businesses whose zip codes placed them in Silicon Valley with those located in New York, Seattle, Washington, D.C., and the San Francisco Bay Area.

The comparisons suggest easier access to VC in Silicon Valley. On average, Silicon Valley businesses are found to complete their first round of financing one to eleven months younger in age than businesses in any other area, as well as complete more rounds of financing by the end of the survey period. The analysis reveals that Silicon Valley start-ups raised more money in each deal than businesses in other areas, although later analysis shows this only held true during the Internet bubble period.

Controlling for industry, year of founding, age in 2001, and ownership status, Zhang further examines the effect of location on size of deals, rounds of financing of a start-up, and its age at the end of its first round of financing. The results show that Silicon Valley start-ups still received their first round of financing earlier than companies started at around the same time in other areas, and that such companies would still also complete more rounds of financing than their contemporaries.

Companies founded later have easier access to VC—earlier completion of first round, more rounds of financing, and larger deals, suggesting some effects may be caused by this trend toward greater accessibility of VC. A robustness experiment, in which data from 1999 to 2001 are removed, however, reveals that Silicon Valley firms received more rounds of financing earlier even before 1999, and that the difference is larger before then, suggesting a convergence in VC accessibility during the Internet bubble.

These differences lead to statistically and economically significant results; firms started in Silicon Valley are more likely to seek a merger or acquisition, start an IPO, begin making a profit, employ more workers, and go out of business. These differences in both success and failure suggest that investments in Silicon Valley are less likely to produce only average payoffs.

What may lead to the better access to VC in Silicon Valley? Zhang suggests competition between investors, the close proximity of entrepreneurs and venture capitalists which results in reduced asymmetric information and increased likelihood of joint investments, the presence of other support services for company creation, and the presence of venture capitalists with technical knowledge contributes to the better access to VC.

Zhang summarizes that Silicon Valley offers easier access to VC for new firms and that this easier accessibility leads to higher rates of both success and failure among Silicon Valley businesses. This capital, however, is not just money; a number of factors both make VC in Silicon Valley more accessible and possibly more helpful to the entrepreneurs in Silicon Valley than in other areas.

ACCESS TO HOUSEHOLD SAVINGS

Chapter 3, "Do Household Savings Encourage Entrepreneurship? Household Wealth, Parental Wealth, and the Transition In and Out of Entrepreneurship," by Erik Hurst and Annamaria Lusardi, presents the relationship between accumulated savings and entry into entrepreneurship.

Venture capital, examined in the previous chapter, is only one type of capital that can play a role in development of entrepreneurship. Other forms of capital, such as savings, also might be significant.

Many empirical papers by leading economists show that, despite progress in the development of financial markets, liquidity constraints are still an important deterrent to business ownership.

In this chapter, Hurst and Lusardi examine the underlying reasons for the correlation between wealth and entrepreneurship in depth. Using primary data from the Panel Study of Income Dynamics (PSID) in the late 1980s and the early 1990s, their results show that the evidence that liquidity constraints have prevented U.S. households from starting businesses during the last two decades is, in fact, very weak. In other words, the relationship between wealth and business ownership does not necessarily imply the existence of binding liquidity constraints.

A few researchers test for liquidity constraints by using inheritances as a proxy for liquidity. Their results suggest that those who receive inheritances are subsequently more likely to start businesses, arguing that liquidity constraints limit business ownership.

Acclaiming this as a superior method of testing for liquidity constraints, Hurst and Lusardi nevertheless propose a new measure of liquidity: capital gains on housing. While inheritances are not evenly distributed over the wealth distribution, gains from increased housing prices apply to all homeowners. Moreover, households can easily access the increase in wealth by borrowing against home equity. When using this alternative measure of liquidity, they find the relationship between wealth and business entry is highly nonlinear. A positive relationship is found only for households at the very top of the wealth distribution—after the 95th percentile.

Data from the Panel Study of Income Dynamics (PSID), the Health and Retirement Study (HRS), the National Longitudinal Survey of Youth (NLSY), and the National Survey of Small Business Finances (NSSBF) are used to perform the empirical analysis, which covers different groups of the population for the late 1980s and the 1990s.

Data from the PSID in 1989 show that entrepreneurs are much richer than other households and that they account for the main share of wealth in the economy. Entrepreneurs account for approximately 13 percent of the population, but they alone account for 42 percent of total household wealth. Entrepreneurs tend to be concentrated in the upper end of the total wealth distribution. In the PSID, entrepreneurs make up 28 percent of households in the 80th–90th percentile of the wealth distribution, 32 percent of households in the 90th–97th percentile of wealth distribution, and 62 percent of households in the top 3 percent of the distribution.

Another finding in the 1989 PSID is that many business owners report low amounts for their business equity. More than 30 percent of business owners (similar percentages shown in the other data sets) report having zero business equity.

Demographic characteristics differ between non–business owners and business owners. Data from the HRS show that business owners are more likely to be male, white, and married; come from a more educated family; score higher on tests of cognitive ability; and display stronger economic ties with family and relatives than non–business owners.

Data from the 1987 NSSBF suggest that the median household that starts a business needs little initial capital. The median wealth utilized by those starting a business was $34,600 between 1980 and 1998. 75 percent of small businesses were started with less than $95,000. Hurst and Lusardi suggest that liquidity constraints should be more likely to bind for those households that require a higher amount of capital to start a business.

Hurst and Lusardi further examine the impact of parental wealth on child business ownership. They find that up to the 97th percentile of the wealth distribution, parental wealth does not significantly predict child business ownership. Having a parent who is an entrepreneur affects a child's entrepreneurial probability much more than having rich parents. Data on capital requirements for start-ups in different industries and among different groups, on the timing of inheritances, and on the experience of households that enjoyed capital gains on their homes demonstrate that high levels of liquidity are neither essential for starting a small business nor for the survival of businesses.

According to Hurst and Lusardi, the documented positive relationship between household wealth and the likelihood of starting a business is premature. In their view, throughout most of the wealth distribution (up through $200,000 in household wealth), there is no discernible relationship between the two. A strong and positive relationship is found only for households at the very top of the wealth distribution. This chapter concludes that the borrowing constraints are not empirically important in deterring the majority of small business formation in the United States.

EFFECT OF TAXES ON ENTREPRENEURS

Tax burden is a potential impediment to entrepreneurial entry and survival. How tax policies affect entrepreneurs has attracted increasing attention among researchers. Given small businesses' importance to the national economy, policymakers have attempted to reform tax policies in favor of entrepreneurs and small businesses to assist their development.

Chapter 4, "Federal Tax Policy and Small Business," by Donald J. Bruce and Tami Gurley-Calvez, looks at recent trends of tax treatment in small business activity, and how marginal income tax rates affect an individual's decision to enter, remain in, and exit entrepreneurial activities.

Using an empirical analysis of twelve-year panel data drawn from the University of Michigan Tax Research Database covering the years 1979 to 1990, their results suggest that increases in marginal tax rates (MTRs) on entrepreneurship income decrease the probability of entry, increase the likelihood of exit, and decrease the duration of entrepreneurial activities. In contrast, increases in marginal tax rates on wage income increase the probability of entry, reduce the probability of exit, and increase the duration of entrepreneurship. The magnitudes of the entry, exit, and duration effects are found to be larger for marginal tax rates on entrepreneurial income than on wage-and-salary income.

Where most previous studies assumed that higher tax rates lead to higher self-employment, more recent studies have suggested that the differential tax structure has different effects on entrepreneurship. Some claim higher taxes increase tax avoidance and evasion, and hence entrepreneurial activity, while others claim higher taxes hinder entrepreneurial growth.

Bruce and Gurley-Calvez analyze year-to-year tax returns to examine how entrepreneurs would fare as wage workers, or how exiting entrepreneurs would fare by continuing their business to discover how marginal tax rates affect behavior.

Including factors such as an age proxy, household size, liquidity constraints, and risk attitudes as control variables, the study discovers that a low marginal tax rate on wage-earners induces less entry into entrepreneurship, and that a low entrepreneurship MTR results in an increase in the probability of entering entrepreneurship. Similarly, reducing the wage MTR increases the likelihood of exiting entrepreneurship, and reducing the entrepreneurship MTR reduces exit rates.

However, the effect caused by changing the entrepreneurship marginal tax rate is estimated to be twice that of the effect caused by changing the wage marginal tax rate. This suggests that, all other things being equal, cutting both the wage and entrepreneurship MTRs equally and simultaneously should increase the likelihood of entrepreneurial entry and reduce the likelihood of entrepreneurial exit.

In light of these findings, Bruce and Gurley-Calvez consider the possible effects of the Simplified Income Tax (SIT) and Growth and Investment Tax (GIT) plans, proposed by President Bush's 2005 tax reform panel. They conclude that the simplification of the tax code may have mixed effects, but that it would have a positive effect on entrepreneurial activity, even without proposals specifically targeting small business growth.

While targeted tax-rate decreases have been shown to increase entrepreneurial activity, the authors note that the larger effect of tax changes on entrepreneurs means that attempts to aid the owners of small businesses need not be targeted; an equal reduction in both marginal tax rates would encourage entrepreneurship as well, demonstrating that policymakers are capable of encouraging small-business growth in an equitable manner.

MEXICAN IMMIGRANT ENTREPRENEURS

Data from the 2000 census and more recent 2004 March Current Population Survey (CPS) show that Mexican-Americans will likely be the largest ethnic group in the country within the next decade. However, the Mexican immigrant self-employment rate, 5.3 percent for males, is well below that of the native non-Hispanic white rate of 11.1 percent and below that of most other immigrant groups as well. Historically, increased entrepreneurship and self-employment have been the precursors to assimilation into American society for other ethnic groups, so this low rate among Mexican-Americans suggests difficulties in their participation in American life.

Chapter 5, "Mexican Immigrants and the Entrepreneurship Gap," by Robert W. Fairlie and Christopher M. Woodruff, addresses the low self-employment rates among Mexican-born immigrants.

Previous studies show that minority-owned businesses aid the economic growth of surrounding neighborhoods, and that, as minority business owners are more likely to hire minority workers than white business owners, increases in minority-owned businesses increase employment opportunities among minority groups. Other studies suggest that business ownership is a first step toward political influence, a valuable tool to minority groups.

In this chapter, Fairlie and Woodruff examine possible reasons for the relatively low self-employment rates for Mexican-born immigrants compared to other immigrant groups. Using data from 5 percent public-use microsurvey data of the U.S. population census and the Legalized Population Survey in 1988 and 1990, they examine several factors that may influence low self-employment rates: sectoral composition of self-employment, English-language ability, legal status, educational attainment, and wealth.

If Mexican-born immigrants often find work in sectors with traditionally low rates of self-employment, this would partially explain the gap in self-employment between them and other ethnic groups. Data from the census, however, show that Mexican immigrants work disproportionately in sectors with higher self-employment rates, especially in agriculture and construction. Thus, sectoral distribution does not explain the lower rates of self-employment among Mexican-born immigrants; in fact, this suggests the gap between Mexican immigrants and other immigrant groups is greater than it first appears.

English-language ability may also affect self-employment. Fairlie and Woodruff find that self-employment in Hispanics is higher in sub-Standard Metropolitan Statistical Areas (SMSAs) with larger Hispanic populations, where immigrants who speak English poorly are able to run businesses more easily when their clients speak their language, a language effect; or where business owners better understand the tastes and habits of their own ethnic group, an enclave effect. By dividing public-use microareas (PUMAs) by the percentage of Hispanics, Fairlie and Woodruff separate the enclave effect from the language effect, and determine that similar language is a more important factor in self-employment in enclaves than cultural advantages are.

More importantly, they discover that in enclaves in the 98th percentile with regard to percentage of the population of Hispanic origin, where 86 percent of the population is of Hispanic descent, the self-employment rate among Mexican-born men is higher than 12 percent, suggesting that Mexican immigrants are not lacking in entrepreneurial ability, but rather that the barriers to Mexican-American entrepreneurial entry exist largely outside the borders of Hispanic enclaves.

One of these barriers may be legal status. An estimated 4.8 million Mexican immigrants illegally lived in America in 2000. Lack of access to legal, banking, and other institutions may hinder a significant portion of the Mexican-born population from entrepreneurial entry. Using data from the Legalized Population Survey, Fairlie and Woodruff find that after the Immigration Control and Reform Act of 1987, the self-employment rate among the Mexican-born males increased by 2.6 percentage points. Estimates from the 1990 census support this conclusion.

Data from the census also imply that educational attainment is positively associated with the likelihood to start a business for Mexican-born male immigrants, and negatively associated for female immigrants, although the authors warn that these associations are only suggestive.

According to Fairlie and Woodruff, Mexican-born immigrant men face a 9 percentage point gap between them and non-Hispanic white immigrant men in the self-employment rate, and Mexican-born immigrant women have a 3.5 percentage point gap. Among men, education and English-language ability each account for 1 percentage point of the gap and legal status may explain another percentage point.

However, U.S.-born non-Hispanic whites have a self-employment rate 6 percentage points higher than U.S.-born Mexican-Americans, a difference unexplained by English-language ability, legal status, or by the effects of an average extra 1.1 years of education among non-Hispanic whites. Fairlie and Woodruff conclude that differences in wealth appear to be the driving factor behind the persistent difference in self-employment rates, which causes Mexican-Americans to lag behind other ethnic groups in economic and political assimilation.

ENTREPRENEURS AND PENSIONS

Concerns about the reliability and solvency of Social Security have led private pension plans to become a useful way to secure post-retirement income for American workers. However, due to the rapidly rising costs of pension benefits, nearly half of full-time year-round private-sector workers in the United States are not covered by a pension. Pension coverage rates are particularly low at smaller firms. For this reason, improving pension coverage at small firms has been a goal for many policymakers for years.

In chapter 6, "Improving Pension Coverage at Small Firms," William E. Even and David A. Macpherson discuss possible reasons for the lower pension coverage rate among small firms. Using data from the March Current Population Survey (CPS) from 1989 to 2005, the 1983–2001 Survey of Consumer Finances (SCF), and the Health and Retirement Survey (HRS), Even and Macpherson examine the recent trend in pension coverage rates, the type of pension plan offered, and the generosity of pension plans across firm size.

Even and Macpherson find that pension offering is driven mostly by the differing characteristics of workers and firms, rather than difficulty in administering pension plans. The largest source of the gap comes from differences in earnings between workers, with higher-paid workers being more likely to be covered by pension plans.

An analysis of the costs and benefits of offering a pension reveals how, intuitively, differences in firms and employees drive the likelihood of pension offerings. Because pensions are a form of deferred compensation, they are likely to be offered when either the company wants to retain an employee or when employees prefer such postponed pay.

Savings instruments such as the Simplified Employee Pension and the Savings Incentive Match Plan for Employees attempt to reduce administrative costs of pension plans. However, surveys conducted by the Employee Benefits Research Institute in 2001 show that many small firms, those likely to be constrained by high administrative costs, do not offer pensions because of employee preferences or revenue uncertainty. While over one-third of small firms consider administrative costs "major," few list it as the most important reason for not offering a pension.

The CPS data reveal that pension coverage rates rose over the past fifteen years, largely due to increases in coverage by small firms. Even and Macpherson find that the coverage gap between small and large firms is largely explained by differences in workforce characteristics, although higher per capita administrative costs for small firms has been suggested as a cause for differences unexplained by workforce characteristics.

The CPS and the SCF data suggest that both explained and unexplained portions of the coverage gap across firm size declined over time due to a decrease in the difference in workforce characteristics or a decrease in the importance of those differences toward causing the coverage gap. Even and Macpherson conclude that the most important of these characteristics, contributing to the largest portion of the gap, is differences in employee earning. Thus, the most important reason for the closing of the gap between 1988 and 2004 was either reduction in earnings differentials or the diminishing importance of earnings differentials in the coverage gap.

Even and Macpherson present the effects of firm size and workforce characteristics on types of pension plans offered. They view a shift toward defined contribution (DC) and away from defined benefit (DB) retirement plans as affecting the labor market and coverage rates.

Data from the SCF and the HRS indicate that firms have shifted away from DB-only plans in the 1990s, particularly at large firms. Reasons for choosing one plan or the other are discussed. DB plans are more attractive where training and employee replacement is costly, while DC plans are more portable and less costly to operate. Ultimately, this suggests that which plan a firm adopts depends on the firm's characteristics and the preferences of the employees.

According to Even and Macpherson, employee characteristics form the largest determinant of the size gap in coverage. Both large and small firms increased coverage by DC-only plans, but for small firms, this was due to an increase in pension coverage, while in large firms it was due to a decrease in the percentage of workers with only a DB plan or both a DB and DC plan. Small firms are shown to be more likely than large firms to offer only a DC plan. Large firms are more likely than small firms to offer either a DB plan or both a DB and DC plan.

Changes in earnings led to a shift to DC plans, especially at large firms. Differences in the level and distribution of earnings explain most of the differences in plan offering at small firms and large firms. Earnings differentials are particularly important causes for the greater probability among small firms to offer a DC-only plan.

Even and Macpherson refer to the HRS and the SCF data to further examine if firm size affects the level of plan generosity, and summarize that for both DB and DC plans, firm size has no significant effect on generosity.

Concluding that the coverage gap in American pension plans at small and large firms is due largely to differences in worker characteristics, Even and Macpherson see that the solution to increase coverage rates at small firms is to encourage workforce demand for pension coverage, rather than the focus of reducing administrative costs for employers. And as earnings differentials have the largest effect on coverage, plans such as tax incentives to encourage low-earnings workers to enter into pensions would be effective at further reducing the gap.

AN ENTREPRENEUR'S EXPERIENCE

An entrepreneur must overcome substantial barriers to start a new business and keep it up and running. Many people describe an entrepreneur as a risk-taker by nature. What makes entrepreneurs take risks and how does one become a successful entrepreneur?

In chapter 7, "Success Stories from the Telecom Industry: How to Become an Entrepreneur," Eric Meltzer, a managing director of Curtis Financial Group and a telecommunications investment banker with twenty years of experience, offers stories of business success and failure, both his own and those of other entrepreneurs.

Meltzer believes the key personal attributes of successful entrepreneurs are creativity, flexibility, ambition, confidence, fearlessness of failure, leadership skills, and the ability to distinguish between potential risks. He also stresses the importance of networking and relationship building in raising capital and accessing the latest industry information.

Meltzer further argues that a successful entrepreneur should possess necessary experience to see the opportunity, and the best way to obtain such experience is via on-the-job-training rather than formal school training. He points out that lacking a specific goal, lacking near-term revenue visibility, and lacking relevant experience and contacts are common traits of unsuccessful entrepreneurs. In this chapter, Meltzer predicts the future of wireless communications as a tool describing his own experiences in entrepreneurship.

CONCLUSION

Policymakers have sought to create a better environment for small business formation and sustainability. They must begin by removing barriers to entrepreneurship. The first six chapters in this book will address the potential obstacles to entrepreneurship and give recommendations on how to overcome them.

Silicon Valley's effects on business creation, being more than monetary, agree with evidence that access to capital is not the largest concern facing entrepreneurs, but rather access to people and institutions to help create and sustain a business. The low self-employment rate among Mexican-born immigrants suggests the importance of non-monetary factors such as English language ability and legal status, as demonstrated by the higher rates of entrepreneurship in Mexican immigrants within areas of large Hispanic populations.

This is not to say money is unimportant to entrepreneurs. Marginal tax rates, both for wage-earners and entrepreneurs, have an important effect on entrepreneurial entry and exit, which suggests that the costs faced by business owners play an important role in their decisions to start businesses. However, wise policymakers realize that equal tax rate reductions encourage business growth without treating entrepreneurs favorably. And in the case of pension coverage, policymakers' goal ought to be targeting employee demand rather than employer provision of pensions.

Policymakers seeking to encourage entrepreneurship must therefore recognize both what new policies will lead to their desired outcome and how to encourage the right people to make those decisions. These following chapters will illustrate what policies can expand American entrepreneurship and who ought to be encouraged to make those decisions to make it happen.

2

Easier Access to Venture Capital in Silicon Valley

Some Empirical Evidence

JUNFU ZHANG*

INTRODUCTION

The rapid growth of Silicon Valley in the second half of the twentieth century is astonishing. Prior to the 1950s, the tract of farmland curling around the southern part of the San Francisco Bay was known only as the Santa Clara Valley, famous for its orange groves and plum trees. In the late 1950s, this region started to develop into a center of semiconductor manufacturing, which inspired its current name. By 2000, Silicon Valley housed more than twenty-five thousand technology firms that provided six hundred seventy thousand well-paying jobs in the technology sector.[1] Today, it is known as the capital of the personal computer revolution and the subsequent Internet revolution. Policymakers throughout the world aspire to clone Silicon Valley in their own regions.[2,3]

It is worth noting that Silicon Valley's economic success had little to do with local government policies that were devised to encourage the technology sector.[4] Most accounts of Silicon Valley's genesis emphasize key players in this region, such as Frederick Terman, who encouraged Stanford University faculty and students to create businesses; William Shockley, who brought transistor technology and talented young engineers to the San Francisco Bay Area; the "Traitorous Eight," who left Shockley's company and started their own business; and Stanford University, which provided not only commercializable inventions but also a high-quality labor pool.[5] Federal spending on defense electronics, which financed many of the early technology companies in this region, is perhaps the only government policy that directly helped Silicon Valley in its early years.[6]

Yet, despite the lack of directed local policy support during the emergence of Silicon Valley, policymakers seem convinced that specific policies are needed to replicate the region's success. In the 1990s, as the Internet boom was taking place, state and local economic development agencies across the United States laid out strategic plans to foster their own high-tech sectors. Their actions suggest that they have in fact recognized two important features of the Silicon Valley economy.

First, Silicon Valley grows through business creation. The economic dynamics in this region perfectly illustrate Schumpeter's process of "creative destruction." Silicon Valley constantly produces new companies (and thus new industries): defense electronic companies in the 1950s, semiconductor companies in the 1960s, personal computer and workstation companies in the 1970s and 1980s, and Internet-related companies in the 1990s.[7] Each generation of companies adds new layers to the regional economy and eliminates many older layers. Although a few Silicon Valley companies, such as Hewlett-Packard and Intel, have persisted over a long period of time, they are the exception rather than the rule. In previous research, I compiled a list of the top forty high-tech firms in Silicon Valley in 1982 and 2002. An overwhelming majority of the companies on the 1982 list have declined in prominence; half of them no longer exist. Only four firms on the 2002 list were survivors from the 1982 list (Hewlett-Packard, National Semiconductor, Intel, and AMD). In fact, more than half of the 2002 top firms were not even founded before 1982. In only two decades, the high-tech economy in Silicon Valley completely changed.[8]

Second, Silicon Valley's venture capital (VC) industry played an important role in fostering business creation. Starting in the 1960s, the development of the VC industry paralleled the rapid growth of high-tech industries in this region. VC has helped fund every wave of innovation in Silicon Valley: the establishment of the semiconductor industry in the 1960s, the inception of the personal computer industry and the biotech industry in the 1970s, the boom in the workstation and networking industries in the 1980s, and the commercialization of the Internet in the 1990s.[9] Venture capitalists in Silicon Valley not only provide capital, but also offer mentoring and guidance to entrepreneurs.[10] Almost every highly successful company started in Silicon Valley during the past three decades received local VC support.

Having witnessed the VC industry's role in business creation in Silicon Valley, many policymakers in other locales decided that they had to help provide risk capital to potential entrepreneurs in order to assist their own high-tech economies. In this study, I examine the accessibility of VC in Silicon Valley and explore whether and how Silicon Valley has benefited from its strong VC industry. Although there is a large amount of qualitative anecdotal evidence on this issue, this study represents one of the first attempts to approach this question with quantitative evidence. I hope that some of the findings may be helpful for local policymakers in the process of formulating their own policies in support of VC investment.

STATE VENTURE CAPITAL POLICIES

Federal policy played an important role in the development of the VC industry in the United States. Many policies, such as the Small Business Act of 1958, the 1978 Revenue Act, the 1979 Employee Retirement Income Security Act (ERISA) "Prudent Man" rule, the 1980 Small Business Investment Incentive Act, the 1980 ERISA "Safe Harbor" regulation, and the 1981 Economic Recovery Tax Act, are believed to have increased the overall VC investment in start-up companies.[11] In contrast, state and local policies played a very limited role. In particular, the formation of the largest VC clusters, such as those in Boston and Silicon Valley, was not a direct consequence of state policies. It was not until very recently that state governments started to devise policies to improve the availability of VC to local start-ups. In fact, state VC policies have arisen in response to the concentration of VC investment in areas such as Silicon Valley. It is believed that venture capitalists tend to overlook investment opportunities outside of VC centers and that local policies are necessary for boosting the supply of VC in regions underserved by private VC firms.[12]

At the state level, at least four types of policies have been implemented to improve the accessibility of venture capital.[13]

1. *Direct investment in VC funds.* Thirteen states directly invest in VC funds that invest in start-up companies within the state. For example, New Mexico

invests in VC funds that have an office in the state or support start-up companies in the state. By late 2004, the New Mexico State Investment Council had invested about $150 million in VC funds.[14] In October 2003, the state of Indiana joined with local universities and corporations to set up the Indiana Future Fund, worth $73 million, to invest in VC funds that support life science start-up companies in the state.[15] West Virginia put $24 million in seven capital companies that invest in emerging companies in the state. Kentucky invested $11 million in VC funds that committed to use at least three times that amount to support companies in the state.[16]

2. *Investment of state pension funds in VC.* Some states allow state pension funds to be invested in VC funds. For example, in mid-2003, Oregon required its investment council to put $100 million of state pension funds in within-state VC investments.[17] In 2004, Florida decided to invest up to $1 billion of its state employee pension fund in VC. Out of the first installment of $350 million, $75 million was earmarked for Florida companies.[18]

3. *Direct investment in technology companies.* Some states make seed money available to support early-stage technology companies. Thirteen states directly invest in technology companies. Georgia, for example, in order to support start-up technology companies in the state, set up an $8 million Seed Capital Fund at the Advanced Technology Development Center headquartered at the Georgia Institute of Technology. Maryland established the Maryland Venture Fund in 1994 to make direct equity investment in early-stage technology companies in the state. In 2004 alone, the Maryland Venture Fund invested $4.6 million.[19]

4. *Tax credits to encourage investment in VC.* Eighteen states provide tax credits to encourage investment in VC funds. For example, Alabama, Florida, New York, Texas, and Wisconsin all give tax credits to insurance companies for their investment in certified capital companies. Arkansas, Illinois, Iowa, Michigan, South Carolina, and Utah each created a so-called fund of funds backed by tax credits to invest in VC funds.[20] Some states, such as Iowa, Kansas, North Dakota, Oklahoma, and West Virginia, offer tax credits to individuals who invest in VC funds. Nine states, including Arkansas, Hawaii, New York, and Vermont, encourage investment by wealthy individuals (or "angel investors") by giving tax credits to individuals and/or corporations who invest in emerging technology companies.

Thus, at the state level, a number of venture capital policies have already been widely adopted, and many other policies are likely being considered. Given that these developments are largely inspired by the perceived role of VC in Silicon Valley's success, it is important to understand how VC investment actually works in Silicon Valley and to what extent its VC industry in fact helped the local economy.

WHAT IS KNOWN ABOUT VENTURE CAPITAL IN SILICON VALLEY

The rapid economic growth in Silicon Valley in the 1980s and 1990s has generated a large body of research that aims to understand the Silicon Valley economy.[21] Naturally, the role of the VC industry in Silicon Valley is an important component of this research agenda. This section briefly reviews the existing literature and summarizes what is known about the VC industry in Silicon Valley.[22]

Although today's Silicon Valley is regarded as the premier center of VC investment in the world, the VC industry in the United States originated elsewhere. Boston's American Research and Development (ARD, founded in 1946) is generally believed to be the country's first nonfamily VC organization.[23] In the San Francisco Bay Area, professional VC activities started later than in the Boston area. In 1957, when Robert Noyce and seven fellow engineers left Shockley Semiconductor Laboratories to start their own business, they had to look to the East Coast for investment.[24] The first West Coast VC firm, Draper, Gaither & Anderson, was not founded until 1958.

Kenney and Florida (2000) provide a detailed account of the history of the VC industry in Silicon Valley and highlight the key players (both individuals and VC firms) at different stages of development. The authors emphasize that the VC industry in Silicon Valley developed as a result of local economic growth:

Venture capital in Silicon Valley grew by a process of combination, division, and incessant networking. Successful enterprises gave rise to wealthy entrepreneurs who would become venture capitalists, and existing venture funds gave rise to new venture funds in a virtuous circle of investment, growth, and capital accumulation. . . . Venture capital evolved with Silicon Valley's technology base, drawing from it and nurturing it by providing the funds for new initiatives. In this process it became integral to the entire region's dynamism and fueled the creation of an economy based on new firm formation.[25]

Kenney and Florida also observe that unlike VC firms in other parts of the country, VC firms in Silicon Valley invest most of their venture funds in local businesses and rarely seek opportunities outside of the region. They argue that the impressive pool of innovative entrepreneurs within the region is the cause of this phenomenon.

In Banatao and Fong (2000), two partners at the renowned Mayfield Fund highlight the unique features of the local VC industry. In their account of how venture capitalists help shape the Silicon Valley economy, they point out that technologists are respected in the Silicon Valley VC world not only because technology companies are the primary recipients of VC investment, but also because assessing the promise of these companies requires technical expertise. Thus it is more and more common in Silicon Valley that those employed in the VC industry have an engineering background and that they have worked at established technology companies.

Banatao and Fong (2002) also identify several important changes that occurred in Silicon Valley's VC industry during the 1990s. For instance, compared to early generations of VC firms, current firms get less involved with their portfolio companies. This likely occurs because today's venture funds are increasingly large, meaning that each venture capitalist has more start-up companies to manage. Also, the traditional role of VC firms in start-up companies is increasingly being played by angel investors. Finally, there is currently a trend for venture capitalists and entrepreneurs to focus more on developing exit strategies and less on building sustainable companies, though this may be only a short-term tendency at the end of the Internet bubble period.

Hellmann (2000) contends that entrepreneurs in Silicon Valley are like athletes in that they compete in games for the reward of wealth and glory.[26] Venture capitalists in the region, on the other hand, are like coaches. They decide which athlete to play, develop a winning strategy, and provide training and motivation, which is to say that venture capitalists decide which entrepreneurs get supported, help these entrepreneurs improve business plans, and provide guidance and mentoring to help the entrepreneurs succeed. Venture capitalists may help sharpen the start-up's strategy, identify and attract top executives, make connections to important customers or suppliers through social ties, and establish strategic alliances with other companies. In other words, venture capitalists bring much more than money to the table.[27]

Saxenian (1994) explores Silicon Valley's success through comparison with Route 128 in the Boston area. This influential and authoritative analysis, which is based on more than one hundred interviews with business executives, venture capitalists, and entrepreneurs, finds that differences between the VC industries in these two regions explain the relative lack of entrepreneurship in Boston's technology industry. Saxenian observes that Silicon Valley's VC industry was established by engineers and entrepreneurs, whereas Route 128's VC industry was established by "old-line East Coast financiers" and managed by "professional bankers." Silicon Valley's venture capitalists are younger and more willing to take risks, while Route 128's venture capitalists are typically older, as well as "more formal and conservative" in making investment decisions. Because of their backgrounds and previous experiences, Silicon Valley's venture capitalists, more than their counterparts in the Boston area, are capable of helping start-up companies deal with the problems they face. Silicon Valley's venture capitalists are also especially engaged in formal collaborations among themselves and tend to have stronger ties to the local technology industry.[28]

Castilla (2003) compares the network structure of VC firms in Silicon Valley and the Boston area using PricewaterhouseCoopers' Money-Tree-Historical Data from the years 1995–1998. He finds that the network among VC firms in Silicon Valley is denser than among Boston area firms, as measured by their likelihood to coinvest in a start-up company. Castilla also finds that VC firms in Silicon Valley are more likely to invest in local companies than those in the Boston area. These findings confirm some of the earlier observations by Saxenian (1994) and Kenney and Florida (2000).

Zook (2005) examines how the VC industry shaped the geography of the Internet industry. Like Saxenian (1994), this study characterizes the VC industry based on interviews with venture capitalists and entrepreneurs in Silicon Valley. Zook argues that venture capitalists identify target industries, select promising start-up companies to support, and help them to succeed. In this process of VC investment, he identifies two types of tacit knowledge as crucial: knowledge about technology, strategies, and markets, which he labels "know-how"; and knowledge of key individuals and organizations, which he labels "know-who." While the former is accumulated through training and work experience, the latter is derived from social connections and informal contacts. Precisely because of their informal nature, both types of knowledge tend to be localized and enabled by physical proximity.

Zook (2005) argues that Silicon Valley boomed during the Internet revolution because the local venture capitalists excelled in brokering knowledge to assist companies in which they invested; they provided general advice and strategy building, set metrics and accountability, and made connections for companies.[29] Like other scholars, Zook emphasizes that VC investment is much more than just the money provided to the start-up. He contends that the Internet bubble formed and burst in the San Francisco Bay Area partly because VC in the later period of the Internet boom was rarely "smart money," which comes with invaluable know-how and know-who, but instead mostly "dumb money"—that is, nothing more than the monetary investment.[30]

Overall, existing studies of Silicon Valley's VC industry are largely based on qualitative evidence, likely because few quantitative data are available.[31] All of these studies suggest that venture capitalists in Silicon Valley are more than mere money providers, that they are deeply involved in the companies they invest in, and that they affect the companies' performances in many ways.

DATA

The data used in this study are acquired from VentureOne, a leading VC research company based in San Francisco, which began tracking equity investment in 1992. The firm regularly surveys VC firms, gathers information about venture-backed companies through direct contacts, and searches secondary sources such as company press releases and initial public offering (IPO) prospectuses.[32] VentureOne intends to capture all early-stage financing events of venture-backed companies located in the United States.[33] It claims to have the most comprehensive database extant on venture-backed companies. While VentureOne maintains its database primarily for commercial purposes, its rich information has attracted many academic researchers.[34]

For each VC deal, VentureOne keeps a record of its size, the stage of financing it represents, and its closing date; the VC firms involved; and detailed information about the firm that received the investment, including its address, start year, and industry. In addition, VentureOne tracks the venture-backed company and updates the information about its number of employees, business status, and ownership status until the VC support is discontinued because of bankruptcy of the venture-backed company, an IPO, or a merger and acquisition (M&A).

The version of the data used in this study covers VC deals completed between the first quarter of 1992 and the fourth quarter of 2001. It includes 22,479 rounds of VC financing involving 11,029 venture-backed firms. Among these firms, 83.5 percent were founded in or after 1990.

VentureOne categorizes each venture-backed firm in one of sixteen industry segments. Internet-related industries—such as communications, software, consumer/business services, and information services—attracted the majority of VC investment. Altogether, these four industries account for 71.3 percent of total VC investment over the decade. VC investment also tends to concentrate geographically. California received over 44 percent of the total investment in the United States. Massachusetts, a distant second, accounted for about 10 percent of the total. The top ten states account for 82.5 percent of the U.S. VC investment during the period of analysis.

While no variable in the VentureOne database indicates expressly whether a firm is in Silicon Valley, area code and zip code variables for each company can be used to generate geographic definitions. I used the zip code variable to identify whether a firm is located in a city in Silicon Valley, following the definition used by many regional studies, such as the annual Silicon Valley Index released by the Silicon Valley Network.[35] Such studies have historically defined Silicon Valley as being composed of Santa Clara County and adjacent cities in Alameda, San Mateo, and Santa Cruz Counties.[36] For the purpose of comparison, I also defined other important technology centers such as New York, Seattle, and Washington, D.C. The whole San Francisco Bay Area, including both the San Francisco–Oakland and the San Jose metropolitan areas, has developed into an integrated regional economy. This area encompasses Silicon Valley but has a substantially larger technology sector than Silicon Valley. Thus, I also use the rest of the Bay Area as an additional region for comparison. These areas are defined using the area code variable.[37]

ACCESS TO VENTURE CAPITAL IN SILICON VALLEY

Although Silicon Valley is not the birthplace of the U.S. VC industry, it has grown into the country's premier VC investment center. According to the directory of VC firms published by VentureOne, 159 VC firms have headquarters or offices in Silicon Valley, and an additional eighty-five firms are located in nearby cities such as San Francisco and Oakland. To put this into perspective, the entire state of Massachusetts, which is also famous for its abundance of VC, has only ninety-four VC firms listed in the same directory.[38] In this section, I will analyze the VentureOne data to explore how these many firms influence VC investment and access to VC, as well as how access to VC in Silicon Valley compares to that in other regions, and how it affects the performance of start-ups.

Trends of VC Investment

Panel (a) of figure 2.1 shows the trends of nominal VC investment in the United States and Silicon Valley from 1992 to 2001. Both series chart eight years of exponential growth followed by a severe crash. VC investment in Silicon Valley experienced 68 percent growth during the 1992–1995 period, increasing from $0.80 billion to $1.34 billion. In the next three years, total VC investment grew by 195 percent. The astounding growth of the late 1990s was unprecedented: VC investment in Silicon Valley increased by 175 percent in 1999 and 97 percent in 2000. In nominal dollars, Silicon Valley's VC investment in 2000, $21.5 billion, was twenty-seven times larger than it was in 1992. The burst of the Internet bubble is also reflected in VC investment. In 2001, total VC investment in Silicon Valley fell to $6.5 billion, a 70 percent decline. Yet in spite of this big falloff, the 2001 total still represents the third highest recorded level of VC investment in Silicon Valley.

Total VC investment in the whole country followed a similar trend over these ten years. At its peak in 2000, total U.S. VC investment reached $88.9 billion, twenty-five times as much as the total in 1992. The sharp decline of investment in 2001 also occurred for the nation as a whole. However, the $28.0 billion invested in 2001 is still the third largest amount in U.S. VC investment history, second only to venture investments in 1999 and 2000.

Panel (b) of figure 2.1 shows that during the 1992–2001 period, VC investments in Silicon Valley represented between 19 and 26 percent of total VC investments in the United States. In 1992, 22.9 percent of the U.S. total investment occurred in Silicon Valley; this percentage dropped persistently until reaching 19.7 percent in 1995. However, VC investment in Silicon Valley relative to the nation as a whole regained its momentum in the next two years, peaking at 25.7 percent of the U.S. total in 1997. In the next four years, Silicon Valley's share declined slightly but remained above 22 percent.

Access to Venture Capital in Silicon Valley and Other Regions: Simple Comparison

Not only did Silicon Valley start-ups receive a large amount of VC between 1992 and 2001, but they also seemed to have easier access to it. Table 2.1 compares Silicon Valley with the rest of the San Francisco Bay Area, Boston, New York, Seattle, Washington, D.C., and the remainder of the United States, using three access measures: average age of start-up at the first round of VC, total rounds of financing per start-up, and money raised in each deal.[39] (In this study, venture capital "deal" and venture capital "round" are used interchangeably.)

As was mentioned in the section on data, 83.5 percent of the firms in the VentureOne database were started in or after 1990. Most of the firms founded before 1990 are companies that have existed for a long time and that obtained VC support during the 1992–2001 period to supplement or restart their operations. I shall exclude firms founded before 1990 and focus solely on venture-backed start-ups for the remainder of the analysis in this study.

The data indicate that Silicon Valley firms are financed more quickly than those in other regions. As table 2.1 shows, Silicon Valley start-ups on average raised their first round of VC at the age of 11.48 months. In the rest of the San Francisco Bay Area, the average age is 12.80 months, only slightly higher. The average age is 16.53 months in Boston and 16.26 months in Seattle. In New York and Washington, D.C., it takes even longer (17.14 and 22.15 months, respectively) to secure the first round of VC. The rest of the nation has an average of 19.33 months. The differences between Silicon Valley and the rest of the Bay Area, Boston, New York, Seattle, Washington, D.C., and the remainder of the nation are all statistically significant.[40]

Silicon Valley start-ups also enjoy an advantage over those in other regions in the total number of rounds of VC financing they complete, as table 2.1 shows. On average, a Silicon Valley start-up completed 2.61 rounds of VC financing during the 1992–2001 period. Start-ups in all other regions received fewer rounds of capital, although the statistical significance of these differences varies. Boston and the rest of the Bay Area are not very far behind Silicon Valley. However, in New York and Washington, D.C., the number of VC rounds per start-up is only 2.08, lower than Silicon Valley as well as the national average.

Silicon Valley start-ups also receive larger investments in each VC deal than those in many other regions. Table 2.1 shows that the average size of a VC deal is $10.37 million in Silicon Valley, while it is only $8.84 million in Boston. The rest of the Bay Area shows an average almost identical to Silicon Valley's. New York has a slightly higher average than Silicon Valley, but this difference is not statistically significant. Boston and Seattle, also rich in VC investment, have average deal sizes far below the average in Silicon Valley.

Overall, simple comparisons between Silicon Valley and other regions suggest easier access to VC in Silicon Valley: on average, start-ups in Silicon Valley receive VC at a younger age, complete more rounds of financing, and raise more money in each deal.

Access to Venture Capital in Silicon Valley and Other Regions: Regression Analysis

To explain VC accessibility further and control for factors not taken into account in the simple comparison above, I run three OLS regressions. The dependent variables in the regressions are start-up age at the first round of VC, total rounds of VC completed by a start-up, and the size of a VC deal (measured in millions of 1996 dollars). I use start-up location dummies as the explanatory variables, with Silicon Valley as the reference group. The coefficients of the location dummies, indicating the difference between Silicon Valley and other regions, are the coefficients of interest. The control variables in the regressions include the following:

1. *Industry dummies.* Industry composition may explain the differences observed in table 2.1. If start-ups in the communications industry get access to VC easily, and if Silicon Valley hosts a larger share of communications start-ups, then one would expect easier access to capital in Silicon Valley. Thus *industry dummies* are included in all three regressions.

2. *Year dummies.* As figure 2.1 shows, total VC investment increased rapidly during the 1990s. Thus it is possible that Silicon Valley start-ups receive more money at a younger age only because many of them were founded in the late 1990s, a period when VC was in greater abundance. Thus *start year dummies* are included in the regressions to explain start-up age at the first round VC and total rounds of VC completed. In the regression for the size of a VC deal, the closing year of the VC deal is a more appropriate control than the start year of the firm. Thus *closing year dummies* are used

in this regression. However, one still suspects that the start year of the firm matters for the deal size. Thus I include in this regression another dummy to indicate whether the firm *started after 1995*, when the Internet boom began.

3. *Start-up age.* Older start-ups are expected to have completed more VC deals and raise more money in a single deal. Thus I include *start-up age in December 2001* (when the database was last updated) in the regression for total VC deals and *start-up age at VC round* in the regression for deal size.

4. *Ownership status dummies.* In the regression for total rounds of VC financing, it is appropriate to take into account the liquidity events that trigger the ending of VC financing for some start-ups. As discussed in the data section, if a start-up is out of business, acquired by another company, or completes an IPO, it is no longer a "venture-backed company" and VentureOne automatically stops tracking it. Because of this, liquidity events such as IPO, M&A, and bankruptcy are all likely to affect a firm's total rounds of VC financing completed. To control for such effects, I use the *ownership status dummies* in the regression to indicate whether a start-up has completed an IPO, been acquired, or gone out of business. The remaining group, start-ups that are alive and privately owned, is used as the reference group.

5. *VC round dummies.* A seed round of VC financing occurs at a very early stage of a start-up's existence, when its need is limited and its growth potential is unclear. Thus deals in the seed round tend to be smaller. Later rounds take place after a start-up has grown larger, and such deals should naturally involve a larger amount of investment. *VC round dummies* are therefore relevant in explaining the size of the deal. I use the "other rounds" as the basis for comparison, which include classes such as restart, venture leasing, and corporate investment.

The OLS regression results indicate that Silicon Valley start-ups still have easier access to VC even after controlling for the factors listed above. The results of these regressions are reported in table 2.2 and explained below.

Model (1) shows that Silicon Valley start-ups still have quicker access to VC even after controlling for industry and founding date. Since Silicon Valley is the reference group, any coefficient of a location dummy variable in table 2.2

indicates the difference between that region and Silicon Valley. Model (1) shows that start-ups in Silicon Valley complete the first round VC at a younger age than those in any other regions and that all the differences are statistically significant. For example, Silicon Valley firms have a 4.3-month advantage over those in the Boston area, a 7.9-month advantage over those in the New York area, and an 11.5-month advantage over those in Washington, D.C. This head start should give first-mover advantage to many Silicon Valley firms.

Model (2) shows that even after controlling for start year and industry, start-ups in Silicon Valley completed more rounds of VC financing. With the exception of the rest of the Bay Area, the estimated coefficients for all the location dummies are negative and statistically significant, suggesting that the total rounds of VC per firm outside of the Bay Area are all significantly smaller than the average in Silicon Valley. In Washington, D.C., total rounds per firm are 0.49 less than in Silicon Valley, the largest difference between any region and Silicon Valley. Start-up age has a negative coefficient in model (2), reflecting the fact that older firms were founded during the early years when VC was relatively scarce.[41]

A comparison between models (1) and (2) suggests that regions where start-ups receive VC at a younger age are the same as the regions where start-ups complete more rounds of financing. This result is expected, because given that two start-ups are observed over exactly the same time period, the one receiving the first round of VC at a younger age will have more time to complete later rounds. In an alternative specification of model (2), I added start-up age at the first round VC as an independent variable to explain the total rounds of VC per firm. Indeed, this age variable has a negative and statistically significant coefficient, confirming the fact that start-ups getting VC at a younger age tend to complete more rounds. However, including this age variable does not affect the significance of some of the location dummies. In particular, start-ups located in New York, Washington, D.C., and the rest of the nation (not in any of the high-tech centers examined) still have significantly fewer rounds of VC financing per firm than in Silicon Valley, although the size of the difference in each case becomes smaller. Thus, start-ups in Silicon Valley do enjoy some locational advantage compared to those in many other regions in terms of total VC deals they can secure.

Model (3) shows that start-ups founded after 1995 receive significantly larger investments in each deal and, more generally, that older start-ups tend to complete bigger deals. Negative coefficients of location dummies again indicate that Silicon Valley start-ups are associated with larger deal size, although for the rest of the Bay Area and New York, the difference is not statistically significant. On average, a start-up in Silicon Valley raises $1.5 million more in each deal than start-ups in Boston, $1.3 million more than those in Seattle, and $2.0 million more than those in Washington, D.C. Round class dummies are all statistically significant. Not surprisingly, later deals tend to be larger than earlier ones: a deal after the second round is on average $12 million larger than a deal in the seed round.

Although coefficients of year dummies are not presented in table 2.2, some of the results are worth mentioning. Compared with start-ups founded in 1992, those founded later had access to VC at younger ages. The start year dummies show a clear pattern that the later the founding year, the faster the start-up obtained VC. This reflects the fact that VC was increasingly available in the late 1990s.[42] Start-ups founded later completed fewer rounds of VC financing, which is expected because they were too young to complete several rounds. Compared to deals closed in 1992, those closed in the 1993–1998 period are not significantly different in terms of size. But those completed in the next three years are significantly larger. In 1999 or 2001, an average venture capital deal raised $3–4 million more than a deal in 1992. In 2000, the peak year of venture capital investment, a deal was $8 million larger.

Since the last three years in our sample period (1999–2001) are around the peak of the Internet boom, one naturally wonders whether some of the results are driven by the enormous amount of VC investment during that period. Although year dummies were included in the regressions to control for the effect, it is important to take a closer look at this issue. Thus I did a robustness check by dropping the observations in the later years. To examine the age of start-ups at the first round of VC and the total rounds of VC financing per firm, all start-ups founded during the 1999–2001 period were excluded from the regression (dropping 35 percent of the observations). Similarly, for the deal size equation, I excluded all deals completed during the1999–2001 period from the regression (dropping 57 percent of the observations). The results are presented in table 2.3 and discussed below.

Silicon Valley start-ups still receive the first round of VC at a significantly younger age than start-ups in other regions. In fact, a comparison between model (1) in table 2.2 and model (1) in table 2.3 reveals that the difference between Silicon Valley and other regions becomes larger when the sample is truncated. This suggests that in terms of quick access to VC, the gap between start-ups in Silicon Valley and those in other regions was actually closing during the Internet boom. Model (2) in table 2.3 shows that start-ups in Silicon Valley still complete more rounds of VC financing than those in other regions, with the exception of the rest of the San Francisco Bay Area and Seattle. Again, the difference between Silicon Valley and other regions is actually larger when start-ups founded in the last three years are excluded.

Interestingly, the result for deal size is different. After excluding the deals completed in the last three years, the results reversed for some regions. Using the full sample (model (3) in table 2.2), VC deals appear to be larger in Silicon Valley than in Seattle and Washington, D.C.; but the opposite is true once the latest deals are dropped (model (3) in table 2.3). And both results are statistically significant. Boston is the only region that has significantly smaller VC deals in both samples. Thus the result that start-ups in Silicon Valley raise more money in each round of VC financing is not robust; it might be a phenomenon that is unique to the period of the Internet boom.

The data show, then, that even after controlling for relevant variables, Silicon Valley start-ups tend to receive VC at a younger age and complete more rounds of financing than others. They also appear to raise more money in each round, but this is not necessarily the case before the Internet boom.

Access to Venture Capital and Performance of Start-Ups

One naturally wonders whether this easier access to VC matters for Silicon Valley. In a separate paper, I investigated whether the performance of Silicon Valley start-ups is related to the easier access to VC and found that easier VC accessibility has a wide-ranging and statistically significant effect.[43] Specifically, start-ups receiving VC at a younger age are more likely to go out of business, more likely to be acquired by another firm, more likely to go public, and more likely to attain profitability, and they tend to have more employees than other firms. All these effects are statistically significant at the 1 percent level. These results are also economically significant. For example, as shown in table 2.2, the average start-up age at the first round of VC in Silicon Valley is 4.3 months younger than in the Boston area. All else being equal, regression results in Zhang (2007) imply that the odds of survival for a start-up in Silicon Valley are 7.4 percent lower than for one in the Boston area.[44] Also because of this quicker access to VC, start-ups in Silicon Valley are expected to have 11.3 percent higher odds of being acquired, to have 10.9 percent higher odds of completing an IPO, to have 4.8 percent higher odds of making a profit, and to have nine more employees than start-ups in the Boston area.

The size of the first round of VC also has a statistically significant effect on three start-up performance measures. Start-ups receiving more money at the first round are more likely to complete an IPO, more likely to make a profit, and more likely to have more employees. All these findings suggest that Silicon Valley start-ups do benefit from the easier access to VC. These results particularly help to explain why start-ups in this region have higher rates of IPO and M&A.[45]

ACCESS TO VENTURE CAPITAL: SIMPLY MORE MONEY OR MORE THAN SIMPLY MONEY?

What these results do not explain, and what I now wish to explore, is why VC in Silicon Valley is more accessible. One possible reason is simply that Silicon Valley has more money. There is a large cluster of VC firms in Silicon Valley and thus a larger supply of VC in this region than any other region in the country. The proximity of entrepreneurs to this major source of VC money facilitates the investment process in many ways. For example, it may take entrepreneurs less time to identify potential investors because they are nearby. It may be easier for entrepreneurs and venture capitalists to communicate with each other, making it easier to complete the evaluation and screening process. In addition, the abundance of VC in Silicon Valley may have intensified competition among VC firms for potential investments, forcing all involved to move quickly if they want a share of a promising start-up. And quicker access to VC could be a result of fierce competition among investors.

Not only is there a larger supply of VC in Silicon Valley, there may also be a higher demand for it. For example, Silicon Valley is known for high costs of living and doing business. This implies that start-ups in this region have to pay higher rents and wages and thus need more cash to stay in business. More rounds of financing and larger deal size in Silicon Valley may simply reflect the higher operating costs in this region.[46]

On the other hand, one could argue that the easier access to VC in Silicon Valley is not just a result of more money. The dense social networks among venture capitalists and potential entrepreneurs as a result of a high concentration of VC firms and high-tech industries, the well-developed innovation-supporting industries, and the greater tolerance for risk-taking may all contribute to the easier access of start-ups to VC in Silicon Valley.

First of all, the physical closeness of potential entrepreneurs to a large number of venture capitalists may make access to VC easier by allowing these groups to establish informal connections through common social or business contacts, and in turn to gain one another's trust. Asymmetric information is a common problem when venture capitalists invest in an unknown entrepreneur's start-up; but where entrepreneurs and venture capitalists have personal connections and mutual trust, as they are more likely to do in Silicon Valley, the problem of asymmetric information is mitigated and the investment process accelerated.[47] Indeed, venture capitalists with greater trust in an entrepreneur's ability are also likely to invest more money in his or her start-up.

Second, the high concentration of VC firms in Silicon Valley facilitates access to VC because it facilitates joint investment partnerships. It is common practice for several VC firms to form a syndicate to invest in a start-up in order to share the risks involved and also to share business information.[48] It is simply easier to form a syndicate in a VC cluster such as Silicon Valley, which could also accelerate the process of VC investment.

Third, a concentration in Silicon Valley of well-developed industries that support innovation may also make access to VC easier. These industries include legal services, human resource services, investment banking, management consulting, and accounting, which together with VC firms form a whole clustered community that facilitates company creation.[49] Because VC investment in start-ups is about creating new companies, its pace is affected by other supporting services. For example, a round of VC financing is sometimes contingent on whether or not a professional manager can be found to help the founders expand the business. The experienced executive search firms in Silicon Valley may expedite this process and thus the investment process itself.

The quicker access to VC in Silicon Valley may also imply that venture capitalists in this region are more willing to take risks. After interviewing individuals who had worked in both the Boston area and Silicon Valley, Saxenian (1994) concluded that East Coast venture capitalists were more formal and conservative in their investment strategies. An entrepreneur in Silicon Valley told Saxenian:

When I started Convergent [Technologies], I got commitments for $2.5 million in 20 minutes from three people over lunch who saw me write the business plan on the back of a napkin. They believed in me. In Boston, you can't do that. It's much more formal.[50]

Another Silicon Valley entrepreneur said:

There is no real venture capital in Massachusetts. The venture capital community is a bunch of very conservative bankers. They are radically different from the venture capitalists in Silicon Valley, who have all been operational people in companies. Unless you've proven yourself a hundred times over, you'll never get any money.[51]

While it is tempting to attribute Silicon Valley's quick investment to its unique risk-seeking culture, this explanation raises a further question. What determines the Silicon Valley culture? Anecdotal evidence suggests that many venture capitalists in the region were previously successful entrepreneurs or experienced engineers. This prior experience gives them a good sense of whether a new idea is viable, which may in turn allow them to depend more on instinct and less on paperwork to evaluate business plans. In contrast, venture capitalists in other regions have previously been employed in banking and are more likely to have a business background than a technical background. Such venture capitalists will necessarily follow more formal routines in evaluating business plans and will naturally be more conservative in making investment decisions.

A final possible explanation of quicker access to VC in Silicon Valley could be that start-ups in the region simply represent great business plans with better growth potential, and that they therefore require less time for venture capitalists to screen. While this notion may have some intuitive appeal, it is hard to believe that great business plans are so concentrated in the San Francisco Bay Area. As shown in Zhang (2007), start-ups receiving VC at a younger age are more likely to go out of business, suggesting that these firms are not more viable than other businesses.

Venture capital is more than simply money. To understand the importance of the VC industry in local economic development, one should conceptualize VC as a combination of monetary, human, and social capital. Human capital can be understood as the venture capitalist's grasp of technology, market, and business, along with his or her track record and reputation in company creation and venture investing. Human capital may also include the ability and experience of the professionals in other supporting industries, such as lawyers and accountants who specialize in venture investment. Social capital consists of the venture capitalist's social and business contacts and connections, the level of trust between entrepreneurs and investors, and the culture of risk-taking.[52]

The regional advantage created by Silicon Valley's local VC industry is not likely the sole result of more money. Instead, as I have argued, the advantages of Silicon Valley may be the consequence of the unique interaction of monetary, human, and social capital. This view is consistent with both the anecdotal evidence from previous studies and the empirical evidence presented in this analysis.

CONCLUSION

State policymakers are convinced that the local VC industry played a crucial role in Silicon Valley's economic success. As a result of this belief, they endorse policies that improve access to VC as necessary to stimulating entrepreneurship in their own regions. However, such policies should be based on an informed understanding of whether and how Silicon Valley has benefited from its strong VC industry.

I find strong evidence that access to VC is easier for start-ups in Silicon Valley than for those in the rest of the country. Specifically, I find that start-ups in Silicon Valley complete the first round of VC financing at a younger age and complete more rounds of financing in any given period of time. During the Internet boom, start-ups in Silicon Valley also tended to raise more VC in each round of financing. In a separate study,[53] I find that this easier access to VC can have a significant effect on the performance of Silicon Valley start-ups. In particular, start-ups receiving VC at a younger age are more likely to complete a public offering, are more likely to make a profit, and tend to have more employees (i.e., grow faster). On the other hand, start-ups accessing VC more quickly are more likely to go out of business. Thus a higher success rate and a higher failure rate should leave fewer mediocre investments in Silicon Valley than in other regions.[54]

While the evidence is strong that start-ups in Silicon Valley have easier access to VC and that they benefit from it, it is unclear what factors are responsible for this easier access. On the one hand, it is possible that Silicon Valley's abundance of capital alone makes a big difference; on the other hand, the easier access is also consistent with alternative explanations that stress the nonmonetary value of VC. As anecdotal evidence suggests, venture capitalists in Silicon Valley may be more inclined to take risks, more experienced in creating new companies, more savvy about technology, better supported by related service industries, and more capable of mobilizing other resources that are crucial for building companies. The abundance of VC in Silicon Valley suggests a causal connection between the higher supply of monetary capital and the region's economic success prior to the burst of the Internet bubble. The recognition of this connection explains why so many states have sought to boost local VC supply. However, it is still unclear to what extent Silicon Valley's success is attributable to the availability of monetary capital and to what extent it is a result of the human and social capital embedded in monetary capital.[55] Empirical work has yet to be done to disentangle the causes of the easier access to VC in Silicon Valley and to give a definitive answer to this question.

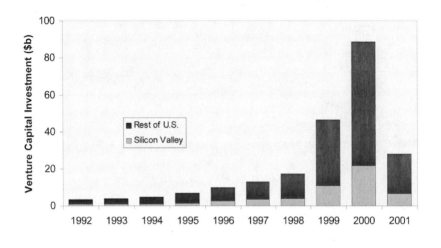

(a)

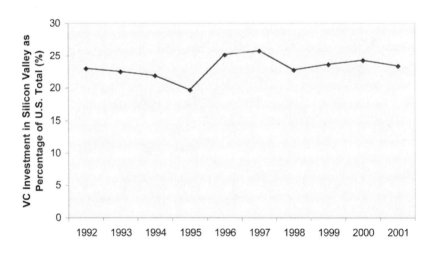

(b)

Source: Author's calculations based on VentureOne data.

FIGURE 2.1.
Total VC Investment in Silicon Valley and United States, 1992–2001

Table 2.1. Access to Venture Capital, 1992–2001

	Silicon Valley	Rest of SF Bay	Boston	New York	Seattle	Washington, D.C.	Rest of U.S.
Start-up Age at First Round of Venture Capital (months)							
Mean	11.48	12.80**	16.53***	17.14***	16.26***	22.15***	19.33***
Std. dev.	16.28	16.49	21.53	21.01	19.50	25.40	23.36
No. of obs.	1,757	833	869	567	271	323	3,641
Rounds of VC per Start-up							
Mean	2.61	2.48**	2.53*	2.08***	2.42**	2.08***	2.23***
Std. dev.	1.50	1.47	1.47	1.20	1.41	1.25	1.37
No. of obs.	1,819	871	899	601	283	344	3,924
Venture Capital Raised per Deal (millions, 1996 dollars)							
Mean	10.37	10.36	8.84***	10.98	9.33*	9.70	9.54***
Std. dev.	16.55	14.47	11.28	16.93	14.59	17.26	19.14
No. of obs.	4,561	2,072	2,193	1,181	651	681	8,372

* Statistically different from Silicon Valley at the 10 percent significance level by one-tailed t-test.
** Statistically different from Silicon Valley at the 5 percent significance level by one-tailed t-test.
*** Statistically different from Silicon Valley at the 1 percent significance level by one-tailed t-test.

Table 2.2. Access to Venture Capital: OLS Regression Results

	Model (1) DV: age at first VC	Model (2) DV: rounds of VC	Model (3) DV: size of VC deal
Constant	19.17***	5.247***	4.759*
	(3.020)	(0.500)	(2.467)
Started after 1995			2.132***
			(0.484)
Start-up age at VC round			0.015**
			(0.008)
Start-up age in December 2001		-0.026***	
		(0.004)	
Location dummies			
Silicon Valley		Reference Group for Comparison	
Rest of San Francisco Bay Area	2.539***	-0.029	-0.068
	(0.738)	(0.055)	(0.437)
Boston	4.288***	-0.127**	-1.452***
	(0.720)	(0.053)	(0.425)
New York	7.871***	-0.379***	-0.331
	(0.847)	(0.063)	(0.542)
Seattle	5.592***	-0.136*	-1.292*
	(1.129)	(0.083)	(0.681)
Washington, D.C.	11.48***	-0.491***	-2.004***
	(1.047)	(0.077)	(0.678)
Rest of U.S.	7.716***	-0.344***	-0.708**
	(0.517)	(0.038)	(0.311)
Start year dummies	Yes	Yes	
Closing year dummies			Yes
Industry dummies	Yes	Yes	Yes
Ownership status dummies		Yes	
Venture capital round dummies			
Seed round			-7.019***
			(0.548)
First Round			-2.847***
			(0.357)
Second Round			1.850***
			(0.386)
Later rounds			4.889***
			(0.411)
R^2	0.350	0.210	0.134
Number of observations	8,261	8,252	19,181

Note: Standard errors are in parentheses. Size of VC deal is measured in millions of 1996 dollars. Yes = Dummy variables are included in the regression as controls.
* significant at the 10 percent level; ** significant at the 5 percent level; *** significant at the 1 percent level.

Table 2.3. Access to Venture Capital: OLS Regressions Using a Truncated Sample

	Model (1) DV: age at first VC	Model (2) DV: rounds of VC	Model (3) DV: size of VC deal
Constant	14.65***	7.885***	2.417*
	(3.766)	(0.677)	(1.330)
Started after 1995			0.392
			(0.332)
Start-up age at VC round			0.007
			(0.007)
Start-up age in December 2001		-0.048***	
		(0.005)	
Location dummies			
Silicon Valley	Reference Group for Comparison		
Rest of SF Bay Area	3.586***	0.050	-0.283
	(1.122)	(0.080)	(0.335)
Boston	6.399***	-0.138*	-0.982***
	(1.039)	(0.075)	(0.306)
New York	12.35***	-0.528***	1.097**
	(1.350)	(0.096)	(0.481)
Seattle	7.696***	-0.190	1.891***
	(1.698)	(0.121)	(0.544)
Washington, D.C.	16.69***	-0.689***	1.274**
	(1.586)	(0.113)	(0.596)
All other regions	11.04***	-0.441***	0.265
	(0.768)	(0.055)	(0.230)
Start year dummies	Yes	Yes	
Closing year dummies			Yes
Industry dummies	Yes	Yes	Yes
Ownership status dummies		Yes	
Venture capital round dummies			
Seed round			-2.974***
			(0.379)
First Round			0.419
			(0.284)
Second Round			2.181***
			(0.310)
Later rounds			3.715***
			(0.328)
R^2	0.269	0.117	0.105
Number of observations	5,357	5,349	8,174

Note: For models (1) and (2), start-ups founded during 1999–2001 are dropped from the sample; for model (3), VC deals completed during 1999–2001 are dropped from the sample. Size of VC deal is measured in millions of 1996 dollars. Standard errors are in parentheses. Yes = Dummy variables are included in the regression as controls.
* significant at the 10 percent level; ** significant at the 5 percent level; *** significant at the 1 percent level.

NOTES

*Parts of this chapter are adapted from "Access to Venture Capital and the Performance of High-Tech Start-Ups in Silicon Valley," *Economic Development Quarterly*, Vol. 21, 124–47, May 2007. The author has benefited from comments by Kannika Damrongplasit, Diana Furchtgott-Roth, Young-Choon Kim, Colin Mason, Charles Ou, David Salzman, Xue Song, Brandon Wall, Mark Walsh, and seminar participants at the Hudson Institute.

1. Junfu Zhang, *High-tech start-ups and industry dynamics in Silicon Valley* (San Francisco: Public Policy Institute of California, 2003a).

2. David Rosenberg, *Cloning Silicon Valley* (New York: Pearson Education, 2002).

3. As Ethernet inventor and 3Com founder Bob Metcalfe famously observed, "Silicon Valley is the only place on Earth not trying to figure out how to become Silicon Valley" (Metcalfe, 1998). Indeed, Silicon monikers appeared all over the globe. Outside the United States, examples include the "Silicon Fen" in Cambridge, England; the "Silicon Plain" in Kempele, Finland; the "Silicon Plateau" in Bangalore, India; the "Silicon Wadi" of Israel; and the "Silicon Island" of Taiwan. Within the United States, there are the "Silicon Alley" in New York City; the "Silicon Gulch" in Austin, Texas; the "Silicon Mountain" in Colorado Springs, Colorado; the "Silicon Forest" in Portland, Oregon; the "Silicon Desert" in Phoenix, Arizona; and many others. For a long list of such nicknames, see <http://www.officetimes.com/silicon.htm> (accessed October 21, 2005).

4. One could argue that Frederick Terman's efforts in encouraging business creation at Stanford should count as local "policy," although not implemented by the local government.

5. See, for example, Saxenian (1994); or Lecuyer (2000).

6. AnnaLee Saxenian, *Regional advantage: Culture and competition in Silicon Valley and Route 128* (Cambridge, MA: Harvard University Press, 1994); and Stuart W. Leslie, "The biggest 'angel' of them all: The military and the making of Silicon Valley," *Understanding Silicon Valley: The Anatomy of an entrepreneurial region*, ed. Martin Kenney (Stanford, CA: Stanford University Press, 2000), 48–67.

7. Doug Henton, "A profile of the Valley's evolving structure," *The Silicon Valley edge: A habitat for innovation and entrepreneurship*, ed. Chong-Moon Lee, William F. Miller, Marguerite Gong Hancock, and Henry S. Rowen (Stanford, CA: Stanford University Press, 2000), 46–58.

8. Starting in 1994, Silicon Valley's local newspaper, the *San Jose Mercury News*, compiled an annual list of the top 150 firms in Silicon Valley. Up until 2003, on average, each year's list included twenty-three new firms, reflecting the high rate of turnover in Silicon Valley (Zhang, 2003a).

9. Dado P. Banatao and Kevin A. Fong, "The valley of deals: How venture capital helped shape the region," *The Silicon Valley edge: A habitat for innovation and entrepreneurship*, ed. Chong-Moon Lee, William F. Miller, Marguerite Gong Hancock, and Henry S. Rowen (Stanford, CA: Stanford University Press, 2000), 295–313.

10. Thomas F. Hellmann, "Venture capitalists: The coaches of Silicon Valley," *The Silicon Valley edge: A habitat for innovation and entrepreneurship*, ed. Chong-Moon Lee, William F. Miller, Marguerite Gong Hancock, and Henry S. Rowen (Stanford, CA: Stanford University Press, 2000), 276–94.

11. William D. Bygrave and Jeffry A. Timmons, *Venture capital at the crossroads* (Boston: Harvard Business School Press, 1992).

12. Scott Wallsten, "The role of government in regional technology development: The effects of public venture capital and science parks," *Building high-tech clusters: Silicon Valley and beyond*, ed. Timothy Bresnahan and Alfonso Gambardella (Cambridge: Cambridge University Press, 2004), 229–79.

13. This overview relies heavily on the summary of state biotechnology initiatives compiled by the Biotechnology Industry Organization (2004). For some earlier reviews on this topic, see Florida and Smith (1992) and Barkley, Markley, and Rubin (1999).

14. Andrew Webb, "Venture group to promote startups," *Albuquerque Journal*, 9 October 2004.

15. See Indiana Future Fund's website at <http://www.indianafuturefund.com/> (accessed December 12, 2005).

16. Biotechnology Industry Organization, "Laboratories of innovation: State bioscience initiatives 2004," Washington, D.C., 2004.

17. Jeffery Kosseff, "House OKs venture capital bill," *Oregonian*, July 11, 2003, 1(B).

18. Stephen Pounds, "Venture investors keep eye on Scripps," *Palm Beach Post*, May 2, 2004, 1(F).

19. See Maryland Venture Fund Annual Report at <http://www
.choosemaryland.org/assets/document/Finance%20Annual%20Report.pdf>
(accessed November 10, 2005).

20. The state government encourages institutional investors such as banks and
insurance companies to invest in the fund by offering tax credits to cover potential
losses or to guarantee a certain rate of return.

21. See, for example, Saxenian (1994); Kenney (2000); Koepp (2003); Zhang
(2003b); and Bresnahan and Gambardella (2004).

22. There is a rich literature on venture capital in general, which will not be
reviewed here. See Gompers and Lerner (1999) and the references therein.

23. Bygrave and Timmons, *Venture capital*; and Martin Kenney and Richard Florida,
"Venture capital in Silicon Valley: Fueling new firms' formation," *Understanding
Silicon Valley: The Anatomy of an entrepreneurial region*, ed. Martin Kenney
(Stanford, CA: Stanford University Press, 2000), 98–123.

24. The New York–based Fairchild Camera and Instrument Corporation provided
the capital to their start-up, thus named Fairchild Semiconductor, which later spun
off many semiconductor companies and became a legend in Silicon Valley's history
(Saxenian, 1994; Von Burg and Kenney, 2000).

25. Martin Kenney and Richard Florida, "Venture capital in Silicon Valley: Fueling
new firms' formation," *Understanding Silicon Valley: The Anatomy of an
entrepreneurial region*, ed. Martin Kenney (Stanford, CA: Stanford University Press,
2000), 98–123.

26. Schumpeter would certainly have agreed with this metaphor. See, for example,
Schumpeter (1934, 93), where he likens economic competition to "boxing-matches."

27. Examining a data set of 173 start-up companies in Silicon Valley, Hellmann and
Puri (2002) find that venture capitalists clearly provide support in building up the
internal organization of the company. In particular, start-ups backed by venture
capital are more likely or faster to become professionalized than those that are not.
They are more likely to use professional recruiting services; their human resource
policies are more likely to be influenced by investors; they adopt stock option plans
more quickly; and they take less time to appoint a vice president of sales and
marketing.

28. Saxenian, *Regional advantage*, 64–65. Some of Saxenian's claims, which are based
on interview evidence or personal observations, remain to be substantiated by other

types of data. Most of the interviewees Saxenian cites were talking from their experiences in the 1980s or even earlier, and it is not clear whether these features of Silicon Valley's VC industry persisted in the 1990s during the Internet revolution.

29. Matthew A. Zook, *The geography of the Internet industry* (Malden, MA: Blackwell Publishing, 2005), 87–94.

30. Zook, *Geography of the Internet*, 112–16.

31. One quantitative study is Horvath (2004), which compares Silicon Valley with other regions using the PriceWaterhouseCoopers survey data on VC deals completed during the 1995–2000 period. The paper, as the author admitted, is only "an exercise of presenting data." Its goal is to show some basic facts about VC investment in different regions. For example, the paper shows that although Silicon Valley remained the leading recipient of VC investment, many other regions were catching up during the second half of the 1990s. It also shows that VC investment in Silicon Valley was more evenly distributed across stages of investment (including seed, early, expansion, and profitable). Although the author occasionally commented on these facts and offered some interpretation, he made no attempt to propose or test any theory about Silicon Valley or high-tech clusters in general.

32. VentureOne Corporation, *Venture capital industry report* (San Francisco, 2001).

33. VentureOne defines a venture capital firm as "a professional, institutional venture capital limited partnership that generally manages over $20 million in assets and invests in privately held companies" (VentureOne 2000, 4). Once a company receives some investment from venture capital firms, it becomes a "venture-backed company" and enters the VentureOne database. Once in the database, VentureOne tracks the company's financing from all sources, including bank loans and IPOs. While I do not count bank loans or money raised through an IPO as venture capital, I do include equity investment made by non-VC corporations or angel investors as venture capital in my calculations.

34. See for example, Gompers and Lerner (2000); Cochrane (2005); Gompers, Lerner, and Scharfstein (2005); and Zhang (2003a, 2006, 2007) for some empirical work using the VentureOne data.

35. The most recent editions of the Silicon Valley Index are available at <http://www.jointventure.org/publications/index/indexofsiliconvalley.html> (accessed September 19, 2005).

36. More specifically, this definition of Silicon Valley includes the whole of Santa Clara County, plus Fremont, Newark, and Union City in Alameda County; Atherton,

Belmont, East Palo Alto, Foster City, Menlo Park, Redwood City, San Carlos, and San Mateo in San Mateo County; and Scotts Valley in Santa Cruz County.

37. The rest of the San Francisco Bay Area: area codes 408, 415, 510, 650, and 925, excluding Silicon Valley; Boston: area codes 508, 617, 781, and 978; New York: area codes 201, 212, 347, 516, 646, 718, 732, 845, 908, 914, 917, and 973; Seattle: area codes 206, 253, 360, and 425; Washington, D.C.: area codes 202, 240, 301, 571, and 703.

38. VentureOne Corporation, 2000.

39. Access to venture capital can be measured along many dimensions. The choice of measures here is entirely dictated by data availability.

40. One-tailed t-tests reject the null hypothesis (the mean for a region equal to that of Silicon Valley) at the 5 percent confidence level for the rest of the Bay Area and at the 1 percent confidence level for all other regions.

41. One might expect start-ups to complete more VC deals if they have existed for a long time. That is, start-up age should have a positive effect. This effect is picked up by the start year dummies, which show that start-ups founded later completed significantly fewer rounds of VC financing (coefficients not shown in table 2.2).

42. Although there was a sharp decline in VC investment in 2001, it was not because of an insufficient supply of capital. In fact, many of the VC firms had to refund some money to their investors because too much money was chasing too few ideas after the burst of the Internet bubble (see, for example, "The VCs Don't Want Your Money Anymore," *BusinessWeek*, July 29, 2002).

43. See Junfu Zhang, "Access to venture capital and the performance of high-tech start-ups in Silicon Valley," *Economic Development Quarterly*, Vol. 21, 124–47, May 2007.

44. The odds of survival are defined as the ratio of probability of surviving to the probability of not surviving. When estimating logit models, as I did in Zhang (2007), it is convenient to interpret the coefficients in terms of odds ratio.

45. Total rounds and the size of later deals are not included in the regression analysis in Zhang (2007) because they are seemingly endogenous, in that later investment decisions are often based on the observed performance of the start-ups. To a lesser extent, start-up age at the first VC round and the size of the first VC deal may also be endogenous, in that better start-ups receive more money at an earlier stage. However, this is unlikely to be the case given that those receiving more VC at an earlier stage are found to have a higher failure rate.

46. Of course, higher costs alone do not justify more investment; only higher expected returns in excess of the higher costs can attract more VC.

47. Toby Stuart and Olav Sorenson, "Social networks and entrepreneurship," *Handbook of entrepreneurship research: Disciplinary perspectives*, ed. Rajshree Agrawal, Sharon Alvarez, and Olav Sorenson. (Berlin: Springer-Verlag, 2005), 211–28.

48. Bygrave and Timmons, *Venture capital*; and Olav Sorenson and Toby E. Stuart, "Syndication networks and the spatial distribution of venture capital investments," *American Journal of Sociology* 106 (2001): 1546–88.

49. See Lee et al. (2000) for discussions of the role of many of these industries in Silicon Valley.

50. Sarxenian, *Regional advantage,* 65.

51. Sarxenian, *Regional advantage,* 65.

52. There is no doubt that entrepreneurs see all the nonmonetary value of VC. For example, recent research by Hsu (2004) finds that entrepreneurs with multiple offers from investors would forego a large amount of capital in order to be associated with more experienced and well-connected venture capitalists. See Cohen and Fields (2000) for a detailed discussion of Silicon Valley's social capital networks.

53. Zhang, "Access to venture capital and the performance of high-tech start-ups in Silicon Valley," *Economic Development Quarterly*, Vol. 21, 124–47, May 2007.

54. Note that a higher failure rate coupled with a higher success rate may generate a higher financial return for venture capitalists because the gain from a highly successful investment is usually more than enough to compensate for the loss of many failures.

55. Of course, this is not to say that only the human and social capital embedded in VC matters in the high-tech economy. For example, the human capital incorporated in university inventions, corporate R&D, and a high-quality labor force are all crucial for the development of a regional high-tech economy.

Do Household Savings Encourage Entrepreneurship?

Household Wealth, Parental Wealth, and the Transition In and Out of Entrepreneurship

Erik Hurst and Annamaria Lusardi[*]

INTRODUCTION

Entrepreneurs have historically played an important role in economic growth.[1] Business ownership is central to a range of issues in both economic theory and public policy, and many countries have programs and institutions that aim to encourage it. For example, the United States established the Small Business Administration (SBA) in 1953 to monitor and promote business ownership. One of the focuses of the SBA has been entrepreneurs' access to capital. The SBA has provided nearly twenty million small businesses with direct or indirect help since 1953. During the 1990s alone, the SBA helped close to 435,000 small businesses receive more than $94.6 billion in loans.[2]

Many empirical papers by leading economists show that, despite the attempts of governmental agencies and the development of financial markets, liquidity constraints are still an important deterrent to business ownership. Several papers referenced in this work find that wealth is positively correlated with the propensity to start a business. That is, the wealthier the household, the more likely it is to start a business. These papers all conclude that liquidity constraints prevent would-be entrepreneurs from starting their businesses.[3]

We show that the evidence that liquidity constraints have prevented U.S. households from starting businesses during the last two decades is, in fact, very weak. Using additional empirical specifications, a much richer set of data, and exploration of the variations in economic conditions during the past two decades, we are able to examine in depth the underlying reasons for the correlation between wealth and entrepreneurship. Although, like other authors, we find a positive correlation between initial household wealth and the probability that a household will subsequently start a business, we also show this is no proof that liquidity constraints bind entrepreneurs in starting their businesses.

We use several data sources to perform our empirical analysis: the Panel Study of Income Dynamics (PSID), the Health and Retirement Study (HRS), the National Longitudinal Survey of Youth (NLSY), and the National Survey of Small Business Finances (NSSBF), which cover different groups of the population for the late 1980s and the 1990s. Using these sources, we first document some important facts about business owners. We then demonstrate that the relationship between wealth and business ownership does not necessarily imply the existence of binding liquidity constraints. The data sets give us a better understanding of who the entrepreneurs are and provide evidence that the correlation between wealth and business entry is, at least in part, due to differences between business owners and non–business owners in abilities, preferences, and family backgrounds.

We show that, contrary to the predictions of a model of entrepreneurship with liquidity constraints, the relationship between wealth and business entry is highly nonlinear. Over most of the distribution of wealth, there is no discernible difference in the propensity to become a business owner. It is only at the very top of the wealth distribution (top 5 percent) that a positive relationship between wealth and business entry can be found. According to the model we examine, moreover, liquidity constraints should be more stringent for firms requiring high initial capital. We divide businesses into industries with high- and low-starting-capital requirements and find no evidence that wealth matters more for businesses requiring higher initial capital.

A few researchers test for liquidity constraints differently: rather than using wealth, they use inheritances as a proxy for liquidity. They show that those who receive inheritances are subsequently more likely to start businesses, again arguing that liquidity constraints limit business ownership. This ap-

proach certainly represents a superior method of testing for liquidity constraints. However, inheritances are not randomly distributed in the population. In fact, they are more likely to be received by those at the top of the
wealth distribution, thus capturing the nonlinear relationship between wealth
and business entry we find in our work. Moreover, inheritances may simply
proxy for talents and ability; those with talented parents are also more talented themselves and inherently display a higher propensity toward business
ownership. Since talents are positively correlated with wealth, wealthier parents tend to have children who are more likely to start a business. To prove this
claim, we show that not only past inheritances but also future inheritances
(inheritances received *after* a business is started) are correlated with business
entry. We also show that the recipients of inheritances already have large
amounts of wealth, often much more than are needed to start a business.

We propose a new measure of liquidity: capital gains on housing. Housing
prices have increased over time and across regions in the United States, often
delivering large capital gains to homeowners. The increase in wealth deriving
from capital gains is spread throughout the wealth distribution and does not
affect only those at the top of the wealth distribution. Moreover, households
can easily access this increase in wealth by borrowing against home equity.
When using this alternative measure of liquidity, we do not find any evidence
that those households who benefit from an increase in their home equity are
more likely than others to start a business.

Data

As mentioned above, we use several data sets to gain deeper insight into the
characteristics of entrepreneurs. Although our empirical analysis is based
mainly on one data set, the PSID, we rely on other data sets to provide information that cannot be captured by the PSID alone, and that allow us to study
different age groups and the distinct characteristics that set entrepreneurs
apart from the rest of the population.

We use data from the PSID for the late 1980s and the early 1990s to address
the role of household wealth in propagating business ownership. The PSID is
a large-scale panel survey that tracks socioeconomic variables of a given family over time. It reports detailed information about wealth at five-year inter-
vals and collects information on parental wealth for both the head of the
family and the spouse in 1988. Significantly for our work, in every year the

PSID asks its respondents to report whether they own a business. This data set allows us to examine entrepreneurs in the entire population and, given its panel aspect, to examine the transition into and out of entrepreneurship.

We also use data from the 1992 HRS, a data set that reports information about the cohort born between 1931 and 1941, thus allowing us to examine older entrepreneurs. This data set provides information not only on wealth but also on a rich set of demographic and economic characteristics, including the respondent's expectations about the future and relationship with the family of origin. To study younger entrepreneurs, we use data from the NLSY-Cohort97. This data set reports information on a cohort of parents with teenage children (age twelve to sixteen) in 1997. Finally, we use data from the 1987 NSSBF, which provides a direct measure of the capital needed to start a business, a critical piece of information for our work.

Simple Facts about Entrepreneurship and Wealth

Who is an entrepreneur is one of the critical questions researchers face. Given our focus on wealth and business equity, we define entrepreneurs here as those households that report owning a business. This definition is similar to that used in several other studies.[4]

We report below some descriptive statistics that guide our evaluation of the effects of wealth on the transition into and out of entrepreneurship. Using data from the PSID in 1989, we find that entrepreneurs are much richer than other households and account for the lion's share of wealth in the economy. Entrepreneurs account for approximately 13 percent of the population, but they alone account for 41.8 percent of total household wealth.[5] Median wealth holdings of those households that own a business are more than three times the amount of wealth held by those that do not own a business ($179,189 versus $47,116).[6] Differences are even bigger in mean wealth holdings ($486,909 versus $119,313). Note that this is not simply due to the size of business equity; wealth is substantially larger for entrepreneurs relative to the rest of the population even when subtracting business equity.

Differences in wealth magnify for older entrepreneurs. Using HRS data, we find that 19.2 percent of households own a business in 1992 and that their median and mean wealth holdings are three to four times bigger than those of the rest of the population, even when subtracting business equity (median nonbusiness wealth is $85,000 for nonentrepreneurs versus $204,000 for entrepreneurs, and means are $161,800 and $419,500, respectively). This result is not simply due to the fact that older entrepreneurs are more likely to be successful ones. Even young entrepreneurs are much richer than the rest of the population. Data from the NLSY in 1997 indicate that 12.4 percent of parents with teenage children (the population sampled in the NLSY) own a business, and that their median wealth is more than three times that of their nonentrepreneur counterparts (median nonbusiness wealth is $29,100 for nonentrepreneurs versus $98,000 for entrepreneurs, and means are $74,600 and $205,800, respectively).

The positive correlation between wealth and entrepreneurship becomes obvious when the data are examined more closely. Table 3.1 shows the percentage of entrepreneurs in the overall household wealth distribution in the 1989 PSID, 1992 HRS, and 1997 NLSY samples. Results are consistent across the three samples. Entrepreneurs tend to be concentrated in the upper end of the total wealth distribution. In the PSID, entrepreneurs make up 27.7 percent of households in the 80th–90th percentile of the wealth distribution, 31.9 percent of households in the 90th–97th percentile of wealth distribution, and 62.1 percent of households in the top 3 percent of the distribution. Likewise, they make up 80.6 percent of households in the top 3 percent of the wealth distribution in the HRS and 80.7 percent of households in the top 3 percent of the wealth distribution in the NLSY. These results clearly show that there is a strong and positive relationship between household wealth and entrepreneurship.

A second feature to note in our household data sets is that many business owners report low amounts for their business equity. Table 3.2 shows that more than 30 percent of business owners in the 1989 PSID report having zero business equity, and results are similar in the other data sets. While the fraction of zero business equity decreases as we move up in the wealth distribution, approximately 10 percent of the business owners in the 80th–97th percentile in the wealth distribution report zero business equity (table 3.1). Further differences among business owners appear when we look closely at business equity in table 3.2 (each of these surveys asks their respondents how much their business would be worth if they sold off all their assets and paid off all their debts). While some entrepreneurs have more than $1 million in business equity, the majority of entrepreneurs have $20,000 or less in business equity. As expected, the distribution of business equity is highly skewed to the right. Thus, empirical samples will contain entrepreneurs whose businesses vary greatly by size.

Note that zero business equity does not necessarily characterize small entrepreneurs or entrepreneurs who remain small. Approximately 20 percent of entrepreneurs who reported zero business equity in the PSID in 1989 ended up having more than $94,000 of business equity in 1994. Some authors, such as Gentry and Hubbard (2004), exclude business owners with less than $5,000 of business equity from their sample. In practice, this corresponds to excluding a large number of business owners (38 percent of the business owners in the PSID sample).

Data from the HRS already show that the correlation between business ownership and wealth may have sources other than liquidity constraints. Table 3.3 reports the means of demographic variables for all non–business owners, all business owners, and the top 25 percent of business owners in the non-business wealth distribution (net worth minus business equity). It is obvious from the table that business owners are quite different from non–business owners and, furthermore, that wealthy business owners are quite different from less wealthy business owners.[7] Not only are business owners more likely to be male, white, and married than non–business owners, but they are also more likely to come from a more educated family (i.e., to have at least one parent with a high school diploma). Business owners also score higher on tests of cognitive ability (i.e., think more quickly and are better able to make analogies) and display stronger economic ties with family and relatives (i.e., are more likely both to receive money from and give money to family and relatives). Most important, compared to the rest of the population, they display different motives to save: they are less likely to be covered by a pension, and report a greater intention to bequeath an inheritance. These motives, per se, rationalize why they should hold more wealth than other households.

Even among business owners, differences are sharp. Wealthy business owners are more likely to have a college degree or postgraduate degree, and they score even higher on tests of cognitive ability than business owners in general. If educational status and cognitive abilities proxy for entrepreneurial talents, then our data show a correlation between wealth and these talents. There are also differences in family background; wealthy entrepreneurs are more likely to come from a family with higher levels of education, to have received money or major assets from relatives as well as inheritances, and to give financial help to their family in the future. They are also more likely to wish to leave a sizeable inheritance to their heirs.

Simple Facts about the Capital Needed to Start a Business

Data from the 1987 NSSBF provide a direct measure of the capital needed to start a business. Between 1980 and 1988, the median wealth utilized by individuals starting a business was $34,600. Close to 25 percent of small businesses were started with less than $8,000, and 75 percent of them were started with less than $95,000. Thus, it appears that the median household that starts a business needs little initial capital.

Meyer (1990) examines a similar question from the 1982 Characteristics of Business Owners data and reports even smaller figures for the capital needed to start a business. He shows that 63 percent of nonminority male business owners and 78 percent of black business owners indicated that they needed less than $5,000 to start their business (approximately $8,700 in 1996 dollars). Similar results are reported by Bhidé (2000), who examines the initial capital used by successful start-ups. Bhidé analyzes a sample of firms from *Inc. Magazine*, which tracks the five hundred fastest growing U.S. companies. He reports that 26 percent of the firms in his subsample started with less than $5,000 in up-front capital. Of all five hundred companies listed in *Inc.*, more than a third started their businesses with less than $10,000, and two-thirds with less than $50,000.

Note that, if liquidity constraints exist, they should be more likely to bind for those households that require a higher amount of capital to start a business. In a later section, we use NSSBF business equity information to segment the firms into two groups for analysis, firms that require low starting capital and firms that require high starting capital. We look first, however, at whether the fact that wealth is positively correlated with starting a business implies that liquidity constraints affect the decision to start a business.

ASSESSING THE IMPORTANCE OF LIQUIDITY CONSTRAINTS

We use data from the whole population to assess whether liquidity constraints prevent would-be entrepreneurs from starting a business. We use a variety of tests to assess the importance of liquidity constraints.

Wealth and the Transition into Entrepreneurship

To examine the relationship between household wealth and the transition into business ownership, we use data from the PSID for the time period 1984–1994. Of course, empirically testing the effects of liquidity constraints on entrepreneurship requires us to define both terms. We view liquidity constraints as the inability of households to borrow to finance their entrepreneurial projects. If starting capital is nontrivial, the inability to borrow constrains low-wealth households from starting a business, implying that the likelihood of small business formation should increase with wealth. Most important, if liquidity constraints are driving the positive correlation between household wealth and starting a business, then this relationship should vanish at high levels of wealth as the constraint ceases to bind. While we define entrepreneurs as those owing a business (irrespective of business wealth), as a robust check we also include in our definition of entrepreneurs those who are self-employed.[8]

To examine the role of initial wealth in the decision to start a business, we created a pooled sample of non–business owners from the 1989 and 1994 waves of the PSID. A household is defined as entering entrepreneurship if either the head of household or the spouse becomes a business owner in the subsequent one-year period. To eliminate households in which the head is still in school or is close to retirement, we restrict our sample to nonretired household heads between the ages of twenty-two and sixty. Our total sample has 7,645 observations.

As do other studies, we find that the effect of wealth on business entry is positive and statistically significant. However, the effect is economically small.[9,10] Increasing household wealth by $100,000 increases the probability of starting a business by less than one-half of one percentage point. With the base probability of becoming an entrepreneur in the subsequent year 4.5 percent, an increase in wealth of $100,000 increases the probability of business ownership only by 10 percent, from roughly 4.5 percent to 5 percent. Relative to both the mean and the median values of wealth for this sample, $100,000 represents a very large change in wealth.[11] It should be noted that our estimated magnitudes are similar to results reported by other authors who use different data sets, different sample periods, or different definitions of entrepreneurship.[12]

Furthermore, contrary to the theoretical predictions discussed above, we do not find the incremental impact of another dollar of wealth on the probability of starting a business to be a decreasing function of wealth. In fact, the predicted probability of starting a business estimated from the nonlinear model does not vary with wealth over most of the wealth distribution. We can demonstrate this point by rerunning our empirical specification discussed above, but replacing the level of net worth with a fifth-order polynomial.[13] These results are shown graphically in figure 3.1.[14] The estimated probability of starting a business for someone with $20,000 in wealth is nearly identical to the estimated probability of starting a business for someone with $200,000 in wealth (the estimates are 0.029 and 0.031 with standard errors of 0.003 and 0.005, respectively). It is only at the very top of the wealth distribution—above the 95th percentile (approximately $300,000 of wealth)—that the probability of starting a business becomes large. Given that the median amount of business capital needed to start a business is less than $23,000, our empirical findings cast doubts on whether liquidity constraints are driving the positive correlation between wealth and business start-ups. The positive association between wealth and business entry found in the linear model is simply driven by households at the top of the wealth distribution.

Parental Wealth and the Transition into Entrepreneurship

If liquidity constraints are important, there may be other means of acquiring the capital needed to start a business besides drawing on private savings. For example, households who come from wealthier families may be able to receive loans or financial support from their parents. In our analysis of how parental wealth affects entrepreneurship, we restrict our analysis to younger households because, for most of the older households, there is no information on parental wealth in the PSID. Our results indicate that parental wealth is a significant predictor of whether the child becomes an entrepreneur between 1989 and 1994.[15] As reported in table 3.4, when parental wealth increases by $100,000, the probability that the child becomes a business owner increases by 0.005 percent (an increase of 5.7 percent over the base probability of entering).

Upon further examination, it appears that the significance of parental wealth is not driven by the existence of binding liquidity constraints. We break down the parental wealth distribution into wealth quartiles and find a strong nonlinear relationship between wealth and business start-ups (see table 3.4, column II). The only parental wealth category that significantly predicts the probability that a child will become a business owner is the one for parents who have wealth in the top 3 percent of the parental wealth distribution. Having such rich parents increases the probability that the child will become a business owner by 7.2 percentage points over someone who has a parent with wealth in the bottom quintile of the parental wealth distribution. None of the other parental wealth categories significantly predicts child business ownership (up to the 97th percentile of the wealth distribution). Moreover, the coefficients are essentially flat between the 40th and 97th percentiles of the parental wealth distribution. Thus the lack of impact of parental wealth (more precisely, modest to large amounts of wealth) on the decision to start a business suggests that liquidity constraints are not an important deterrent to business ownership. However, one of the most striking results shown on table 3.4 is the relationship between parents who are entrepreneurs and children who are entrepreneurs. This table makes clear that having a parent who is an entrepreneur affects a child's entrepreneurial probability much more than having rich parents (i.e., parents whose wealth is between $100,000 and $200,000).

Wealth, the Transition into Entrepreneurship, and Business Type

Our findings thus far show that over most of the wealth distribution the probability of starting a business is flat, and that wealth appears to matter only for those households at the top of the wealth distribution. One possible explanation for this pattern is that little wealth is required to enter most entrepreneurial activities, but high capital requirements may render some activities accessible only to the very wealthy. In the presence of liquidity constraints, wealth should matter more for starting a business that requires a large initial capital investment than for starting one that requires a small initial capital investment. Using data from the NSSBF, we segment industries in the PSID by the amount of capital needed to start a business. On average, starting a business in the construction or service industries requires less than $20,000 in initial capital. Firms in all other industries require starting capital that ranges from double to triple that amount.[16] In the 1993 PSID data, 52.8 percent of businesses reported being in a low-starting-capital industry (service or construction). The number is close to the fraction of firms in the construction and service industries reported in the 1987 NSSBF (41.2 percent).

If liquidity constraints are a deterrent to business formation, we would expect a stronger positive relationship between wealth and business entry for those in a high-starting-capital industry than for those in a low-starting-capital industry. Our results show this is not the case.[17] The probability of starting a business in a high-starting-capital industry as a function of wealth is strikingly similar to the probability of starting a business in a low-starting-capital industry. The probability of starting a business in either a high- or a low-starting-capital industry does not increase until wealth reaches the top 5 percent of the distribution (above $280,000 in household wealth). Additionally, the marginal effect of wealth on the probability of starting a business in a high-starting-capital industry is nearly identical to that of starting a business in a low-starting-capital industry. A $10,000 increase in wealth decreases the probability of starting a business in a high-starting-capital industry, on average by 0.04 percentage points, whereas the comparable marginal effect for starting a business in a low-starting-capital industry is 0.06 percentage points. Moreover, there is no statistical difference between someone with $15,000 in wealth and someone with $150,000 in wealth. Thus, we do not find any effect of wealth on the probability of business ownership, even when looking at industries where the constraints should bind the most.

Wealth and the Transition into Entrepreneurship in Subsamples of Households More Likely to be Liquidity Constrained

In this subsection, we look at the effect of initial wealth as well as change in wealth on the decision to become an entrepreneur for those groups of non–business owners who are more likely to be liquidity constrained, such as young, black, and female entrepreneurs.[18] All of these groups have substantially lower earnings than their more advantaged counterparts. Women earn about two-thirds of what men earn,[19] while blacks, unconditionally, earn about two-thirds to three-quarters of what whites earn,[20] and have substantially lower levels of assets than whites.[21] Theory predicts that there should be a greater positive relationship between wealth and the transition into entrepreneurship when liquidity constraints are more likely to bind. To test this prediction, we look at wealth changes in addition to wealth levels.

When we consider the transition into entrepreneurship for young households in the PSID (younger than forty in 1989), we find that net wealth is not statistically significant (table 3.5). This result is not sensitive to the age cutoff imposed on the data since the result remains insignificant when we restrict our samples to households less than thirty-five years of age or thirty years of age. Wealth and the change in wealth are also not statistically significant for black entrepreneurs or for female entrepreneurs (table 3.5). These findings are consistent with the results presented in other papers. Meyer (1990), for example, using several data sets and focusing on black entrepreneurs, does not find any evidence that financial resources play a role in explaining the transition into entrepreneurship. This is an interesting result given that minority business owners are thought to be more likely to be liquidity constrained. Similarly, Dunn and Holtz-Eakin (1995) finds only weak evidence that wealth affects entrepreneurship among the young (both male and female young entrepreneurs). Coleman (2004) also finds limited evidence of liquidity constraints for female entrepreneurs.

Inheritance and the Propensity to Start a Business

One problem with these types of tests, as mentioned before, is that wealth may proxy for something else (for example, talents). Several authors have recognized this problem and propose alternative measures of liquidity. Both Blanchflower and Oswald (1998) and Holtz-Eakin, Joulfaian, and Rosen (1994a) used inheritances in place of wealth. They show that those households that receive inheritances are more likely to start a business and succeed in entrepreneurship. These findings have been generally interpreted—both by economists and the SBA—as supporting the relevance of liquidity constraints to entrepreneurship.

But there are several ways to interpret the correlation between wealth and the transition into and out of entrepreneurship. First, tax reasons cause many small and mid-size businesses to be transferred at the time of death; many families simply pass on their business to their heirs. Thus, the correlation between the receipt of inheritances and entrepreneurship may capture simply the correlation in intergenerational wealth and occupations, and not the existence of liquidity constraints.[22]

Second, the receipt of an inheritance is not necessarily a random event. Households that receive inheritances are much more likely to come from wealthy families. Thus, the correlation may capture simply the nonlinear relationship between wealth and business entry we discussed before. Moreover, given the strong intergenerational correlation in education and saving preferences, households receiving inheritances may simply display different entrepreneurial propensities than households that do not receive inheritances.

We can provide several pieces of evidence supporting these claims. First, people who receive inheritances generally already have enough money to start a business.[23] Second, and more important, if inheritances represent just liquidity, inheritances received in the past should predict current business entry, whereas future inheritances should not. Using data from the PSID, we find that, as in the previous work, inheritances do indeed correlate with starting a business. However, not only past inheritances matter; future inheritances (inheritances received after starting a business) are also correlated with the probability of starting a business today.[24] This shows that the timing of inheritances is not crucial for new business formation, and thus that the receipt of inheritances is proxying for something other than changes in household liquidity. In the next section, we propose an alternative measure of liquidity.

Housing Capital Gains and the Transition into Entrepreneurship

During the mid-1980s, U.S. housing prices increased considerably, often delivering large capital gains to many households. To capture changes in wealth experienced by most households, not simply those at the top of the wealth distribution, we explore regional changes in housing prices as a better and more exogenous measure of liquidity.

Two considerations with respect to the housing capital gain variable are noteworthy. First, if potential entrepreneurs intend to use home equity to surmount liquidity constraints, it is not important whether households perceive these changes in housing prices to be transitory or permanent. As long as lenders are willing to lend to households on the basis of their housing equity, households can borrow against their increased housing equity to relax any liquidity constraints they face. This notion is supported by empirical evidence that lenders are willing to lend (and households are willing to borrow) when households experience large capital gains on housing.[25] Second, regional movement in business conditions could change both housing prices and the desire of households in a given region to become business owners. If this latent unobserved variable results in a positive correlation between housing prices and the propensity to start a business, our approach will be biased toward finding an effect of wealth on business creation.

We find that the correlation between housing capital gains and business start-ups is not statistically different from zero.[26] Thus, when we consider a more exogenous variable than wealth or inheritances to measure liquidity constraints, our estimates offer little support in favor of liquidity constraints. Those households who become wealthier because of capital gains on their homes are no more likely to start a business than those who enjoy lower or zero wealth increases.

Liquidity Constraints and Business Survival

Having explored the effect of liquidity constraints on the formation of businesses, we now ask whether liquidity constraints affect the survival of businesses.

If entrepreneurs cannot borrow to attain their profit-maximizing levels of capital, they may start under-capitalized businesses that are less likely to be profitable. Thus, entrepreneurs who have substantial personal financial resources may be more likely to survive. As reported below, our results show otherwise.

We again explore the panel aspect of the PSID. As we did after our previous tests, we find that neither the one-year survival nor the five-year survival is significantly correlated with personal wealth (see table 3.6). We then investigate the relationship between business survival and parental wealth and find a significant positive correlation. However, parental wealth is significant for the one-year survival only for those at the top 20 percent of the parental wealth distribution. For the five-year survival, parental wealth is significant for those in the middle of the parental wealth distribution and those above the median value of parental wealth. These results are broadly consistent with the work of Holtz-Eakin, Joulfaian, and Rosen (1994a). While they find that the coefficient of household wealth is significant statistically, it is essentially zero. According to their finding, a $100,000 inheritance increases the probability of survival by only 0.009 percentage points, where the base survival rate for their sample was 0.730.

Our findings show both that personal wealth does not correlate with business survival, and that although parental wealth correlates with business survival positively, it is mainly driven by the wealthy.

CONCLUSION

Several studies have documented the positive relationship between wealth and the likelihood of starting a business. This association has been read as evidence that liquidity constraints are a deterrent to new business formation. But this conclusion is premature. Throughout most of the wealth distribution (up through $200,000 in household wealth), there is no discernible relationship between household wealth and the probability of starting a business. Only for households at the very top of the wealth distribution is there a strong and positive relationship between wealth and business entry.

Data on capital requirements for start-ups in different industries and among different groups, on the timing of inheritances, and on the experience of households that enjoyed capital gains on their homes provide further evidence that high levels of liquidity are not essential for starting a small business. They also show that the survival of businesses is not affected by the wealth of the entrepreneurs.

Our results do not imply that any given household wanting to start a small business has unlimited access to credit at reasonable borrowing rates. Given optimal lender behavior and common sense, such results would be implausible. We do conclude, however, that even if some households that want to start small businesses are currently constrained in their borrowing, such constraints are not empirically important in deterring the majority of small business formation in the United States. This finding may simply reflect the fact that the starting capital required for most businesses is sufficiently small. We provide evidence to this effect throughout the chapter. Alternatively, even if the required starting capital for some small businesses is high, existing institutions and lending markets in the United States appear to work sufficiently well at funneling funds to households with worthy entrepreneurial projects.

Linear Wealth Model (Solid Line), Nonlinear Wealth Model (Dotted Line), and Wealth Dummy Model (Dashed Line)

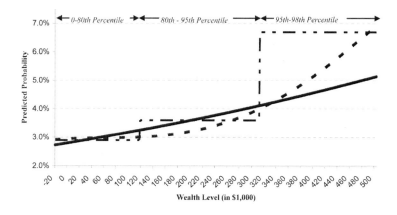

Notes: Sample includes all PSID non-business-owning households in the pooled 1989/1994 sample. This figure displays the predicted probability of starting a business using a nonlinear wealth model using a 5th order polynomial in wealth.

FIGURE 3.1.
The Predicted Probability of Entrepreneurship as a Function of Wealth

Table 3.1. Percentage of Entrepreneurs and Entrepreneurs with Zero Business Equity in the PSID, HRS, and NLSY Wealth Distributions

PANEL A:	1989 Panel Study of Income Dynamics (PSID)	
Wealth Distribution (upper cutoff in parentheses)	Percentage of Entrepreneurs in the Wealth Distribution	Percentage of Entrepreneurs (out of total entrepreneurs) with Zero Business Equity in the Wealth Distribution
Quintile 1 ($2,800)	4.0 (19.7)	35.6 (48.2)
Quintile 2 (25,400)	5.9 (23.6)	44.6 (49.9)
Quintile 3 (75,500)	10.5 (30.6)	19.8 (39.9)
Quintile 4 (199,000)	12.4 (32.9)	20.3 (40.3)
80th–90th percentile (359,200)	27.7 (44.8)	12.1 (32.6)
90th–97th percentile (793,800)	31.9 (46.4)	12.2 (32.9)
Above 97th percentile	62.1 (48.6)	6.2 (24.2)

Notes: Data from the 1989 full sample of PSID respondents. Data weighted using PSID core sample weights.
Standard deviations are in parentheses. All dollar values reported in 1996 dollars.

PANEL B:	1992 Health and Retirement Study (HRS)	
Wealth Distribution (upper cutoff in parentheses)	Percentage of Entrepreneurs in the Wealth Distribution	Percentage of Entrepreneurs (out of total entrepreneurs) with Zero Business Equity in the Wealth Distribution
Quintile 1 ($20,132)	4.4 (20.6)	54.4 (50.2)
Quintile 2 (74,900)	7.7 (26.7)	37.0 (48.5)
Quintile 3 (151,100)	14.3 (35.0)	28.4 (45.3)
Quintile 4 (309,100)	22.6 (41.8)	19.9 (40.0)
80th–90th percentile (541,900)	32.8 (47.0)	11.6 (32.1)
90th–97th percentile (1,433,800)	53.0 (50.0)	9.0 (28.7)
Above 97th percentile	80.6 (39.6)	3.9 (19.3)

Notes: Data from the 1992 full sample of HRS households. Data weighted using HRS sample weights.
Standard deviations are in parentheses. All dollar values reported in 1996 dollars.

PANEL C: 1997 National Longitudinal Survey of Youth (NLSY)		
Wealth Distribution (upper cutoff in parentheses)	Percentage of Entrepreneurs in the Wealth Distribution	Percentage of Entrepreneurs (out of total entrepreneurs) with Zero Business Equity in the Wealth Distribution
Quintile 1 ($1,500)	2.9 (16.7)	46.2 (50.8)
Quintile 2 (20,500)	3.8 (19.2)	46.0 (50.6)
Quintile 3 (58,700)	8.7 (28.2)	33.0 (47.3)
Quintile 4 (147,700)	10.9 (31.3)	25.0 (43.5)
80th–90th percentile (279,700)	22.7 (42.0)	14.8 (35.7)
90th–97th percentile (716,900)	34.4 (47.6)	10.5 (30.8)
Above 97th percentile	80.7 (39.6)	4.3 (20.4)

Notes: Data from the 1997 full sample of NLSY parents. Data weighted using NLSY97 sample weights.
Standard deviations are in parentheses. All dollar values reported in 1996 dollars.

**Table 3.2.   Distribution of Business Equity for Business
Owners in the PSID, HRS, and NLSY**

PANEL A: 1989 Panel Study of Income Dynamics

Percentile of Business Wealth for Business Owners	Business Wealth Value
20th Percentile	$0
40th Percentile	6,300
50th Percentile	18,900
60th Percentile	44,000
80th Percentile	125,800
90th Percentile	352,300
97th Percentile	1,258,100
Mean	$219,000
Percentage with Zero Business Equity	30.1
Percentage with Less than $5000 in Business Equity	38.0
Number of Households	1,100
Percentage of Total Sample that are Business Owners	13.1

Notes: Data from the 1989 PSID. Sample restricted to include all PSID respondents who reported owning a business in 1989. Data weighted using PSID core sample weights. All values are in 1996 dollars.

PANEL B: 1992 Health and Retirement Study

Percentile of Business Wealth for Business Owners	Business Wealth Value
20th Percentile	$560
40th Percentile	22,370
50th Percentile	53,680
60th Percentile	83,880
80th Percentile	251,640
90th Percentile	559,200
97th Percentile	1,677,600
Mean	$249,200
Percentage with Zero Business Equity	18.6
Percentage with Less than $5000 in Business Equity	25.3
Number of Households	1,038
Percentage of Total Sample that are Business Owners	19.22

Notes: Data from the 1992 HRS. Sample restricted to include all HRS respondents who reported owning a business in 1992. Data weighted using HRS sample weights. All values are in 1996 dollars.

PANEL C: 1997 National Longitudinal Survey of Youth

Percentile of Business Wealth for Business Owners	Business Wealth Value
20th Percentile	$0
40th Percentile	10,760
50th Percentile	34,230
60th Percentile	90,760
80th Percentile	422,500
90th Percentile	880,200
97th Percentile	1,799,520
Mean	$505,210
Percentage with Zero Business Equity	19.65
Percentage with Less than $5000 in Business Equity	30.23
Number of Households	546
Percentage of Total Sample that are Business Owners	12.4

Notes: Data from the 1997 NLSY. Sample includes all NLSY respondents who reported owning a business in 1997. Data weighted using NLSY sample weights. All values are in 1996 dollars.

Table 3.3. Means of Descriptive Variables for Nonentrepreneurs, Entrepreneurs, and Wealthy Entrepreneurs in the 1992 HRS Sample

Variables	(I) Non-Business Owners	(II) All-Business Owners	(III) Wealthy Businsss Owners	t-stat: Diff (I) (II)	t-stat: Diff (II) -(III)
	(1,038 obs)	(4,790 obs)	(237 obs)		
Age of Respondent	54.9	54.6	55.5	2.71	-4.09
Percentage Male	47.2	59.6	66.6	-7.43	-2.42
Percentage Hispanic	8.8	3.5	0.9	6.28	2.86
Percentage Black	11.8	4.1	1.8	10.21	2.32
Percentage with High School Diploma	37.5	31.7	23.1	2.43	3.00
Percentage with Some College Education	18.9	28.2	28.0	-7.13	0.32
Percentage with College Education	11.1	14.2	19.1	-3.71	-2.93
Percentage with More Than a College Education	8.6	14.1	22.8	-5.74	-4.79
Percentage Married	62.4	82.5	85.6	-13.04	-1.71
Percentage in Excellent Health	23.4	34.7	44.1	-8.30	-3.03
Percentage Who Are the Most Risk Averse	61.6	60.2	61.1	0.47	-0.53
Percentage Who Are the Least Risk Averse	11.9	13.3	14.4	-0.43	-0.63
Score on Ability to Think Quickly (5 is highest score)	3.7	4.0	4.1	-9.95	-2.18
Score on Memory Test (# of words one can recall)	13.0	14.2	14.4	-7.91	-1.28
Score on Analogy Test (# of correct answers)	6.30	7.00	7.2	-8.25	-1.93
Percentage Who Experienced Unemployment in the Past	34.3	22.2	10.8	7.91	4.92
Percentage Who Experienced Negative Financial Shocks in Past	32.6	35.7	24.9	-1.85	3.78
Percentage w/at Least One Parent w/High School Diploma	44.7	59.7	66.7	-10.15	-2.95
Probability of Giving Financial Help to Family in Next 10 Years	39.1	43.9	49.2	-4.11	-2.54
Percentage Who Received an Insurance Settlement	5.5	4.5	3.5	0.94	0.017
Percentage Who Received Money or Major Assets from Relatives	7.1	12.3	19.3	-6.22	-4.13
Percentage Who Received Inheritances	18.4	26.8	32.3	-7.47	-2.55
Percentage Who Expect to Leave a Sizeable Inheritance to Heirs	39.3	55.0	80.1	-9.61	-9.40
Percentage Who Have a Pension	54.3	31.1	31.2	12.12	0.061
Total Family Income	46,920	78,083	138,128	-18.17	-14.54
Business Equity	0	249,204	590,740	-25.90	-9.58

Notes: Data is from the 1992 sample of HRS households. Data weighted using HRS sample weights. All values are reported in 1996 dollars. Because of missing values, the means of some variables are reported for smaller sample sizes than the one reported in this table. "Wealthy business owners" refers to business owners who are in the top quartile of business owners' nonbusiness wealth distribution.

Table 3.4. Who Becomes an Entrepreneur? The Effect of Parental Wealth and Occupation in Younger Households: Linear Probability Regressions

Variables	I	II
Include a full set of income and demographic controls?	Yes	Yes
Household's Own Nonbusiness Net Worth in 1989 (in $100,000)	0.008	0.009
	(0.007)	(0.007)
Dummy: Husband's/Wife's Father is a Business Owner	**0.048**	**0.049**
	(0.023)	**(0.023)**
Total Net Worth of Both Husband's and Wife's Parents (in $100,000)	**0.005**	
	(0.003)	
Dummy: Parental Wealth 20th–40th percentile	-	0.024
	-	(0.020)
Dummy: Parental Wealth 40th–60th percentile	-	0.002
	-	(0.018)
Dummy: Parental Wealth 60th–80th percentile	-	0.021
	-	(0.019)
Dummy: Parental Wealth 80th–90th percentile	-	0.032
	-	(0.021)
Dummy: Parental Wealth 90th–97th percentile	-	0.025
	-	(0.024)
Dummy: Parental Wealth > 97th percentile	-	**0.072**
	-	**(0.039)**

Notes: This table reports linear probability estimates of the transition into business ownership in the subsequent year. Regressions include controls for demographics (age, education, family composition), current and past income, employment status, past business ownership, and whether the husband's and wife's parents are alive. Sample includes all PSID non–business owners in 1989 between the ages of twenty-two and forty-five who were not retired. The top 1 percent of both household and parental wealth distribution was truncated. The number of observations is 2,829. Standard errors are in parentheses. Coefficients in bold are significant at the 10 percent level.

Table 3.5. Who Becomes an Entrepreneur? The Effect of Household Wealth: Linear Probability Regressions on Alternate Samples

OLS Regressions/Samples:	Coefficient on Household Wealth I	Coefficient on Changes in Household Wealth II
Dependent Variable: Households That Become Business Owners By 1994		
a. Young Sample	1.12 E-7	-2.19 E-7
	(1.11 E-7)	(2.71 E-7)
b. Black Sample	4.83 E-8	-2.39 E-7
	(1.78 E-7)	(1.97 E-7)
c. Female Sample	-1.04 E-7	1.69 E-7
	(8.31 E-8)	(2.04 E-7)

Notes: This table reports the results of a regression of the probability that a household enters entrepreneurship between 1989 and 1994 on household wealth in 1989 and many other demographic and income controls for young, black, and female-headed households. In column II, it reports the results of a similar regression, but using changes in wealth rather than wealth levels. Regressions include controls for demographics (age, education, family composition), current and past income, employment status, and past business ownership. The sample used to perform the regression in column I is restricted to all nonretired households in the PSID between the age of twenty-two and forty who did not own a business in 1989. The sample used to perform the regression in column II is restricted to all nonretired households in the PSID between the age of twenty-two and forty who did not own a business in 1989, who were in the sample in 1984, and who did not own a business during that year. Young households are defined as households whose head is between the age of twenty-two and forty in 1989 (2,452 observations for regression I and 2,083 observations for regression II). Black households are those where the head of the household is black (1,351 observations for regression I and 1,261 observations for regression II). Female households refer to households where the head is female (821 observations for regression I and 757 observations for regression II). Standard errors are in parentheses.

Table 3.6. Who Survives as Entrepreneur? The Effect of Personal and Parental Net Worth: Linear Regressions of One-Year and Five-Year Business Survival Probabilities

Variables	One-Year Survival Regressions		Five-Year Survival Regressions	
	1	II	III	IV
Include Demographic and Income Controls?	Yes	Yes	Yes	Yes
Household's Own Nonbusiness Net Worth in 1989	1.50 E-7	–	1.20 E-7	–
	(2.08 E-7)	–	(1.45 E-7)	–
Dummy: Household Wealth 20th–40th percentile	–	-0.028	–	0.029
	–	(0.058)	–	(0.040)
Dummy: Household Wealth 40th–60th percentile	–	0.079	–	0.088
	–	(0.061)	–	(0.045)
Dummy: Household Wealth 60th–80th percentile	–	0.104	–	0.020
	–	(0.069)	–	(0.049)
Dummy: Household Wealth 80th–90th percentile	–	0.101	–	0.158
	–	(0.086)	–	(0.073)
Dummy: Household Wealth 90th–97th percentile	–	0.136	–	0.075
	–	(0.105)	–	(0.081)
Dummy: Household Wealth > 97th percentile	–	-0.093	–	0.080
	–	(0.156)	–	(0.101)
Dummy: Husband's/Wife's Father Is a Business Owner	-0.026	-0.026	0.029	0.027
	(0.073)	(0.073)	(0.063)	(0.063)
Total Net Worth of Both Husband's and Wife's Parents	2.91 E-7	–	1.42 E-7	–
	(7.76 E-8)	–	(6.10 E-8)	–
Dummy: Parental Wealth 20th–40th percentile	–	-0.138	–	-0.024
	–	(0.063)	–	(0.039)
Dummy: Parental Wealth 40th–60th percentile	–	0.049	–	0.013
	–	(0.068)	–	(0.042)
Dummy: Parental Wealth 60th–80th percentile	–	0.010	–	**0.082**
	–	(0.068)	–	**(0.048)**
Dummy: Parental Wealth 80th–90th percentile	–	**0.110**	–	**0.149**
	–	**(0.067)**	–	**(0.056)**
Dummy: Parental Wealth 90th–97th percentile	–	**0.170**	–	0.087
	–	**(0.085)**	–	(0.071)
Dummy: Parental Wealth > 97th percentile	–	**0.282**	–	0.112
	–	**(0.167)**	–	(0.116)
Mean of Dependent of Variable	0.458	0.458	0.167	0.167

Notes: This table reports the results of a regression of the probability of one-year survival (whether new business owners remained in business one year later) and five-year survival (whether new business owners remained in business five years later) on household wealth, parental wealth, and other controls. The controls include age, age squared, marital status, race, educational attainment, average income for the three years prior to becoming a business owner, income squared, time dummies for the year the household became a business owner, and a dummy for whether the household's parents are alive. All demographic controls were dated as of the year the household became a business owner. The sample is restricted to all PSID households who became a business owner between 1984 and 1989, were not business owners two years before starting the business, and remained in the sample for at least five years after starting the business. Personal and parental wealth are truncated at the top 1 percent. The number of observations is 931. Standard errors are in parentheses. Coefficients in bold are significant at the 10 percent level.

NOTES

* This chapter was originally written as a paper to be presented at a conference on savings and entrepreneurship organized by the Hudson Institute in Washington, D.C. It draws heavily on our work published in the April 2004 issue of the *Journal of Political Economy*. We thank our discussant, Petra Todd, and conference participants for many suggestions and comments. Financial support from the Polsky Center for Entrepreneurship at the University of Chicago Graduate School of Business via a grant from the Ewing Marion Kauffman Foundation is gratefully acknowledged. Yuni Yan provided excellent research assistance. Any errors are our responsibility.

1. As we discuss later, there is no clear-cut definition of entrepreneurs. We here use *entrepreneurs* and *business owners* interchangeably.

2. See SBA's overview and history at <http://www.sba.gov/aboutsba/history.html>.

3. See Gentry and Hubbard (2004) and the references therein.

4. See, for example, Gentry and Hubbard (2004), Quadrini (1999), and Cagetti and DeNardi (2004).

5. Total household wealth is defined as the sum of savings and checking accounts, bonds, stocks, IRAs, housing equity, other real estate, business equity, and vehicles, minus all debt.

6. All dollar amounts in this paper (including the tables) are reported in 1996 dollars unless otherwise indicated.

7. Differences between entrepreneurs and nonentrepreneurs found in the HRS data are similar to differences found in the PSID and NLSY samples. For brevity, we report only the HRS results. We focus on the HRS sample because of the richness of data on attitudes toward risk, motives to save, and intergenerational transfers.

8. The main results of this paper are unaffected by whether we classify entrepreneurs as business owners or as self-employed.

9. Erik Hurst and Annamaria Lusardi, "Liquidity constraints, household wealth and entrepreneurship," *Journal of Political Economy* 112 (April 2004): table 3.2, column 1.

10. Household net worth excludes business equity. In addition to wealth, the controls included in the regression include a quadratic in age; a series of education, race, and family structure dummies; a quadratic in household labor income; dummies for whether the household head is currently unemployed or was unemployed any time in the prior five years; and a dummy for whether the household was a business owner any time in the prior five years.

11. Hurst and Lusardi, "Liquidity constraints," table 3.1.

12. Evans and Jovanovic (1989); Evans and Leighton (1989); Holtz-Eakin, Joulfaian, and Rosen (1994b); Fairlie (1999); Quadrini (1999); and Gentry and Hubbard (2004).

13. Hurst and Lusardi, "Liquidity constraints," table 3.2, column II.

14. This figure is the same as figure 1 in Hurst and Lusardi (2004). To create the figure, we fitted the regression using the mean levels of all the other control variables aside from net worth. We also plotted two separate specifications in figure 1: a linear specification and a specification where we included dummies for being in either the 80th–95th percentiles of the wealth distribution or the top 5 percentiles of the wealth distribution. See Hurst and Lusardi (2004) for additional details.

15. This is true after controlling for parental self-employment status, which is a very significant predictor of whether the child becomes an entrepreneur.

16. Hurst and Lusardi, "Liquidity constraints," table A1.

17. Hurst and Lusardi, "Liquidity constraints," figure 2.

18. Fairlie, forthcoming.

19. U.S. Bureau of the Census, 2004.

20. U.S. Bureau of the Census, 2003.

21. Robert W. Fairlie, "The absence of the African-American owned business: An analysis of the dynamics of self-employment," *Journal of Labor Economics* 17 (January 1999): 80–108.

22. Kerwin Kofi Charles and Erik Hurst, "The correlation of wealth across generations," *Journal of Political Economy* 111 (December 2003): 1155–82.

23. Douglas Holtz-Eakin, David Joulfaian, and Harvey S. Rosen, "Sticking it out: Entrepreneurial survival and liquidity constraints," *Journal of Political Economy* 102 (February 1994a): 53–75.

24. Hurst and Lusardi, "Liquidity constraints," table 3.3.

25. Erik Hurst and Frank P. Stafford, "Home is where the equity is: Liquidity constraints, mortgage refinancing and consumption," *Journal of Money, Credit, and Banking* 36, no. 6 (2004): 985–1014.

26. Hurst and Lusardi, "Liquidity constraints,' table 3.3.

4

Federal Tax Policy
and Small Business

DONALD J. BRUCE AND TAMI GURLEY-CALVEZ*

INTRODUCTION

Entrepreneurs are in the hearts and minds of policymakers, largely because of their importance to the economy. Since small businesses provide much of the energy behind job creation and overall economic growth, researchers and policymakers alike are increasingly concerned about potential barriers to entrepreneurial entry and survival. Recent work has considered such important potential obstacles as access to start-up financial or human capital. Recognizing the limited policy solutions to overcoming so-called liquidity constraints, researchers have placed increasing emphasis on tax policies affecting entrepreneurs.

In this chapter, we describe the tax treatment of entrepreneurs in the United States and examine recent trends in small-business activity. We then ask the critical question of whether small businesses should be tax favored. Regardless of one's stance on this issue, the effectiveness of any tax policies intended to encourage entrepreneurial activity ultimately hinges on the extent to which potential entrepreneurs actually respond to those policies.

We discuss recent empirical research on the extent to which tax rate changes influence small-business start-up and survival rates. We draw on a

rich twelve-year panel of individual tax return data (from 1979 to 1990) to explore this issue, since the Internal Revenue Service (IRS) Statistics of Income
data reveal that nearly four out of every five businesses pay taxes through the
individual tax system (see below). Our chapter concludes with an exploration
of the small business implications of recent proposals from the President's Advisory Panel on Federal Tax Reform.

MEASURING ENTREPRENEURIAL ACTIVITY

The Small Business Administration (SBA) generally defines small businesses
as those with fewer than five hundred employees, although more detailed
small-business size standards exist at the industry level. According to the SBA,
small businesses represent 99.7 percent of all employers, employ half of all
private-sector employees, pay 45 percent of total payroll costs, and generate
between 60 and 80 percent of new jobs.[1]

Most casual observers consider small businesses—and entrepreneurs
more specifically—to be much smaller than the SBA standards. Researchers
continue to debate the relative merits of various measures of entrepreneurial
activity, and it is doubtful whether any universally acceptable measure will
ever exist. The vast majority of the economic research in this area has relied
on self-reported self-employment status from individual survey data. A
growing number of studies, including ours, have turned to tax return data
where entrepreneurial status can be inferred from the presence of income
from a small business or profession (Schedule C), partnership or small-
business corporation (Schedule E), or other sources such as rent and royalty
income (Schedule E).

As shown in figure 4.1, the number of individual income tax returns with
a Schedule C has been increasing in recent years, more than doubling between
1980 and 2005. Further, while only about 10 percent of individual returns included a Schedule C in 1980, more than one in seven did so in 2005.

The next few figures display the overall importance of small businesses using tax-based measures. In figure 4.2, we see that noncorporate entities (including Schedule C sole proprietorships, partnerships, and subchapter S
corporations) are a very large and growing share of the total number of business tax returns. Corporate tax returns fell from just over 10 percent of all returns in 1994 to about 8 percent in 2002. Nonfarm sole proprietorships have
consistently represented more than 70 percent of the total, although that share

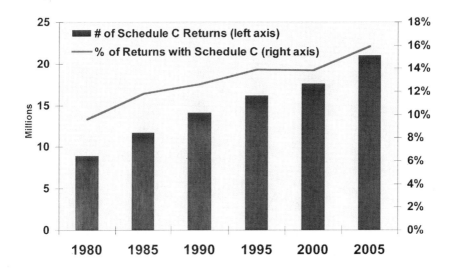

Source: IRS Statistics of Income.
Note: 2005 entries are estimates.

FIGURE 4.1.
Recent Trends in Schedule C Returns, 1980–2005

has fallen slightly with the advent of limited-liability partnerships and corporations in recent years.

Despite the impressive numbers of sole proprietorships, they represent only a small share of total business income. As shown in figure 4.3, sole proprietorships typically contribute less than 5 percent of total business receipts. Indeed, all noncorporate forms contribute less than one-third of total receipts. Interestingly, the distribution of taxable profits in figure 4.4 does not necessarily reflect the distribution of total receipts.

As shown in figure 4.4, the corporate share of total taxable profits has declined dramatically from more than 60 percent in 1996 to less than one-half in 2002. Noncorporate forms, especially partnerships, have picked up the slack, likely as a result of the emergence of limited-liability partnerships during this period. While sole proprietors bring in less than 5 percent of total receipts, however, they report more than one-sixth of total taxable profits. Unfortunately, the distribution of total taxes paid is unavailable.

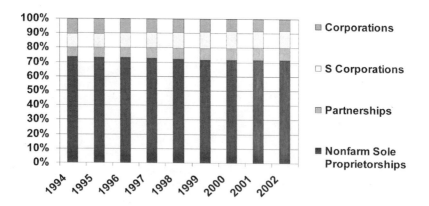

Source: IRS Statistics of Income.

Note: "Corporations" excludes S Corporations, Real Estate Investment Trusts (REITs), and Regulated
Investment Companies (RICs).

FIGURE 4.2.
Distribution of Business Tax Returns, 1994–2002

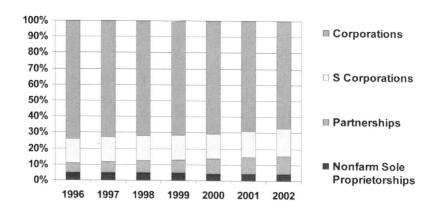

Source: IRS Statistics of Income.

Note: "Corporations" excludes S Corporations, Real Estate Investment Trusts (REITs), and Regulated
Investment Companies (RICs).

FIGURE 4.3.
Distribution of Total Business Receipts, 1996–2002

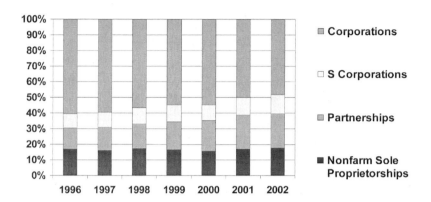

Source: IRS Statistics of Income.
Note: "Corporations" excludes S Corporations, Real Estate Investment Trusts (REITs), and Regulated
Investment Companies (RICs).

FIGURE 4.4.
Distribution of Total Business Taxable Profits, 1996–2002

Taxing Small Businesses

Given that the vast majority of businesses (as judged from tax return data) are nonfarm sole proprietorships and pass-through entities such as partnerships and subchapter S corporations, most businesses and virtually all small businesses pay their taxes through the individual income tax. A lack of third-party withholding and reporting results in an income tax system that effectively treats entrepreneurs differently from wage workers. While a different tax rate structure does not apply to small businesses reporting on individual income tax forms, the ability to deduct certain consumption expenses, such as office supplies and automobiles, as business expenses can result in differential taxation of similarly situated individuals.

Other features, such as differential deductibility of health insurance premiums and differential compliance costs, contribute to the tax wedge between wage workers and entrepreneurs.[2] For example, employees in a large firm typically pay their share of health insurance premiums out of pretax dollars (i.e., before income and payroll taxes are taken out), while health insurance premiums for self-employed workers are only deductible for income (not payroll) tax purposes.

Another important form of horizontal inequity from the income tax comes about if small businesses engage in more tax evasion or avoidance. Entrepreneurs are frequently portrayed as being more likely than other taxpayers to engage in tax evasion, either by underreporting income or over-reporting business expenses.[3] We know better than to attempt to refute this, but it is important to highlight two other important sources of the oft-cited tax gap attributed to small businesses. First, complexity in the tax code and differential compliance costs surely result in many honest mistakes on entrepreneurial tax returns. Second, those same features lead more small business filers to seek paid assistance with their tax returns, thus enabling them to learn more about legal ways to reduce their tax bills.[4]

The payroll tax is receiving more and more attention as a source of differential taxation between wage workers and self-employed workers. For wage workers, the statutory burden of the payroll tax is split evenly between the worker and his or her employer. At today's rates, for example, employers pay 7.65 percent directly and take the other 7.65 percent out of the worker's pay.[5] Self-employed workers are inherently playing both roles, employee and employer, so they have to pay both halves of the tax. Of course, self-employed workers were not actually subject to the payroll tax (implemented for wage workers in 1937) until 1951, and for many years were taxed at favorable rates (see figure 4.5). Changes enacted in 1984 phased in roughly equal treatment of self-employed and wage workers, with the self-employed now responsible for the equivalent of the sum of the employer and employee shares of the payroll tax burden. This exogenous change in the relative tax treatment of the self-employed during the 1980s, part of a large-scale leveling of the tax playing field across various types of taxpayers, will figure prominently in our empirical analysis below.

While the vast majority of recent studies in this literature have focused on income and payroll taxes, it is important to realize that small businesses face many more taxes on a daily basis. Included are the corporate income tax (for those that incorporate), unemployment insurance and worker's compensation taxes, the potentially short-lived estate tax, and a menu of state and local taxes. Cline, Neubig, and Phillips (2006) show that state and local property taxes and sales taxes make up about 60 percent of the total business tax burden at the subfederal level, with more traditional corporate and individual income taxes and payroll taxes making up less than 20 percent of the total.

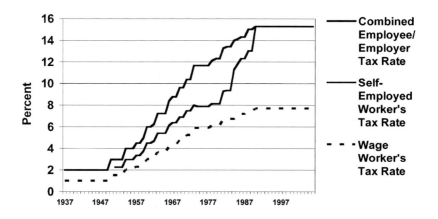

Note: The wage worker's tax rate is half of the combined employee/employer tax rate.

FIGURE 4.5.
Payroll Tax Rates, 1937–2006

Preferential Tax Treatment for Entrepreneurs

Policymakers often fall victim to blind allegiance to the American entrepreneur. Indeed, small businesses have achieved favored political status rivaled only by the Social Security program, the mortgage interest deduction, and schoolchildren. As researchers, we must critically evaluate the case for tax breaks for small businesses. Holtz-Eakin (1995) provides a nice overview of the issues at hand. The author's central conclusion is that the current literature does not provide sufficient evidence to support using the tax code to target subsidies toward small businesses. We highlight his main points here and add a few of our own.

First, small businesses might warrant favorable tax treatment if they create net positive spillover benefits to the economy and to society. While recent research has explored the role of small business in overall job creation and economic growth, little is known about the impact of frequently short-lived small businesses—and common occurrences of bankruptcy—on social well-being. The true net impact of small businesses on the economy has not been assessed, and we will not attempt such a calculation here. Our intent is only to point out that the net impact is not necessarily positive.

Second, favorable tax treatment might be necessary if binding liquidity constraints (i.e., imperfect access to financial capital) result in a supply of entrepreneurial ventures that is less than socially optimal. A raft of recent studies has found that access to financial capital is vitally important in the small business start-up process.[6] A lack of evidence on the socially optimal amount of entrepreneurship makes this evidence less useful, however. On one hand, binding liquidity constraints help ensure that only the most financially viable enterprises are undertaken. On the other hand, many perfectly good ideas have fallen by the wayside as a result of insufficient funding.

On that note, a third possible reason for favorable tax treatment for small businesses involves the extent to which riskiness deters entrepreneurial entry. If entrepreneurial ventures involve inherently greater risk than wage and salary employment, and if potential entrepreneurs are risk averse, then a freely operating market might not generate a sufficient number of new businesses. Domar and Musgrave (1944) show how progressive tax systems can provide insurance against risk by compressing the distribution of after-tax returns. In that sense, our tax system already provides some measure of risk reduction that benefits all potential entrepreneurs.

Fourth, as discussed above, tax code complexity might in itself result in an insufficient amount of entrepreneurial activity if potential entrants are deterred by seemingly insurmountable compliance burdens. Favorable tax treatment may in fact be warranted, if only to offset that barrier to entry. That said, the most complex features of the tax code often reward entrepreneurs by lowering their final tax burdens. The net impact of complexity on entrepreneurial activity is therefore unknown.

As summarized by Holtz-Eakin (1995), the case for favorable tax treatment for small businesses is far from complete. If the current tax system embodies a net disincentive to entrepreneurial risk-taking, however, perhaps a stronger case could be built for removing those distortions. In that sense, rather than provide an explicit subsidy for entrepreneurial activity, the tax code should at least provide a level playing field that does not actively discourage new ventures.

As we will now discuss, the existing body of research yields ambiguous results regarding likely entrepreneurial responses to tax policies. Even if preferential tax breaks are desirable, then, it is not clear that such policies would be effective. Empirical research is needed in order to fully assess the extent to which taxes influence entrepreneurial activity.

PRIOR RESEARCH ON ENTREPRENEURIAL SENSITIVITY TO TAXES

Schuetze and Bruce (2004) provide an exhaustive review of the theoretical and empirical research on entrepreneurial responses to tax policy. We highlight a few of the survey's main themes here but refer readers to it for more information. Research on the effects of tax policy on entrepreneurial activity has flourished in recent years, due in part to the availability of vast longitudinal databases containing multiple years of information for large samples of current and potential entrepreneurs. The ability to track individuals over time, especially when the time period includes a major federal tax reform, has resulted in dramatic increases in the quality of this body of research. Yet, despite the growing empirical literature in this area, facilitated by the widespread availability of rich panel data, consensus has been elusive.

Time-series studies, which have focused on national-level tax policies in the United States and the United Kingdom, have generally concluded that higher federal tax rates cause higher rates of self-employment.[7] The explanation for this result usually rests on the assumption that high tax rates drive workers out of paid employment, or wage jobs, into entrepreneurial ventures where they can more easily avoid or evade taxes. Early cross-section studies have generally supported the early time-series results.[8]

More recent research has cast doubt upon these conclusions.[9] A few studies have used panel data to tackle the important issue of tax rate endogeneity in entrepreneurial decisions while examining transitions into or out of small business activity. Many of these studies have also considered the differential tax treatment of entrepreneurs vis-à-vis wage workers. Two papers very close in spirit to the work described here (Bruce, 2000 and 2002) use the Panel Study of Income Dynamics to show that the differential tax treatment of the self-employed has somewhat counterintuitive effects on self-employment transitions. Specifically, Bruce finds that higher tax rates faced by entrepreneurs might actually increase entrepreneurial entry and survival by increasing tax avoidance and evasion. Gentry and Hubbard (2000) uses the same data as Bruce (2000) but finds that more progressive tax rate schedules serve as a tax on success in self-employment and therefore reduce self-employment rates.

A number of other panel data studies have examined the effects of tax rates on the activities of existing entrepreneurs. Of note are three papers by Carroll et al. (2000a, 2000b, and 2001), which examine a panel of taxpayer data and find that marginal tax rate increases reduce overall firm growth (as measured by receipts), mean investment expenditures, and the probability of hiring employees.

To summarize, the consensus apparent in earlier studies has been called into question by more recent work. Most research has found significant entrepreneurial responses to tax rate changes, but the direction of response has been far from uniform.

A NEW STUDY

Our most recent contribution to the growing literature on entrepreneurial response to tax policy, which we present in detail below, was conducted for the Small Business Administration.[10] Our intent in this study is to improve upon the earlier literature by exploiting a rich panel of individual tax return data to investigate the impact of marginal tax rates on transitions into and out of some form of entrepreneurial activity. We compare the tax rate an individual would face as an entrepreneur with the tax rate he or she would face as a wage worker and ask whether the difference between the two affects behavior.

We begin by exploring the determinants of entrepreneurial entry and exit in a discrete choice framework. We then explore entrepreneurial survival in a duration analysis framework. While the discrete choice models examine year-to-year transitions into and out of entrepreneurship, the duration analysis considers spells of time spent in an entrepreneurial activity. Ours is the first study to apply duration analysis techniques to the question of taxes and entrepreneurial activity.

Data

We use the University of Michigan Tax Research Database for our empirical work. This longitudinal data set, which covers the years 1979–1990, is the best publicly available source of tax return data. In total, the panel includes data from over two hundred thousand tax returns, and approximately six thousand filers are present in the panel for all twelve years. While the time period covered by our data might be considered a bit outdated, it directly overlaps the time period covered by data used in the most similar prior study,[11] allowing for important comparisons to be made. It also spans a number of significant tax policy changes, providing the necessary exogenous variation for identification purposes.

Perhaps the best advantage of using tax return data is our ability to obtain from it precise definitions of entrepreneurship based not on self-reported survey responses but on filing status (e.g., presence of a Schedule C) and reported sources of entrepreneurial income. In addition to filing status and entrepreneurship variables, the data include detailed information on income from all sources, including wages and salaries, sole proprietorships (and other forms of entrepreneurship), dividends, and transfers. These advantages offset the major drawback of using tax return data—a general lack of detailed demographic information.

We focus on the most straightforward definition of entrepreneurship: sole proprietorships as indicated by the presence of a Schedule C, which we refer to as measure 1. We also explore two increasingly broader definitions of entrepreneurship. Measure 2 adds to measure 1 those with income from partnerships or subchapter S corporations. Finally, measure 3 adds to measure 2 those filers with rental or royalty income. Given that our data are at the household (tax filer) level, we divide the sample by marital status throughout.[12]

We define entry as having no entrepreneurial activity (e.g., Schedule C) on one year's tax return but having some entrepreneurial activity on the next year's return. Similarly, exit is defined as having entrepreneurial activity in one year but not the next. We note that exit in no way implies failure, as many small businesses are successful at closure.[13] Entry rates from our data are provided in figures 4.6 through 4.8 and exit rates in figures 4.9 through 4.11. Entry rates generally rose over the course of the 1980s and seem to have reacted to the increased relative payroll taxation of sole proprietors enacted in 1984. Interestingly, exit rates do not display an upward spike around the key payroll tax reform of the mid-1980s. Understanding the impacts of tax rates on these trends requires multivariate analysis, to which we now turn.

Methodology

We begin our multivariate analysis by estimating discrete choice models of the following form to examine the effects of taxes on entrepreneurial activity:

$$D_{i,t+1} = \beta'X_{i,t} + \gamma T_{i,t+1} + \mu_i + \nu_{i,t+1}$$

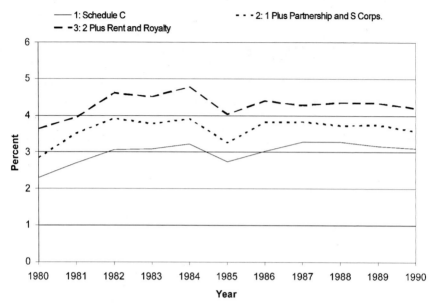

FIGURE 4.6.
Entrepreneurial Entry Rates, 1980–1990

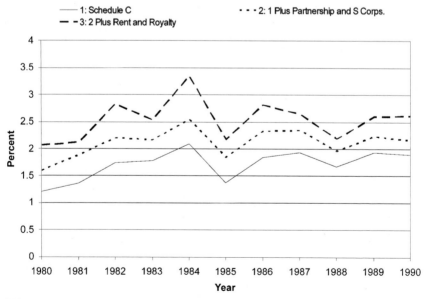

FIGURE 4.7.
Entrepreneurial Entry Rates—Single Filers, 1980–1990

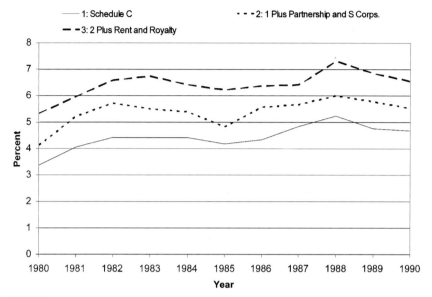

FIGURE 4.8.
Entrepreneurial Entry Rates—Married Filers, 1980–1990

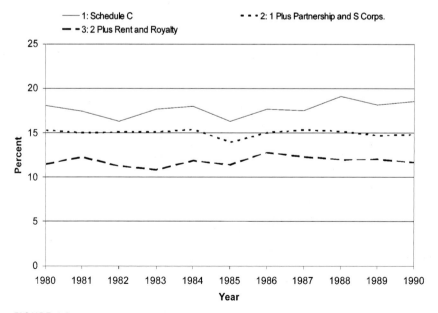

FIGURE 4.9.
Entrepreneurial Exit Rates, 1980–1990

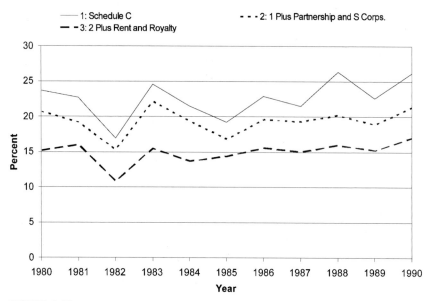

FIGURE 4.10.
Entrepreneurial Exit Rates—Single Filers, 1980–1990

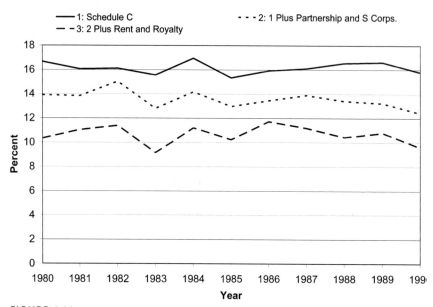

FIGURE 4.11.
Entrepreneurial Exit Rates—Married Filers, 1980–1990

In our entry analysis, $D_{i,t+1}$ is a binary variable that takes a value of 1 if an individual transitions from not having entrepreneurial activity in the first year (t) to having entrepreneurial activity in the next year (t+1), and zero if the household remains nonentrepreneurial in both years. These criteria are reversed in our exit analysis. $X_{i,t}$ is a vector containing a constant and a set of exogenous control variables defined as of time t. Each filer's potential posttransition tax rates are included in $T_{i,t+1}$.

The error term in this equation includes an individual-specific time-invariant random effect (μ_i) to capture unobserved individual heterogeneity, and an independently and identically distributed residual component ($\nu_{i,t+1}$) with zero mean and finite variance. All discrete choice models are consequently estimated as random effects probits, as in Bruce (2000 and 2002). This structure permits us to examine the independent influences of tax rates and other factors on each tax filer's probability of entering or exiting some form of entrepreneurial activity. Unobservable factors—things such as entrepreneurial ability or other idiosyncratic features that influence these probabilities—are controlled for via the individual random effects.

Our focus throughout the analysis is on the relative impacts of the tax rates that individuals would face in each of the two possible outcomes: wage employment and entrepreneurial activity. Since filers' actual employment outcome is all that we can observe in year t+1, we have to estimate their hypothetical tax rate in the alternative outcome. We do this by first predicting alternate-sector income and then estimating the corresponding marginal tax rate using the National Bureau of Economic Research TAXSIM model.[14] For those who are in a wage job in year t+1, we estimate the income they would have earned and the tax rate they would have faced had they entered (or remained in) an entrepreneurial activity.[15] For comparability, we use similarly calculated tax rates in both sectors throughout our analysis. We combine federal marginal income tax rates with state income tax rates (also estimated via TAXSIM) and payroll tax rates (calculated manually) to get a more inclusive composite marginal tax rate for each individual in each of the two outcomes.

Table 4.1 presents some evidence that tax rates play a role in entrepreneurial transitions. This table shows average marginal tax rates (MTRs) for both outcomes broken down by filing status and whether or not the filer entered or exited entrepreneurship (as indicated by the presence of a Schedule C, our measure 1). Looking first at the entry results in the top panel, single filers who did not enter enjoyed lower tax rates in the wage sector than they would have faced in entrepreneurship. The opposite is true among married filers. Both single and married filers who entered enjoyed much lower tax rates in entrepreneurship than they would have faced in the wage sector. Turning to the exit results, entrepreneurial tax rates were lower than wage tax rates for those who did not exit. Single filers who exited would have had higher tax rates on average if they had remained in entrepreneurship, but the opposite is true for married filers who exited.

Additional Independent Variables

In order to measure the true impact of tax rates on entrepreneurial transitions, we follow prior studies in controlling for a number of other possible factors. While age is not included on tax returns, we control for it by including a dummy for the presence of a special exemption for taxpayers or spouses over the age of sixty-five. The number of exemptions claimed for children living at home provides a proxy for household size. We also include the number of children living away from home and the total number of exemptions claimed. For filers who itemize their deductions, we can identify the presence of a mortgage interest deduction, which can be used as a source of information regarding liquidity constraints, as in Bruce and Holtz-Eakin (2001).

Risk attitudes are also thought to be important in whether or not an individual becomes an entrepreneur. In an attempt to capture a household's risk attitude, we include a measure of the balance due on the tax return. It seems plausible that more risk-averse households should be more likely to overwithhold their taxes, thereby receiving a refund from the IRS. Finally, we use aggregations of state identifiers in the tax panel to control for region of residence. Locations (such as Guam) outside of the fifty states and the District of Columbia are represented using an indicator for "other region." Another indicator for "missing region" is also necessary because the state identifiers are omitted for any return with an adjusted gross income of $200,000 or more in order to guarantee confidentiality.[16]

An issue only recently addressed in the literature is the potential endogeneity of the calculated tax rates. In other words, whether or not an individual moves from wage and salary employment to entrepreneurship might have some effect on his or her calculated posttransition tax rates. We address endogeneity by using the approach applied by Bruce (2000 and 2002) in this literature and many other researchers in other areas, which exploits changes in tax rules over time to create instrumental variables. Statistical tests indicate that tax rates are endogenous in our models, so we focus our discussion on instrumental variables results.

Results

Our discrete choice analysis of entrepreneurial entry yields intuitive results. All else equal, cutting the wage-sector MTR is associated with a decrease in the probability of entering entrepreneurship, while cutting the entrepreneurship MTR is associated with an increase in the probability of entry. Further, the effect from the entrepreneurship tax rate is more than double the size of the effect of the wage tax rate, suggesting that equal cuts in both tax rates would increase entrepreneurial entry rates.

Numerically, our empirical results suggest that cutting both the wage MTR and entrepreneurship MTR simultaneously by one percentage point would have the combined effect of increasing the probability of entrepreneurial entry by 0.84 percentage points (-0.58 plus 1.42) for single filers and 1.49 percentage points (-0.51 plus 2.00) for married filers. These effects are quite large when compared to the average entry rates of 1.6 percent for single filers and 4.2 percent for married filers. These results are found to be quite robust to alternative samples, measures of entrepreneurial activity, and other changes in specification.[17]

Results from our discrete choice analysis of entrepreneurial exit are again consistent with conventional wisdom. Specifically, reductions in the wage MTR are associated with increases in the probability of exit, while reductions in the entrepreneurship MTR are associated with reductions in the probability of exit, all else being equal. And again, the effect of the entrepreneurship tax rate is nearly twice the size of that for the wage tax rate. Cutting both the wage and entrepreneurship MTRs simultaneously by one percentage point would reduce the likelihood of entrepreneurial exit by 8.15 percentage points (17.32 minus 9.17) for single filers and 3.83 percentage points (7.81 minus 3.98) for married filers. These effects are also quantitatively important relative to the average exit rates of 23.3 percent and 16.2 percent for single and married filers, respectively.

We supplement our discrete choice framework by estimating duration models that examine spells in entrepreneurship. Rather than treat each two-year transition as a separate but econometrically linked process as in the discrete choice approach, duration models examine the entire spell of entrepreneurial activity at once.[18] Additional data restrictions required for this analysis result in a sample of 184 single filers and 1,065 married filers, who make a total of 142 and 829 exits, respectively, during the tax panel. Filers in our data have only about a 50 percent chance of "surviving" beyond their fourth year. Perhaps unsurprisingly, duration model results are largely consistent with the discrete choice findings described earlier. Specifically, reductions in the wage MTR are associated with shorter spells of time in entrepreneurship, while reductions in the entrepreneurship MTR are associated with longer spells of time in entrepreneurship.

Taken together, our empirical results suggest that the leveling of the tax playing field during the 1980s (when tax rates for entrepreneurs were increased relative to those for wage workers) might have resulted in less entrepreneurial entry and more entrepreneurial exit than would have been observed otherwise. On the other hand, the simultaneous across-the-board marginal tax rate cuts might have resulted in more entry and less exit. An application of these results to the current debate would suggest that policies aimed at reducing the relative tax rates on entrepreneurs would likely lead to increases in entrepreneurial entry and better chances of survival. However, our results also indicate that equal cuts in tax rates on both wage and entrepreneurship incomes could yield similar results in a more efficient and equitable manner.

SIT OR GIT? TAX REFORM ISSUES FACING SMALL BUSINESS

With large-scale federal tax reform again on the minds of policymakers and researchers, it is useful to evaluate recent proposals in terms of their likely impact on potential and existing entrepreneurs. We focus this part of our discussion on the two major proposals submitted in November 2005 by the President's Advisory Panel on Federal Tax Reform (henceforth the tax reform panel).

By now it is well known that the tax reform panel recommended two major scenarios in the way of "fundamental" tax reform: a Simplified Income Tax (SIT) plan and a Growth and Investment Tax (GIT) plan. The SIT consists of a broad menu of changes to the current income tax system that is primarily intended to enhance simplicity and fairness in the tax code, while the GIT is a more far-reaching hybrid that meshes something of a graduated-rate flat tax or subtraction-method value-added tax with a lower-rate tax on capital income. Each of these proposals has much to be desired and should be carefully considered by policymakers.

A few elements that are part of both the SIT and the GIT would directly affect small businesses. One obvious major change is a general reduction in marginal tax rates. Given our empirical findings, this would likely be a net gain for entrepreneurial activity since it would probably increase entry and reduce exit rates. Earlier research described above would also predict gains in small business employment, investment, and growth in receipts as a result of lower marginal tax rates. We are sympathetic, however, to recent criticism of the panel's use of a revenue baseline that might not reflect policy reality. We will therefore not overemphasize the benefits from the lower marginal tax rates in the panel's proposals.

Perhaps the most prominent feature of both proposals is a rather dramatic emphasis on tax code simplicity. Most efforts along these lines will likely be heralded by American entrepreneurs. That said, one simplicity measure in both proposals that is likely to be met with some criticism is the shift to more cash-based accounting. Under the SIT, small businesses would be required to establish a separate checking account for business income and expenses. Nonbusiness transactions would not be permitted in these accounts. While the simplicity gains are apparent in theory, obvious difficulties (especially among very new businesses) in separating business and nonbusiness revenues and purchases would make this provision especially hard to enforce in practice.

At the same time, a possible benefit from the shift to cash accounting is the allowance of full expensing for small business investment (except purchases of structures and land, which would continue to be depreciated but under a simplified system).[19] In terms of recent policy changes, this provision essentially represents expanded and unlimited bonus depreciation. While several efforts are currently under way to study the implications of such a change, researchers have not yet published evidence on the extent to which small businesses undertake new investment in response to expanded depreciation allowances (as opposed to simply changing the timing of investment that would have taken place anyway). The simplicity aspect alone might be enough to encourage new investment, however.

In a potentially more controversial vein, both plans would streamline and enhance individual options for health insurance and savings incentives, such that taxpayers could engage in more tax-free saving activity outside of job-related benefit programs. On one hand, this would reduce the need for new entrepreneurs to provide health insurance and retirement plans to their employees. It would also reduce barriers to entrepreneurial entry in the form of generous wage-job benefits (i.e., loosen the grip of "job lock"). On the other hand, it could reduce health insurance coverage and retirement savings among employees of small businesses who do not elect to take advantage of the new savings provisions.

A prominent provision of the SIT with potentially important ramifications for small businesses is the elimination of tax on domestic dividends and the exemption of three-fourths of capital gains from sales of U.S. stock. This reduction in the taxation of capital income could feasibly result in a surge in the supply of venture capital for new firm formation, while simultaneously increasing the value of investment portfolios that might be used to privately fund new businesses.

A key feature of the GIT is the dramatic reduction in tax distortions regarding organizational form, as all businesses except sole proprietorships would be taxed uniformly. While sole proprietors would be taxed at individual rates up to a maximum tax rate of 30 percent, all other businesses would be taxed at a flat business tax rate of 30 percent. This provision would take the tax code out of important decisions regarding incorporation or other organizational issues.

On balance, we view the tax reform panel's recommendations as potentially beneficial for small businesses, even without the questionable reductions in marginal tax rates. While tax breaks would not necessarily be targeted to small businesses in either of these proposals, the simplification measures in both would create a level playing field and represent a net reduction in tax-related distortions of small-business activity.

CONCLUSION

While consensus has been elusive, a growing body of empirical literature is finding that tax policies have important implications for entrepreneurial activity. The induced behavioral responses, often in the form of good business ideas that either are not pursued or end prematurely, likely result in significant efficiency losses in the economy. Our empirical results suggest that entrepreneurial responses to tax rate changes can be rather large. We stop short of using these results to recommend large-scale tax rate cuts, however, as little is known about how the current stock of entrepreneurs compares to the socially optimal supply.

In any case, tax reform discussions should be careful to consider impacts on small-business activity. Even if tax breaks for entrepreneurs are not desirable, the tax code is probably not the best policy instrument for encouraging or discouraging entrepreneurial activity. Financial markets are surely better suited to evaluating worthwhile projects on a case-by-case basis.

Our general sense is that large-scale tax reform along the lines proposed by the tax reform panel could provide net benefits to America's small businesses. They would almost certainly represent improvements over the current federal tax system, even with marginal rates sufficient to fund more realistic future budgets. Failing sweeping reform of the U.S. tax system, though, some incremental changes are worthy of exploration in the immediate term. For example, despite a gradual increase in the deductibility of health insurance costs for the self-employed, unequal treatment of health insurance costs under the payroll tax persists.

Perhaps most important, entrepreneurs (and all other taxpayers) deserve a greater degree of stability and uniformity in the tax code. The current tangle of short-term tax changes and temporary provisions surely makes small-business planning more difficult than it needs to be, even if those provisions provide tax reductions to affected taxpayers.

Table 4.1. Average Marginal Tax Rates by Filing Status

		Marginal Tax Rates (%)	
Entry		*Did Not Enter*	*Entered*
Single	Wage	30.62	33.19
	Entrepreneurship	32.52	26.72
Married	Wages	36.92	37.82
	Entrepreneurship	34.99	33.05
		Marginal Tax Rates (%)	
Entry		*Did Not Enter*	*Entered*
Single	Wage	31.77	31.89
	Entrepreneurship	26.55	32.00
Married	Wages	36.83	35.94
	Entrepreneurship	31.56	33.87

Note: Entries are posttransition means, and all tax rates are inclusive of federal income and payroll and state income taxes. Entrepreneurship status in this table is defined by the presence of a Schedule C.

Appendix Table 4.1. Variable Definitions and Notes
Variables Used in Econometric Models

Age 65	=1 if there is at least one age 65 exemption in a household.
West	=1 if residence in the following states: Alaska, Arizona, California, Colorado, Hawaii, Idaho, Montana, Nevada, New Mexico, Oregon, Utah, Washington, Wyoming.
Midwest	=1 if residence in the following states: Illinois, Indiana, Iowa, Kansas, Michigan, Minnesota, Missouri, Nebraska, North Dakota, Ohio, South Dakota, Wisconsin.
South	=1 if residence in the following states: Alabama, Arkansas, Delaware, District of Columbia, Florida, Georgia, Kentucky, Louisiana, Maryland, Mississippi, North Carolina, Oklahoma, South Carolina, Tennessee, Texas, Virginia, West Virginia. (This is the omitted reference category.)
Northeast	=1 if residence in the following states: Connecticut, Maine, Massachusetts, New Hampshire, New Jersey, New York, Pennsylvania, Rhode Island, Vermont.
Other Region	=1 for residence classification other than the above, excluding missing residence.
Missing Region	=1 if the state identifier is missing (adjusted gross incomes of $200,000 or more).
Mortgage Interest Ded.	=1 if the household claimed a mortgage interest deduction.
Kids Home	Number of exemptions claimed for children living at home.
Kids Away	Number of exemptions claimed for children living away from home.
Total Exemptions	Total number of exemptions claimed.
Balance Due ($100)	Amount due on the tax return (negative if receiving a refund) divided by 100.

Variables Used to Estimate Tax Rates in TAXSIM

Tax Year	1979–1990. (Late or amended returns are reassigned to the appropriate tax year.)
State	Indicator for fifty states and DC; other residences treated as missing.
Marital Status	Married (includes widow(er)s and married filing separately), single, or head of household.
Dependent Exemptions	Number of dependent exemptions claimed.
Age Exemptions	Number of age and exemptions other than dependents. (Note: Other exemptions were included in this category as there was not a separate place to enter them and placing them in the dependent exemptions category could potentially distort Earned Income Tax Credit eligibility. However, as TAXSIM only allows a maximum value of "2" in this field, all values greater than "2" were set to the maximum.)
Wage and Salary Income of the Taxpayer	Wage and salary income for the household. Self-employment earnings are included in the category as long as the sum of wage earnings and self-employment earnings is not less than zero. When this sum is negative, wage and salary income is set to zero and the remaining negative amount is added to (subtracted from) other income (see below).
Wage and Salary Income of the Spouse	Set to zero for all households (spousal income cannot be distinguished for joint filers).

Dividend Income	Gross dividend income (the gross amount of dividend income is used for 1979–1986 after which there is not a distinction between taxable and total dividend income).
Other Property Income	All income other than wages, self-employment income, dividends, pensions, Social Security benefits, and unemployment compensation. Can be negative. Self-employment income is included only to the extent that losses are not offset by wage earnings (see "Wage and Salary Income of the Taxpayer" for more details).
Taxable Pensions	Taxable portion of reported pension income (addition of amounts reported on Form 1040 and Schedule E for years 1979–1986).
Gross Social Security Income	Gross income from Social Security benefits.
Other Nontaxable Transfer Income	Not reported in the tax return data; set to zero for all observations.
Rent Paid	Not reported in the tax return data; set to zero for all observations.
Property Taxes Paid	Amount paid in property taxes reported as an itemized deduction on Schedule A.
Itemized Deductions	Deductions other than state income tax and property taxes.
Child Care Expenses	Gross amount of child care expenses or the maximum reportable amount, whichever is greater. For 1979–1980 only the credit amount, not gross expenses, was reported. Gross expenditures were estimated by taking the credit amount times 5. When this estimate exceeded the maximum claimable amount, it was set to the maximum.
Unemployment Compensation	Gross unemployment compensation (the gross amount of unemployment compensation is used for 1979–1986 after which there is not a distinction between taxable and total unemployment compensation).

Appendix Table 4.2: Summary Statistics

| | Entry | | | | Exit | | | |
| | Single | | Married | | Single | | Married | |
	Mean	S.D.	Mean	S.D.	Mean	S.D.	Mean	S.D.
Entry 1	0.016	0.125	0.042	0.201				
Entry 2	0.020	0.140	0.052	0.222				
Entry 3	0.024	0.153	0.062	0.241				
Exit 1					0.233	0.423	0.162	0.369
Exit 2					0.197	0.398	0.135	0.342
Exit 3					0.154	0.361	0.106	0.308
Age 65	0.097	0.295	0.121	0.326	0.092	0.289	0.090	0.286
West	0.201	0.401	0.187	0.390	0.279	0.448	0.230	0.421
Midwest	0.248	0.432	0.260	0.438	0.223	0.416	0.250	0.433
Northeast	0.234	0.423	0.205	0.404	0.194	0.395	0.169	0.375
Other Region	0.005	0.072	0.007	0.081	0.003	0.050	0.001	0.038
Missing Region	0.001	0.028	0.005	0.073	0.006	0.076	0.010	0.099
Mortgage Interest Ded.	0.094	0.292	0.398	0.490	0.234	0.424	0.503	0.500
Kids Home	0.286	0.746	1.125	1.280	0.325	0.754	1.227	1.258
Kids Away	0.018	0.182	0.023	0.209	0.036	0.251	0.016	0.179
Total Exemptions	1.407	0.931	3.312	1.352	1.546	0.988	3.392	1.286
Balance Due ($100)	−0.313	2.242	−0.349	9.579	0.305	8.056	0.440	10.654

Note: Means and standard deviations (S.D.) for all variables except entry and exit measures are based on estimation samples used for the measure 1 (Schedule C) models only. See text for additional details.

NOTES

* This chapter draws heavily upon empirical work that was supported by a grant from the U.S. Small Business Administration (SBA) and a dissertation fellowship (for Dr. Gurley-Calvez) from the Ewing Marion Kauffman Foundation, for which the authors are grateful. We thank Daniel Feenberg and Jean Roth at the National Bureau of Economic Research for assistance with TAXSIM; Herb Schuetze, Joe Johnson, and Robert Carroll for helpful comments; Karie Barbour and Beth Howard for expert research assistance; and the Center for Business and Economic Research at the University of Tennessee and the Center for Policy Research at Syracuse University for assistance in procuring the data. The contents of this work are solely the responsibility of the authors and do not necessarily reflect the views of the Government Accounting Office, the Kauffman Foundation, or the SBA.

1. These statistics are updated by the Small Business Administration's Office of Advocacy and can be found in the frequently asked questions section of their website (<http://www.sba.gov/advo>).

2. Crain and Hopkins (2001) estimates that tax compliance costs per employee in small businesses range from 1.8 times greater than large firms in the service industry to 4.5 times greater than large firms in the manufacturing industry.

3. Joulfaian and Rider (1998) find a positive relationship between marginal tax rates and evasion among the self-employed. Slemrod, Blumenthal, and Christian (2001) show evidence that suggested that Schedule C filers were more likely to engage in tax evasion, but the amount of tax revenue at stake was likely to be small.

4. Our panel of tax return data indicates that entrepreneurs are indeed more likely than others to use the services of a paid tax preparer. An examination of data for the years 1982–1988 revealed that 68–76 percent of entrepreneurs used a paid preparer, while only 37–45 percent of nonentrepreneurs used a paid preparer. All differences are statistically significant at the 1 percent level.

5. Most economists would assume, of course, that the employee actually bears most of the economic burden of the payroll tax regardless of the statutory burden.

6. See, for example, Evans and Jovanovic (1989); Evans and Leighton (1989); Holtz-Eakin, Joulfaian, and Rosen (1994a and 1994b); Blanchflower and Oswald (1998); Dunn and Holtz-Eakin (2000); and Bruce, Holtz-Eakin, and Quinn (2000).

7. Long (1982a); Blau (1987); Parker (1996); Robson (1998); and Robson and Wren (1999).

8. Long (1982a and 1982b); and Moore (1983).

9. Fairlie and Meyer (2000); Briscoe, Dainty, and Millett (2000); Bruce and Mohsin (2006); and Parker (2003).

10. Interested readers should consult the full report, available at <http://www.sba .gov/advo/research/rs252tot.pdf>.

11. Donald Bruce, "Effects of the United States tax system on transitions into self-employment," *Labour Economics* 7, no. 5 (2000): 545–74.

12. Returns are compressed into two categories: married (joint), including those whose filing status is married or married filing separately; and single, including returns filed as unmarried (single), head of household, or widowed.

13. Brian Headd, "Redefining business success: Distinguishing between closure and failure," *Small Business Economics* 21, no. 1 (2003): 51–61.

14. TAXSIM can be thought of as a virtual tax form or calculator, which can take limited information from survey data or other sources and estimate tax rates. Variables used in the TAXSIM calculations are outlined in appendix table 4.1. The TAXSIM model is accessible at <http://www.nber.org/taxsim>. For more details, see Feenberg and Coutts (1993).

15. In this case, we estimate both entrepreneurial income and wage income, since many entrepreneurs also report wage and salary income on their income tax returns. Income predictions consist of OLS regressions of observed income for a given sector by year and filing status on a constant, nonlabor income, and a set of household-specific control variables including proxies for age and the number of children in the tax filer's household. These regressions are estimated separately by year and filing status (single and married), and are repeated for each of our three measures of entrepreneurship. Estimated parameters from each regression are used to predict incomes for tax filers in the alternative sector.

16. Dummy variables indicating the year in which the return was filed (time $t + 1$) are also included to account for year fixed effects. Summary statistics, which are provided in the appendix, reveal that roughly one in ten filers claims an age 65 exemption. Filers are fairly evenly distributed across the West, Midwest, and Northeast regions (South is the omitted reference category). Between one-tenth and one-quarter of single filers and about half of married filers claimed a mortgage interest deduction. Unsurprisingly, married filers reported more exemptions on average. Results for our measure of the balance due indicate sufficient variation for

our estimation purposes, with the entry samples receiving refunds on average (negative balance due) and the exit samples owing money on average.

17. Readers are referred to Bruce and Gurley (2005) for additional details on these robustness checks.

18. To avoid problems due to gaps in the panel data, we restrict this part of our analysis to filers who were in the panel for all twelve years and did not change filing status (single versus married).

19. While only small businesses would be able to expense all investment under the SIT, similar provisions in the GIT would apply to businesses of all sizes.

Mexican Immigrants and the Entrepreneurship Gap

ROBERT W. FAIRLIE
AND CHRISTOPHER M. WOODRUFF*

INTRODUCTION

Data from the 2000 census indicate that Mexican-Americans represent 8 percent of the population of the United States. More recent estimates, from the March 2004 Current Population Survey (CPS), put this figure at 9.4 percent. If current trends continue, Mexican-Americans will become the largest ethnic group in the United States within the next ten years. This growth is fueled by a very rapid immigration rate: census data indicate that 46 percent of the Mexican-American population as a whole, and 67 percent of its working-age population, was born in Mexico. Of all individuals living in the United States not born here, more than a quarter were born in Mexico. Understandably, this rapid pace of immigration has generated a growing interest among policymakers and academics in the assimilation of Mexicans and their offspring.[1]

In this chapter, we focus on one aspect of assimilation and economic advancement for Mexican-American immigrants: self-employment rates. While business ownership rates vary tremendously across immigrant groups in the United States, Mexican immigrants have low rates relative to other immigrant groups. Estimates from the 2000 census indicate that 5.3 percent of male Mexican immigrants are self-employed, compared, for example, to 23.3 percent of Korean immigrants. Self-employment rates for Mexican immigrants are also similar to those for the U.S-born of Mexican descent, whereas other immigrant populations generally see a decline in rates of self-employment among offspring born in this country. Finally, Mexican immigrants have low rates of self-employment compared to non-Hispanic whites born in the United States, a group with a self-employment rate of 11.1 percent. In sum, no matter which comparison group is chosen, Mexican immigrants have relatively low rates of self-employment.

Why this should matter for Mexicans' assimilation is suggested by the historical example of earlier immigrant groups in the United States, such as the Chinese, Japanese, Jews, Italians, and Greeks. It has been argued that their economic success in the United States was in part due to their ownership of small businesses.[2] More recently, business ownership among Koreans has purportedly resulted in economic mobility and success for that group.[3]

Census data help to explain these historical examples by suggesting one reason self-employment may be important for economic success. While incomes of Mexican immigrants are lower than incomes of the native born, a disproportionate share of the high-income earners among Mexican immigrants is self-employed. This results from two effects. First, average earnings are somewhat higher for self-employed immigrants. Among Mexican-born men living in the United States, for example, the average earnings among the self-employed are $29,766, compared with earnings of $20,499 among Mexican-born male wage earners; the median figures are $18,000 and $17,000, respectively. Second, the variance in earnings among the self-employed is also higher. Combined with the higher average earnings, higher variance means that while only 4.2 percent of Mexican-born male wage workers earned $50,000 or more in 2000, and only 0.7 percent earned $100,000 or more, by comparison 14 percent of the Mexican-born self-employed earned more than $50,000 and 4.5 percent earned more than $100,000. Thus, while median earnings are similar for the Mexican-born wage workers and self-employed, the self-employed were much more likely to earn salaries above the median level for the United States as a whole.

Self-employment brings benefits not only to immigrant business owners but also to the communities in which they live, as policymakers recognize. Stimulating business creation in sectors with high growth potential (e.g., construction, wholesale trade, and business services) may represent an effective public policy for promoting economic development and job creation in poor neighborhoods.[4] In addition, Hispanic and other minority-owned firms are substantially more likely to hire minority workers than are white-owned firms.[5] Self-employed business owners are also unique in that they create jobs for themselves, and it has been argued that political influence comes with success in small business.[6]

Acknowledging the large differences in self-employment rates that exist across different foreign-born populations, we explore in this chapter four potential explanations for the low incidence of self-employment among Mexican immigrants.

First, we look at whether the Mexican-born are employed in sectors with low rates of self-employment. We compare the sectoral composition of employment among those born in Mexico to that of other immigrants, including both the distribution of employment across sectors and the self-employment rates within sectors.

Second, we examine the impact of English-language ability on self-employment, since Mexican immigrants are less likely than other immigrants to say that they are fluent or near-fluent in English. We also look at the importance of enclave effects; that is, we explore how self-employment rates vary with the percentage of the population in an area born in the same country or narrow region. For this analysis, we define geographic areas using the sub-Standard Metropolitan Statistical Area (SMSA) public-use microareas, which are the narrowest geographic areas available in the public-use data. If English-language ability is a constraint on entry into self-employment, then we should expect to find that enclaves have a particularly large effect on self-employment among those who speak English relatively poorly.

We next explore the possibility that a lack of legal status affects self-employment rates among immigrants. The main evidence on this comes from the Legalized Population Survey (LPS), conducted in 1988 and 1990 after the passage of the Immigration Reform and Control Act (IRCA) in 1987. The LPS is a relatively small sample that allows us to compare Mexican immigrants only with all other immigrants, but it provides some evidence that suggests the importance of legal status for self-employment.

Finally, we examine the effect of educational attainment and wealth. Previous research has shown that the probability that an individual is self employed increases with the individual's wealth level.[7] The evidence on education is more mixed, but we show that educational levels of Mexican immigrants are significantly lower on average than those of either the native-born residents of the United States or of immigrants from most other countries.

For all of these analyses except that on legal status, we use data from 5 percent public-use microsurvey data of the U.S. population census. The census is the only data set with a sample large enough to allow comparison of the Mexican-born with those born in other countries or narrowly defined regions. However, use of the census limits a full examination of other factors, such as wealth. The census is also a cross section, so examination of factors associated with entry into and exit from self-employment is not possible with these data. We will say something about these factors in the discussion following the analysis.

PREVIOUS LITERATURE

The literature on self-employment and entrepreneurship has expanded rapidly in recent years. A smaller literature focuses on African-American self-employment. The findings from this literature indicate that black self-employment rates have remained at approximately one-third of white rates over the entire twentieth century,[8] and that the dearth of black-owned businesses appears to be partly due to relatively low levels of education, assets, and parental self-employment among blacks.[9] Recent evidence also indicates that black-owned businesses experience higher loan denial probabilities and pay higher interest rates than white-owned businesses even after controlling for differences in size and credit history.[10] A loan application filed by a firm owned by blacks is twice as likely to be denied as a comparable application filed by a white owner. The evidence on consumer discrimination against black firms, however, is less clear.[11]

Immigrant self-employment has also been the focus of several recent studies. The findings from this literature indicate that immigrants have historically had higher rates of self-employment than natives in the United States,[12] although in the past few years rates appear to be similar.[13] There is also a literature indicating considerable differences in self-employment rates among immigrants from different countries. Yuengert (1995) finds that immigrants to the United States from countries with higher self-employment rates are more likely to enter self-employment; however, Fairlie and Meyer (1996) find that this effect is not statistically significant. A few recent studies also examine how self-employed immigrants assimilate in their host countries.[14] In the United States, the earnings of self-employed immigrants are predicted to converge with the earnings of natives receiving wages or a salary substantially faster than the earnings of immigrants receiving wages or a salary. The evidence outside the United States is more mixed. Clark and Drinkwater (2000) for the United Kingdom and Andersson and Wadensjö (2003) for Denmark and Sweden find higher self-employment rates for immigrants than for the indigenous populations. In contrast, Kidd (1993) finds that the self-employment rate of the Australian-born sample was higher than for immigrants.

Very few studies in the self-employment literature focus on Hispanics. This omission is surprising because Hispanics now represent the largest minority group in the United States and have rates of business ownership that are only slightly higher than African-American rates. One of the first studies in the literature, Borjas (1986), explores the ethnic enclave hypothesis. He finds that self-employment among Mexicans, Cubans, and "other Hispanics" increases with the percentage of Hispanics in an SMSA. The effect is larger among the immigrant population than among the population born in the United States. More recently, Flota and Mora (2001) find that Mexican-American men in cities on the U.S.-Mexico border have higher self-employment rates than those in other cities. Self-employed earnings, however, are lower for Mexican-American men in border cities than those in nonborder cities, and similar for women. In another recent study, Fairlie (2004) analyzes data from the National Longitudinal Survey of Youth and finds faster earnings growth among self-employed Hispanic men than among Hispanic men earning wages or a salary. Estimates for Hispanics do not reveal a statistically significant difference.

In previous research, we used microdata from the Mexican census and U.S census to explore why self-employment rates differ so much between residents of Mexico and Mexican immigrants in the United States.[15] We found that neither industry composition nor measured characteristics—age and education—explain much of the gap in self-employment rates between the two countries. Instead, the much higher rate of self-employment in Mexico appears to be the result of structural differences in that country's economy.

None of the previous studies in the literature directly explores why Mexican immigrants have low business ownership rates generally and compared to other immigrant groups. We attempt to remedy this deficiency.

DIFFERENCES IN BUSINESS OWNERSHIP AMONG IMMIGRANTS

Business ownership rates among Mexican immigrants are much lower than rates among immigrants from many other countries. Table 5.1 shows rates of self-employment for foreign-born non-Hispanic whites and for immigrants born in Mexico and Asia. For both men and women, rates are much lower for the Mexican-born than for the other immigrant groups. The table also shows rates for U.S.-born non-Hispanic whites and for U.S.-born individuals who identify themselves as being of Mexican or Asian descent. Among the foreign-born, those born in Mexico have markedly lower self-employment rates. The gap is especially large for Mexican-born males. Self-employment rates are 5.3 percent for males born in Mexico, compared with 10.3 percent for Asian-born males and 14.2 percent for the non-Hispanic white foreign-born. Among females, the rates are 5.0 percent, 7.1 percent, and 8.5 percent, respectively. Though self-employment rates among the U.S.-born population of Mexican descent lag behind those of the U.S.-born population of Asian descent and U.S.-born non-Hispanic whites, this gap is considerably smaller than the one separating those born in Mexico from others of foreign birth.

Table 5.2 shows self-employment rates for male and female immigrants from several countries or narrow geographical regions. We chose countries for which the census had data on at least ten thousand individuals. The table includes data on individuals born in Mexico, Poland, a set of eastern European countries,[16] a set of non-English-speaking western European countries,[17] a set of Central American countries,[18] China, India, Vietnam, Korea, and the Philippines. Only immigrants born in the Philippines have lower rates of self-employment than those born in Mexico, though for males, those born in Central America have rates that are almost identical to Mexicans'. Among immigrants from Poland, other eastern European countries, and western European countries, rates of self-employment are in the 12–13 percent range for males and the 7–10 percent range for females. Rates among Asian immigrants vary much more, ranging for males from 4.7 percent among those from the Philippines and 8.3 percent among those from Vietnam to 23.3 percent among those from Korea. Among females, the highest rates are also among those from Korea (15.0 percent) and the lowest among those from the Philippines (3.5 percent), India (6.5 percent), and Vietnam (8.0 percent).

Sectoral Composition

In seeking to account for these differences in self-employment rates among immigrants, we begin by looking at the sectoral composition of self-employment. The top halves of tables 5.3A and B show the industry distribution of employment for males and females, respectively. We show data for immigrants born in Mexico, immigrants born in Asia, non-Hispanic white immigrants, and non-Hispanic whites born in the United States; this last group is a benchmark against which we examine differences among the immigrant groups. The bottom halves of tables 3A and B show self-employment rates by industry for males and females for the same four groups of individuals.

Considering males first, Mexican-born immigrants are overrepresented in agriculture and mining; construction; and arts, entertainment, and recreation. They are underrepresented in education and health services, and public administration. The data on the lower half of the table show that agriculture and construction have self-employment rates among native white non-Hispanics that are far above the average self-employment rate, while rates in education and public administration are far below. Moreover, the data on the bottom half of table 5.3A indicate that the self-employment rates of the Mexican-born are lower than the self-employment rates of the reference group in every sector, though in the transportation sector they are close to the same as the reference group. Multiplying the non-Hispanic white self-employment rate in each sector by the proportion of the Mexican-born workforce in that sector results in a self-employment rate of 15.1 percent. This compares with the actual self-employment rate of 11.8 percent among the reference group and 5.2 percent among the Mexican-born. Hence, Mexican-born immigrants are disproportionately employed in sectors with high rates of self-employment. According to these data, then, sectoral distribution does not explain the lower rates of self-employment among Mexican-born immigrants; rather, it points to a gap even larger than that suggested by the raw data.

For Asian immigrants, on the other hand, sectoral differences do appear to explain a large part of the difference between their own self-employment rates and those of non-Hispanic white natives. As table 5.3A shows, Asian immigrants are underrepresented in construction and overrepresented in arts, entertainment, and recreation; education and health services; and professional services. Construction and professional services both have particularly high self-employment rates, while education and entertainment have rates that are below average. Making the same calculation as above—that is, multiplying the non-Hispanic white native self-employment rates by the percentage of the Asian-born labor force employed in a given sector—produces a self-employment rate of 10.6 percent. This is very close to the actual Asian rate of 10.3 percent. Hence, almost all of the much smaller gap between Asian immigrants and non-Hispanic white natives is explained by sectoral differences. Finally, the distribution of employment among non-Hispanic white immigrants is higher than that of non-Hispanic white natives. Using the employment distribution of non-Hispanic white immigrants and the self-employment rates of non-Hispanic white natives produces a self-employment rate of 11.8 percent, which is identical to the actual rate among the reference group. Hence, sectoral distribution does not explain any of the higher rates of self-employment among immigrant non-Hispanic whites.

As table 5.3B shows, female immigrants from Mexico are overrepresented in manufacturing and in arts, entertainment, and recreation. They are underrepresented in finance, insurance, and real estate and in education and health services. As with males, however, the data suggest that, overall, the sectoral distribution of females is favorable to self-employment rates. Given their distribution, if Mexican-born women had the same self-employment rates as non-Hispanic white natives, their overall self-employment rate would be 7.9 percent, well above the actual rate of 6.5 percent for the reference group. The sectoral distribution of employment is neutral among Asian immigrant women and slightly favorable among non-Hispanic white female immigrants. Using the sectoral distribution of employment among the immigrant group and the non-Hispanic native white self-employment rates results in calculated self-employment rates of 6.6 percent for Asian women and 7.0 percent for non-Hispanic white immigrants. These are comparable to the actual rate of 6.5 percent for native-born non-Hispanic white women.

English-Language Ability and Enclaves

The data shown in table 5.1 indicate that U.S.-born men of Mexican descent are as likely to be self-employed as Mexican immigrants, and U.S.-born women of Mexican descent are more likely to be self-employed than Mexican immigrants.

For non-Hispanic whites and those of Asian descent, the pattern across generations is very different. Immigrants are much more likely to be self-employed than the native born. In other words, the gap between Mexican-Americans and non-Hispanic whites is particularly large for the immigrant populations.

One factor that may help to explain this gap is the differing English-language abilities of immigrants from different countries, about which census data are very informative The census asks member of households where a language other than English is spoken whether they speak English "very well," "well," "not well," or "not at all." We group the last two categories together as indicating difficulty with English, and compare people in this group to those who either report that they speak only English, or report that they speak English very well or well.

Table 5.4 reports the percentage of immigrants by country/region of origin who self-report that they speak English fluently, well, or very well. Slightly over half of men (52 percent) and women (53 percent) born in Mexico report a high level of English competency. These percentages are much lower than those for immigrants from any other country or region. The next lowest level is among immigrants from Central America (62 percent for men and 64 percent for women). Among males, immigrants from Vietnam (72 percent), China (74 percent), Korea (74 percent), and Poland (78 percent) all report English competencies around the same level. Not surprisingly, immigrants from countries that are former colonies of England or the United States have higher rates of English-language competency.

Table 5.5 reports the percentage of men and women with low and high English-language ability who are self-employed. English-language ability is sometimes associated with higher levels of self-employment, and sometimes not. Among men from Mexico, Central America, Poland, eastern Europe, and the Philippines, those who speak English well or fluently are much more likely to be self-employed than those who speak English less well. Among men from Korea and to a lesser extent China, the opposite is true. For women, the association between English-language ability and self-employment rates is much weaker, though there is a strong negative association among female immigrants from Korea. These results suggest a correlation between English-language ability and self-employment for immigrants from many countries.[19] The direction of causation and whether the relationship is driven by an unobserved factor, such as entrepreneurial ability, are difficult to ascertain.[20]

English-language ability may affect self-employment for any of several reasons. A better command of English may help in dealing with government regulators, facilitate communication with customers and suppliers, and increase access to financial, legal, and other institutions. If English is important because it facilitates communication with trading partners, however, then English should be less important in neighborhoods where a large percentage of the population speaks the immigrant's native language, or in ethnic enclaves where specialized, native-language financial and legal services are available. Borjas (1986) has shown that self-employment among Mexicans, Cubans, and "other Hispanics" increases with the percentage of Hispanics in an SMSA. The study also found that this enclave effect is larger among immigrants than among the population born in the United States. Fairlie and Meyer (1996) reach similar conclusions.

Language is one reason that self-employment rates may be higher in enclaves. But language is not the only channel through which ethnic enclaves affect self-employment. Immigrant entrepreneurs may also benefit from knowledge of their compatriots' tastes for goods and services. We attempt to isolate language effects from demand effects by looking at the interaction of language and enclave effects. If enclaves affect self-employment decisions through language, then there should be a stronger relationship between self-employment and enclaves among those who speak English poorly than among those who speak English well. The data on the left side of table 5.6 show exactly this pattern for male immigrants born in Mexico. The sample of Mexican immigrants is large enough to allow us to look at the patterns nonparametrically. We begin by dividing the public-use microareas (PUMAs) into quartiles according to the percentage of the population that identifies itself as being of Hispanic origin. The first row and column of table 5.6 indicate that the self-employment rate among Mexican male immigrants residing in PUMAs in the lowest quartile of Hispanic-origin population, with less than 7 percent of the population of Hispanic origin, is 4.6 percent. In the second and third quartiles, 5.0 and 6.1 percent of the Mexican-born males are self-employed.

We divide the highest quartile more finely into deciles and percentiles. Among those in the 9th decile, self-employment rates are 7.1 percent. In the 98th percentile, 86 percent of the population is of Hispanic origin, and the self-employment rate among Mexican-born men is 12.4 percent. In the 99th percentile, 90 percent of the population is of Hispanic origin, and the self-employment rate of Mexican-born men is 13.3 percent. About 30 percent of the Mexican-born population lives in PUMAs in the upper five percentiles, those with more than 50 percent Hispanic-origin population.

The second column of table 5.6 repeats the same exercise for Mexican-born men who report speaking English fluently, very well, or well. The third column reports the data for Mexican-born men who do not speak English well or at all. In the lowest quartiles, self-employment rates are much higher for those who speak English well. But in the upper decile of the distribution, the rates are actually slightly higher among those who do not speak English well. Enclaves appear to have a much larger impact on self-employment among those who do not speak English well than among those who do. This suggests that language is one of the channels through which enclaves affect self-employment among Mexican-born men.

The right side of table 5.6 shows the same data for Mexican-born women. The enclave effect appears to be smaller for women than for men. But as with men, the effect is much larger among women who speak English poorly than among women who speak English well. Indeed, the enclave effect is not evident at all among women who speak English well.

To see whether the interaction between enclaves and language survives the controls, and to see whether language and enclave effects are important for immigrants from other countries, we include the interaction term in the regressions. While most Hispanics come from countries where the native language is Spanish, Asians and Europeans do not have a single prevalent language.[21] Therefore, for the regressions, we define the enclave variable as the percentage of individuals born in the same country or narrow region. To be consistent, we define enclave similarly for those born in Mexico or Central America for the purposes of the regressions.

The results, reported in table 5.7, confirm for the Mexican-born the associations shown in table 5.6. Both the language and enclave effects are significantly positive for Mexican-born men. The interaction of the two is negative, suggesting that language matters less where the percentage of Mexican-born population in the PUMA is higher. The same is true for females, though the enclave-level effect is not statistically significant.[22]

Table 5.7 reports the results of similar regressions for immigrants from nine other countries or narrow regions. Where the language/enclave interaction effect is not significant, we report the results from the regression without the interaction effect. We find that the positive association between self-employment rates on the one hand and both language and ethnic enclaves on the other holds for male immigrants from Central America, Poland, and eastern Europe. Among male immigrants from western Europe, we find a negative enclave effect, no language effect, and a positive interaction between language and the concentration of immigrants from western Europe. These findings suggest that among western European immigrants, those with low levels of English are more likely to be self-employed when they reside in PUMAs with lower percentages of immigrants from western Europe, but that enclaves have no effect on those who speak English well. We also find negative enclave effects for male immigrants from China, India, and the Philippines. In the last case, there is a positive language effect. For female immigrants, we find positive enclave effects only for those from Central America. The enclave effects are negative for female immigrants from China, Vietnam, India, and the Philippines. Across all immigrant groups, enclave effects are less likely to be significant for female immigrants. This may be due to smaller sample sizes, or to the lesser importance of language among female immigrants who are in the labor force.

The regressions reported on table 5.7 suggest that the effect of enclaves on self-employment differs markedly for immigrants from different countries. Those from Mexico are most like those from Poland and other eastern European countries. Enclave effects appear to be much less important for those from Asia. Whether this is because the process of selection into self-employment is different for these immigrants or because the cohort for these groups is much smaller is difficult to say.

Legal Status

Another explanation we explore here for low self-employment rates among Mexican immigrants is their legal status. The U.S. Immigration and Naturalization Service (INS) places the Mexican-born population residing illegally in the United States in 2000 at 4.8 million;[23] according to Passel, Capps, and Fix (2004), this figure is 5.3 million. These estimates compare with the census total of 9.1 million Mexican-born individuals residing in the United States in 2000, suggesting that half or more of the Mexican-born population resides in the United States without legal documentation. The proportion of the Mexican-born population estimated to be in the United States without legal documentation is much higher than the proportion of Koreans (6.3 percent), Chinese (7.6 percent), Indians (6.8 percent), Poles (10.1 percent), or those from countries that had been part of the former Soviet Union (5.5 percent; all percentages from INS 2003). Of the countries represented on table 5.7, only Central America (26.2 percent) has rates of undocumented residents that come close to those for Mexico. To the extent that legal status affects self-employment rates, the impact is likely to be largest among the Mexican-born population.

The theoretical impact of legal status on self-employment is not clear. Kossoudji and Cobb-Clark (2002) find that Hispanic wage and salary workers gaining legal status through IRCA experienced wage increases. In a standard model of entrepreneurship,[24] this increase in wages would make self-employment less likely among immigrants residing in the country legally. Legal status, however, would also be expected to affect earnings from self-employment through, for example, its effect on the ability to access institutions important to entrepreneurs. Legal residents have access to the court system, should disputes arise with employees or customers. Legal immigrants are also more likely to own property that might be used as collateral, and hence to have access to credit. The theoretical effect of legal status on self-employment rates is thus ambiguous.

We examine the impact of legal status empirically, using IRCA to identify a discontinuous change in the legal status of immigrants. IRCA included an amnesty that allowed immigrants residing illegally in the United States at the time the act was passed to obtain legal status. To qualify under IRCA, immigrants had to prove that they had lived continuously in the country since at least January 1, 1982.[25] One source of data on the impact of IRCA is the Legalized Population Survey. In 1988 and again in 1992, the LPS interviewed immigrants applying for legal status through IRCA; the sample included 892 males and 500 females born in Mexico. Immigrants were asked about employment both at the time they applied for legal status and again in 1992. The LPS data indicate that the self-employment rate of immigrants increased markedly after they were legalized through IRCA. For male immigrants, the rate of self-employment increased from 4.6 percent in 1989 to 8.3 percent in 1992; for females, the increase was from 3.6 percent to 5.1 percent during this same period. Among the Mexican-born males, self-employment increased over the same period from 3.0 percent to 5.6 percent; among females, self-employment increased from 2.2 percent to 3.2 percent. Thus, if half of the resident Mexican-born population lacks legal status, and legal status is associated with a 2.3 percentage point increase in self-employment, then rates of self-employment among the Mexican-born population might be expected to increase by 1.2 percentage points with legalization of the resident population. The data suggest, then, that legal status may be an important factor in explaining the lower self-employment rates among the Mexican-born population.

We also examine the impact of legalization using population census data and specifically using the 1982 entry requirement as a discontinuity in the legal status of immigrants. We compare self-employment rates in 1990 for Mexican-Americans entering the country between 1981 and 1982, and for those entering between 1982 and 1984. To be sure, the sharp line created by the law is made fuzzy by several factors. First, many who met the qualifications failed to apply for legal status either by choice or because they could not document their residence. Second, the deadline for applying for legal status was May 4, 1988. Some of those who applied had not completed the process at the time of the 1990 population census. Nevertheless, IRCA provides a useful natural experiment for exploring the impact of legalized status on business ownership.

Estimates from the 1990 census provide evidence consistent with the LPS. The self-employment rate in 1990 of males born in Mexico who entered the United States in 1980–1981 was 5.4 percent, compared to a rate of 4.3 percent for those who entered between 1982 and 1984. The change during these two periods is large relative to the change in rates of Mexicans entering in the 1975–1979 period and those entering in the 1985–1986 period. The self-employment rates of the former group are only 1.7 percentage points higher than those of the latter group.

An alternative comparison group is immigrants entering the United States from countries that were less affected by IRCA. Estimates from U.S. Immigration and Naturalization Service (1997) indicate that Mexico is by far the largest source country for IRCA applicants; Asian countries have relatively few applicants. For example, almost 2.3 million Mexicans applied for legal status under IRCA, or 53 percent of the Mexican-born population in 1990. In contrast, only 3 percent of the 1990 U.S. population born in Asia was legalized through IRCA. For all non-Mexican immigrants and Asian immigrants we find much smaller declines in self-employment rates between the 1980–1981 and 1982–1984 entry cohorts than for Mexican immigrants. We also find steeper downward trends in self-employment rates across entry cohorts over a longer period of time for the Asian and all non-Mexican immigrants than for Mexican immigrants. Although these results are only suggestive, they are consistent with legal status having a strong effect on rates of self-employment.

Education and Wealth

Self-employment may also be associated with education levels. Fairlie and Woodruff (2007) show that education is positively associated with self-employment levels among the native-born in the United States. Table 5.8 shows that the education levels of immigrants vary markedly by country of origin. Mexican-born male immigrants have an average of six years of schooling, compared with about twelve years among immigrants from Europe and ten to twelve years among Asian immigrants. The average years of schooling of Mexican-born females is slightly higher, around 6.6 years, while the schooling of women immigrants from other countries is similar to that of men from those countries.

Although self-employment rates increase with education among natives in the United States, the connection between education and self-employment is less clear for immigrants. Table 5.8 shows the predicted difference in self-employment rates (taken from the regression coefficients reported on table 5.7) for individuals with twelve and six years of schooling for each country or narrow region examined. The table shows that Mexican-born men with twelve years of schooling are one percentage point more likely to be self employed than Mexican-born men with six years of schooling. This suggests that raising the education level of Mexican-born immigrant men from six years to the median level among native-born non-Hispanic whites (eleven years) would increase self-employment rates by about one percentage point. But while there is a positive association between self-employment rates and education for Mexican-born men, there is a negative association for immigrant men from eastern Europe, western Europe, and the Philippines. Among immigrant women from Mexico, Central America, China, India, and the Philippines, self-employment is negatively associated with education among immigrants. For both men and women, these associations are only suggestive, because we do not account for the effect of education on labor force participation decisions, or for the correlation of education with unmeasured ability that might also affect schooling levels.

Wealth is another factor that has been identified as important in determining whether an individual is self-employed. Wealth may affect entry into and exit from self-employment either because individuals are able to leverage wealth through credit markets or because wealthier individuals are more willing to take risks.[26] Self-employment also affects wealth. For this reason, the causal association of wealth on self-employment requires panel data. Unfortunately, the available panel data sets are too small to allow for analysis of separate immigrant groups other than the Mexican-born. As a result, we are able to provide only some suggestive data on the impact of wealth on self-employment among immigrants.

Data from the six March Current Population Surveys conducted between 1998 and 2003 suggest that wealth levels of individuals born in Mexico are much lower than wealth levels of U.S.-born non-Hispanic whites. The CPS provides data on income earned from assets rather than the level of assets themselves. Mexican-born men report average annual interest income of $102, rental income of $63, and dividend income of $21. By comparison, U.S.-born non-Hispanic whites report interest income of $822, rental income of $241, and dividend income of $425. Just over half (52 percent) of Mexican-born men own the house in which they live, compared with 82 percent of white, non-Hispanic men. The differences for women are slightly larger. Income from interest, dividends, and rents totals $131 for Mexican-born women, compared with $1,384 for U.S.-born non-Hispanic white women. The samples of Asian and European immigrants in the CPS are too small to provide reliable estimates. But the available data suggest that wealth is likely to have an important effect on the rates of self-employment among Mexican-born immigrants.

CONCLUSION

The self-employment rate among Mexican-born immigrant men is nine percentage points lower than the rate among non-Hispanic white immigrant men. The gap for women is smaller but still significant, 3.5 percentage points. We have examined several factors that account for a part of this difference. Among men, English language ability appears to account for about one percentage point of the gap and education for another one percentage point. Data from the Legalized Population Survey suggest that legal status also has an effect on self-employment, with self-employment increasing as legal status is gained. Given the estimates that half of the Mexican-born population counted in the 2000 population census lack legal documentation, we estimate that legal status may explain another percentage point of the gap. English-language ability and legal status combine, then, to explain about a third of the gap between Mexican-born men and U.S.-born non-Hispanic men. Once differences in wealth are taken into account, perhaps half of the gap can be explained.

With respect to self-employment rates, perhaps the most interesting result comes from the analysis of ethnic enclaves. Almost a third of the Mexican-born population lives in PUMAs where more than half of the population identifies itself as being of Hispanic descent. In these areas, self-employment rates are much higher than elsewhere and reach levels comparable to those for Asian and European immigrants. In the PUMAs in the upper two percentiles of Hispanic-origin population, more than 13 percent of men are self-employed.[27] This suggests that Mexican immigrants are not lacking in entrepreneurial ability, but rather that those outside of enclaves face either more barriers or better wage market opportunities, which result in lower levels of self-employment.

While these factors explain a substantial part of the gap between Mexicans and other immigrants, only wealth appears able to explain any part of the gap that remains between those of Mexican descent born in the United States and non-Hispanic whites born in the United States. The gap between these groups remains high, about six percentage points. Since all are citizens by birth, legal status clearly does not differ among the native born. About 95 percent of those of Mexican descent born in the United States report that they speak English fluently, very well, or well, implying that language is much less a factor among the U.S.-born. And education levels among first-generation Mexican-Americans are also markedly higher than those of immigrants born in Mexico. As Blau and Kahn (2007) report, average education levels rise from around nine years for immigrants to 12.6 years among first-generation Mexican Americans. This compares with an average of 13.7 years among non-Hispanic whites. Given the modest association between education and self-employment rates, the remaining difference in education explains only a fraction of the remaining gap. Only differences in wealth can explain any part of this gap.

Table 5.1.   Self-Employment Rates

	Males	Females
Foreign-born:		
Non-Hispanic white	14.20%	8.50%
Asian	10.30%	7.10%
Mexican-American	5.30%	5.00%
U.S.-born:		
Non-Hispanic white	11.10%	6.40%
Asian	6.80%	4.30%
Mexican-American	5.30%	3.40%

Note: Data from 2000 U.S. population census, using sample weights provided in the census.

Table 5.2.   Self-Employment Rates for Immigrants by Country/Region of Birth

	Males	Females
Mexico	5.3%	4.9%
Central America	5.4%	6.6%
Poland	12.4%	10.6%
Eastern Europe	12.6%	6.9%
Western Europe	12.7%	8.2%
China	10.7%	7.2%
Korea	23.3%	15.0%
Vietnam	8.3%	8.0%
India	10.3%	6.5%
Philippines	4.7%	3.5%

Note: Data from 2000 U.S. population census, using sample weights provided in the census.

Table 5.3A. Industry of Occupation and Self-Employment Rates Immigrants and U.S.-Born

MALES

Percentage of Workforce by Industry

	Foreign-born non-Hispanic white	U.S.-born non-Hispanic white	Mexican-born	Asian-born
Agriculture/Mining	8.41	0.70	1.05	2.77
Construction	21.58	3.49	10.59	12.39
Manufacturing	21.68	20.95	17.75	19.00
Wholesale Trade	5.19	4.27	4.35	4.84
Retail Trade	6.76	10.59	10.45	10.23
Transport and Warehousing	3.63	5.27	5.40	5.84
Utilities	0.37	0.51	0.72	1.52
Information	0.89	3.48	3.68	3.22
Finance, Insurance, and Real Estate	1.69	5.58	6.14	5.57
Professional Services	9.35	12.65	12.13	9.52
Education/Heath Services	2.65	13.18	10.93	9.09
Arts and Entertainment	11.95	11.01	8.01	5.24
Other Services	4.86	4.79	4.67	4.26
Public Admin/Armed Forces	0.99	3.53	4.13	6.52
Total	100.00	100.00	100.00	100.00

Percentage Self-Employed by Industry

	Foreign-born non-Hispanic white	U.S.-born non-Hispanic white	Mexican-born	Asian-born
Agriculture/Mining	3.75	21.85	22.80	36.85
Construction	7.30	21.05	27.22	23.39
Manufacturing	1.10	2.58	5.13	3.16
Wholesale Trade	3.05	14.68	17.69	9.04
Retail Trade	7.01	16.90	16.97	10.06
Transport and Warehousing	8.48	10.58	13.41	8.60
Utilities	0.00	0.00	0.00	0.00
Information	2.86	2.88	6.88	5.55
Finance, Insurance, and Real Estate	5.84	10.97	15.24	16.35
Professional Services	11.02	10.33	18.98	22.61
Education/Heath Services	2.93	9.19	9.94	7.45
Arts and Entertainment	2.96	14.33	17.59	10.33
Other Services	11.37	23.17	23.95	19.38
Public Admin/Armed Forces	0.00	0.00	0.00	0.00
Total	5.20	10.30	14.40	11.80

Note: Data from 2000 U.S. population census, using sample weights provided in the census.

**Table 5.3B. Industry of Occupation and Self-Employment
Rates Immigrants and U.S.-Born**

	FEMALES			
	Percentage of Workforce by Industry			
	Foreign-born non-Hispanic white	U.S.-born non-Hispanic white	Mexican-born	Asian-born
Agriculture/Mining	4.94	0.39	0.42	0.71
Construction	1.18	0.63	1.45	1.76
Manufacturing	23.10	16.96	9.95	9.35
Wholesale Trade	5.12	3.05	2.49	2.39
Retail Trade	9.30	10.72	11.90	12.32
Transport and Warehousing	1.55	2.43	2.10	2.32
Utilities	0.15	0.26	0.28	0.48
Information	1.22	2.78	3.08	3.04
Finance, Insurance, and Real Estate	3.57	7.97	8.96	8.94
Professional Services	7.98	9.29	11.64	9.35
Education/Heath Services	16.99	25.93	29.94	32.56
Arts and Entertainment	15.27	10.44	8.22	7.50
Other Services	7.99	6.43	6.37	4.74
Public Admin/Armed Forces	1.64	2.72	3.20	4.54
Total	100.00	100.00	100.00	100.00

	Percentage Self-Employed by Industry			
	Foreign-born non-Hispanic white	U.S. born non-Hispanic white	Mexican-born	Asian-born
Agriculture/Mining	1.48	14.92	22.47	28.67
Construction	7.52	11.78	17.73	15.66
Manufacturing	0.98	1.86	3.81	2.51
Wholesale Trade	2.00	8.96	8.23	5.69
Retail Trade	6.13	11.95	8.25	6.57
Transport and Warehousing	2.79	1.84	3.99	3.99
Utilities	0.00	0.00	0.00	0.00
Information	0.71	1.95	4.90	4.05
Finance, Insurance, and Real Estate	3.23	4.82	7.20	5.97
Professional Services	7.91	8.02	14.63	14.05
Education/Heath Services	5.15	4.24	5.13	4.03
Arts and Entertainment	2.32	11.57	10.07	6.10
Other Services	21.38	23.99	26.87	21.88
Public Admin/Armed Forces	0.00	0.00	0.00	0.00
Total	4.80	7.10	8.60	6.50

Note: Data from 2000 U.S. population census, using sample weights provided in the census.

Table 5.4. English Language Ability of Immigrants: Percentage Speaking Fluently, Very Well, or Well

Country of Origin	Males	Females
Mexico	52.4	53.4
Central America	61.5	63.6
Poland	77.9	81.2
Eastern Europe	83.1	85.5
Western Europe	96.1	96.7
China	73.8	72.7
Korea	74.4	75.2
Vietnam	71.8	66.9
India	96.1	93.4
Philippines	95.8	96.8

Note: Data from 2000 U.S. population census, using sample weights provided in the census.

Table 5.5. Self-Employment of Immigrants by Level of English

	Males		Females	
Country of Origin	Low	High	Low	High
Mexico	4.2	6.3	4.9	5.0
Central America	4.3	6.1	7.3	6.3
Poland	7.3	13.8	12.2	10.2
Eastern Europe	8.3	13.4	6.1	7.0
Western Europe	10.7	12.8	7.2	8.6
China	12.2	10.2	7.6	7.0
Korea	30.4	20.9	22.9	12.4
Vietnam	7.8	8.5	8.0	8.0
India	10.4	10.2	8.0	6.4
Philippines	2.2	4.8	3.0	3.6

Note: Data from 2000 U.S. population census, using sample weights provided in the census.

Table 5.6. Enclaves and Self-Employment: Percentage of Workforce Self-Employed

	Males			Females		
Percentile of Hispanic-origin population	All	Speak English fluently, very well, or well	Speak English not well/ not at all	All	Speak English fluently, very well, or well	Speak English not well/ not at all
Lowest quartile	4.6	6.0	3.2	5.1	6.1	3.9
Second quartile	5.0	6.6	3.2	5.8	6.4	5.1
Third quartile	6.1	7.4	4.7	7.2	7.0	7.7
80th–90th percentile	7.1	8.5	5.6	6.5	6.3	6.7
90th–95th percentile	7.4	8.3	6.6	6.6	6.2	7.1
95th–97 percentile	9.4	9.9	8.8	7.1	5.9	8.4
98th percentile	12.4	11.0	14.2	7.0	6.9	6.9
99th percentile	13.3	12.5	14.3	7.6	5.3	10.2

Notes: Data from 2000 U.S. population census, using sample weights provided in the census. Sample limited to those born in Mexico, working fifteen or more hours per week, and between the ages of twenty and sixty-four.

Table 5.7. Probits for Language and Enclave Effects

Dependent Variable: Self-Employed

Males

	Mexico (1)	Central America (2)	Poland (3)	Eastern Europe (4)	Western Europe (5)	China (6)	Korea (7)	Vietnam (8)	India (9)	Philippines (10)
English language ability	0.0222***	0.016***	0.0591***	0.0381***	0.0232	-0.0115	-0.0155	0.0134**	0.0109	0.0162**
	(0.0022)	(0.0040)	(0.0117)	(0.0076)	(0.0132)	(0.0093)	(0.0112)	(0.0057)	(0.0109)	(0.0058)
Percentage country-of-origin population, PUMA	0.0008***	.0012***	0.002*	0.0035***	-0.0080**	-0.0027**	0.0005	-0.001	-0.0072***	-0.0012***
	(0.0002)	(0.0005)	(0.0011)	(0.0009)	(0.0034)	(0.0012)	(0.0014)	(0.0007)	(0.0019)	(0.0004)
Enclave* English Language	-0.0006***	-0.0011**	–	-0.0035***	0.0082*	0.0030***				
	(0.0001)	(0.0005)		(0.0010)	(0.0042)	(0.0007)				
Pseudo-R-square	0.032	0.038	0.0335	0.0622	0.0543	0.085	0.133	0.045	0.114	0.094
Unweighted observations	153015	34588	6007	17258	33689	18473	10910	16162	19028	19616
Weighted observations	3263007	755858	137648	393344	721181	408398	241624	353829	434075	419079
Dependent mean	0.053	0.054	0.124	0.126	0.127	0.108	0.233	0.083	0.103	0.047

Females

	Mexico (1)	Central America (2)	Poland (3)	Eastern Europe (4)	Western Europe (5)	China (6)	Korea (7)	Vietnam (8)	India (9)	Philippines (10)
English language ability	0.0129***	0.0027	-0.0032	0.0014	0.0181*	-0.0107	-0.0632***	0.0057	-0.0038	0.0066
	(0.0030)	(0.0040)	(0.0138)	(0.0086)	(0.0090)	(0.0078)	(0.0110)	(0.0063)	(0.0107)	(0.0058)
Percentage country-of-origin population, PUMA	0.0001	0.0008*	-0.0003	-0.0001	-0.002	-0.0028***	-0.0011	-0.0013*	-0.0068***	-0.001***
	(0.0001)	(0.0004)	(0.0012)	(0.0007)	(0.0090)	(0.0006)	(0.0010)	(0.0007)	(0.0016)	(0.0003)
Enclave* English Language	-0.0005***	–	–	-0.0015**	–	0.0023***	0.0052***			
	(0.0002)			(0.0008)		(0.0009)	(0.0014)			
Pseudo-R-square	0.02	0.03	0.03	0.04	0.03	0.06	0.10	0.05	0.08	0.04
Unweighted observations	78837	26046	5314	14869	31536	16878	11432	13816	10937	25306
Weighted observations	1656649	562800	119871	334259	657758	373804	256151	301761	246791	540639
Dependent mean	0.050	0.066	0.106	0.069	0.082	0.071	0.150	0.080	0.065	0.036

Notes: Standard errors in parentheses. Sample limited to those born in Mexico, working more than zero hours per week, and between the ages of twenty and sixty-four. Statistical significance indicated by asterisks: *** —significant at <.01; ** —significant at .05; * —significant at .10.

Table 5.8. Education and Self-Employment of Immigrants

Country/ region of origin	Males		Females	
	Avg. years of schooling	Difference in S/E rate, 12 years vs. 6 years	Avg. years of schooling	Difference in S/E rate, 12 years vs. 6 years
Mexico	6.1	0.01	6.6	-0.01
Central America	7.1	0.02	7.7	-0.01
Poland	10.4	0.02	10.5	0.05
Eastern Europe	11.3	-0.02	11.4	0.00
Western Europe	10.8	-0.03	10.7	0.00
China	11.4	0.04	11.0	-0.02
Korea	11.7	0.10	10.8	0.04
Vietnam	9.7	0.02	9.2	0.05
India	12.7	0.01	12.2	-0.01
Philippines	11.3	-0.01	11.5	-0.01

Note: Calculations by the authors using regressions shown on Table 5.7.

NOTES

* We would like to thank Lori Kletzer, David Neumark, Pia Orrenius, and seminar participants at University of California, Davis; the National Bureau of Economic Research (NBER) conference on Mexican immigration; and the Hudson Institute for helpful comments and suggestions on a related NBER conference paper. Daniel Beltran, Kuntal Das, and Jose Martinez provided excellent research assistance. We thank the Ewing Marion Kauffman Foundation for financial support for this project.

1. See, for example, Trejo (1997, 2003), Blau and Kahn (2007), and Cobb-Clark and Hildebrand (2004).

2. See Loewen (1971), Light (1972), Baron et al. (1975), and Bonacich and Modell (1980).

3. Pyong Gap Min, "Some positive functions of ethnic business for an immigrant community: Koreans in Los Angeles," Final Report submitted to the National Science Foundation, Washington, D.C.: 1989; and Pyong Gap Min, "Korean immigrants in Los Angeles," *Immigration and entrepreneurship: Culture, capital, and ethnic networks,* ed. Ivan Light and Parminder Bhachu (New Brunswick, NJ: Transaction Publishers, 1993): 185–204.

4. Timothy Bates, *Assessment of state and local government minority business development programs,* Report to the U.S. Department of Commerce Minority Business Development Agency (Washington, D.C.: U.S. Department of Commerce, 1993).

5. U.S. Census Bureau, *1992 Economic census: Characteristics of business owners* (Washington, D.C.: U.S. Government Printing Office, 1997).

6. Charles Brown, James Hamilton, and James Medoff, *Employers large and small* (Cambridge, MA: Harvard University Press, 1990).

7. See, for example, Hurst and Lusardi (2004).

8. Robert W. Fairlie and Bruce D. Meyer, "Trends in self-employment among black and white men: 1910–1990," *Journal of Human Resources* 35, no. 4 (2000): 643–69.

9. See, for example, Bates (1997), Fairlie (1999), and Hout and Rosen (2000).

10. Blanchflower, Levine, and Zimmerman (2003), and Cavalluzzo, Cavalluzzo, and Wolken (2002).

11. See Borjas and Bronars (1989) and Meyer (1990), for example.

12. Borjas (1986), Yuengert (1995), and Fairlie and Meyer (1996).

13. Robert W. Fairlie, "Does business ownership provide a source of upward mobility for blacks and Hispanics?" *Public policy and the economics of entrepreneurship*, ed. Doug Holtz-Eakin and Havey S. Rosen (Cambridge, MA: MIT Press, 2004), 153–79.

14. See Lofstrom (2002) and Andersson and Wadensjö (2003), for example.

15. Robert W. Fairlie and Christopher Woodruff, "Mexican entrepreneurship: A comparison of self-employment in Mexico and the United States," *Mexican Immigration to the United States*, ed. George Borjas, (Chicago: University of Chicago Press, forthcoming spring 2007).

16. Including Bulgaria, Czechoslovakia, Hungary, Romania, and the countries that made up the former Soviet Union.

17. Including Belgium, Denmark, Finland, France, Germany, Italy, the Netherlands, Norway, Portugal, Spain, and Sweden.

18. Including Belize, Costa Rica, El Salvador, Guatemala, Honduras, Nicaragua, and Panama.

19. Fairlie and Meyer (1996) find that better command of the English language is associated with higher rates of self-employment among males, while the opposite holds among females. English-language ability has also been found to affect earnings in wage labor markets (McManus, Gould, and Welch, 1983; Dustman and van Soest, 2002; and Bleakley and Chin, 2003).

20. One instrument for language ability that has been suggested in the literature is the age of arrival in the United States (Bleakley and Chin, 2003). Because migration to the United States might also be seen as a decision endogenous to entrepreneurial ability, this instrument is valid only among a sample of those arriving in the United States at a young age—that is, as dependents. Among the sample of those arriving at age fourteen or younger, the language and enclave effects are not significant in both linear probability and IV regressions. Hence, we report the language and enclave results as associations rather than causal factors.

21. The census asks individuals what language is spoken at home. We use the country of birth instead because many foreign-born individuals report English as the primary language. The census does not ask about second languages.

22. For U.S.-born males of Mexican descent, neither language nor enclave effects are significant. For U.S-born females of Mexican descent, language has no effect, but self-employment rates are significantly lower in enclaves. These results are consistent with the findings of Borjas (1986) of weaker effects among the native-born of Hispanic descent.

23. U.S. Immigration and Naturalization Service, *Estimates of unauthorized immigrant population residing in the United States: 1990 to 2000* (Washington, D.C.: Office of Policy Planning, 2003).

24. See, for example, Lucas (1978).

25. IRCA allowed for an important exception to the 1982 residence requirement. Special Agricultural Workers (SAWs) had to prove that they had been in the United States and worked on perishable crops for only ninety days between May 1, 1985, and May 1, 1986. 42 percent of those seeking amnesty under IRCA applied through the SAWs program.

26. Evans and Jovanovic (1989) and Blanchflower and Oswald (1998) find links between self-employment and an individual's assets using data from the United States and Great Britain, respectively. Hurst and Lusardi (2004) and Fairlie and Krashinsky (2005) examine the nonlinearity of the effect of wealth on self-employment. Hurst and Lusardi (2004) suggest that the effect is highly nonlinear and is concentrated in the 95th percentile and above in the distribution of wealth. This suggests that risk aversion may be a more important factor than credit constraints in limiting self-employment.

27. Even in these areas, the mean earnings of the self-employed are higher than the mean earnings of wage workers.

Improving Pension Coverage at Small Firms

WILLIAM E. EVEN AND DAVID A. MACPHERSON

INTRODUCTION

The private pension system is a vital component of retirement income for many Americans. However, as recently as 2004, only 52 percent of full-time year-round private-sector workers were covered by a pension in the United States. While this represents a one percentage point increase over the level of coverage in 1988, large numbers of workers remain uncovered.

With growing concerns about the ability of Social Security to continue its current level of generosity, policymakers are considering ways to encourage other forms of retirement saving. Since there is evidence that the ability to save through a private pension plan increases retirement savings, particularly among low-income households, improving pension coverage rates has been an important goal for many legislators.[1]

While numerous variables are useful predictors of whether a worker has a pension, one of the most salient predictors is the size of the firm employing him. In 2004, only 20 percent of workers employed at firms with less than twenty-five employees were covered by a pension, whereas 60 percent of workers employed at firms with a thousand or more employees were covered. Given that more than one of every four workers is employed at firms with less than twenty-five employees, improving coverage at small firms would significantly enhance pension coverage in the United States.[2]

This study examines the source of lower pension coverage rates at small firms. After reviewing some of the hypotheses for why coverage is lower at small firms, we discuss recent trends in coverage rates by firm size. An important finding is that pension coverage rates rose over the past fifteen years, particularly at small firms. This study uses a variety of data sources to determine why pension coverage rose over time, and why the increase was greatest among small firms. Our analysis finds that changes in worker characteristics increased worker demand for pensions over time, particularly at small firms. Although rising worker demand explains most of the increase in coverage at small firms, there is evidence that other factors, such as legislative attempts to improve pension coverage at small firms by reducing administrative costs, contributed to improvements as well.

This study also compares small and large firms in terms of the type of pension plan offered and the generosity of the plans. Both large and small firms shifted away from defined benefit (DB) and toward defined contribution (DC) plans in recent years. The major difference between small and large firms is that large firms are more likely to offer both a DB and a DC plan, whereas small firms are more likely to offer only a DC plan. Although one might expect that scale economies in the provision of pensions and the greater administrative costs of DB plans could account for this pattern, this study shows that differences in the type of workers employed at large and small firms accounts for much of the difference.

Finally, the generosity of pension plans is compared for workers at large and small firms. Among workers covered by a pension, generosity is quite similar at small and large firms. Consequently, the main concern regarding a shortfall of pension wealth for workers at small firms is a lack of pension coverage.

SOME REASONS FOR DIFFERENCES IN PENSION COVERAGE

A company's decision to offer a pension plan depends on the costs and benefits of the pension. Offering a plan entails several costs. First and foremost, employers frequently make contributions to fund the pension. Second, the employer must cover the administrative expense of the plan. The benefits of offering a pension include the fact that a worker will be willing to accept lower wages in return for a pension. Whether the worker is willing to give up more or less than one dollar of wages for a dollar of pension benefits will depend on the worker's saving preferences, the value placed on the access to tax-advantaged saving, and the perception of how much risk is involved in contributing to the pension. Contributing to the pension may be viewed as risky if there is some chance that the firm will go bankrupt and be unable to meet its pension obligations. Alternatively, if the pension is not perfectly portable, the worker is faced with the risk of losing some pension wealth upon a change of employers.

Firms also benefit from offering pensions because by switching compensation from wages to pensions, they potentially improve worker productivity.[3] Since pensions can be designed to backload pay, the pension can be used to screen out quitters and thus conserve on hiring and training costs. Pensions may also reduce monitoring costs, since employees will be more concerned about dismissal when pay is backloaded.

The benefits and costs of a pension differ across employers for several important reasons. First, the amount of wages that a worker is willing to exchange for a pension differs across employee groups. Given the tax advantages of pension saving and the progressive income tax structure in the United States, firms that employ predominantly high-income workers are more likely to offer a pension plan. Also, firms that employ a relatively young workforce are probably less likely to offer a pension because younger workers are generally less concerned about saving for retirement. Second, the per capita cost of administering a plan varies across firms. Several studies document that there are scale economies in the administration of pensions.[4] Consequently, the higher per capita cost of administration will make small firms less likely to offer a pension.

LEGISLATIVE EFFORTS TO IMPROVE COVERAGE AT SMALL FIRMS

To help improve the low pension coverage offered by small firms, Congress specifically designed two pensions that attempt to reduce administrative costs—the Simplified Employee Pension (SEP) and the Savings Incentive Match Plan for Employees (SIMPLE).

Created by the Revenue Act of 1978 for use by firms with twenty-five or fewer employees, the SEP was designed to reduce set-up and administration costs that were thought to impede pension adoption by small companies.

Under the SEP, an individual retirement account (IRA) is established for each eligible employee, and the employee is immediately vested in employer contributions. Employer contributions must be made for each employee who has reached age twenty-one and worked for the employer during at least three of the preceding five years. Employers must contribute the same percentage of compensation for all eligible employees in any given year, but contribution rates may vary from year to year. The maximum employer contribution is the lesser of $30,000 or 15 percent of compensation in a given year.

Employees may make elective contributions to a SEP, subject to the restriction that employer plus employee contributions may not exceed the lesser of $30,000 or 15 percent of compensation. Also, elective contributions are subject to nondiscrimination requirements.

In the Tax Reform Act of 1986, Congress created a salary reduction SEP (SARSEP) that allowed for the SEP to be funded entirely by contributions from the employee rather than the employer. At least half of all eligible employees had to participate for the plan to be qualified. These plans were subjected to the same eligibility, vesting, and nondiscrimination requirements as other defined contribution plans. Congress prohibited the adoption of new SARSEPs in the Small Business Job Protection Act of 1996, though existing plans were allowed to continue enrolling new participants.

The SIMPLE was established for firms with less than one hundred employees under the Small Business Job Protection Act of 1996. Designed to avoid complex nondiscrimination testing and reduce administrative burdens for the employer, the SIMPLE can be either an IRA for each employee or part of a 401(k) plan to which employees make elective contributions. Employee contributions must be expressed as a percentage of compensation and cannot exceed $6,000 per year (indexed). The employer is required to satisfy one of two contribution formulas. Under the matching contribution formula, the employer matches on a dollar-for-dollar basis up to 3 percent of employee compensation. Alternatively, the employer may make a nonelective contribution of 2 percent of compensation for all eligible employees. All contributions must vest immediately.

More recent legislative attempts to improve pension coverage at small firms include the provision in the Economic Growth and Tax Relief Reconciliation Act of 2001 to provide a tax credit of up to $500 for qualifying start-up costs for businesses with up to one hundred employees. The Pension Protection and

Expansion Act of 2003 (which did not pass) proposed two new stimuli for coverage at small firms. First, businesses with more than ten employees that did not offer a pension plan would be required to allow employees to fund an IRA through payroll deductions. Second, small businesses could receive a tax credit for contributions to a new pension plan.

Despite these legislative efforts to improve pension coverage at small firms, there remains a wide gap in coverage rates. Surveys of small firms conducted by the Employee Benefits Research Institute (EBRI) reveal some of the reasons that small firms do not offer pension plans. In a recent survey,[5] firms with one hundred or fewer employees were asked to identify the most important reason for not offering a pension. The three most common answers were: (1) employees prefer wages or other benefits (20 percent), (2) revenue is too uncertain to commit to a plan (18 percent), and (3) a large portion of workers are seasonal or part-time, or there is high turnover among workers (15 percent). The expense of setting up and administering a pension was identified by only 12 percent of firms as the "most important" reason for not offering a pension. However, 34 percent of firms indicated that this expense was a "major" reason. In a more recent survey,[6] small firms currently without a pension identified the following as the four factors that would be most likely to motivate them to add a plan: (1) an increase in business profits, (2) a plan that requires no employer contributions, (3) increased business tax credits for starting a plan, and (4) a plan with reduced administrative expenses.

If there are scale economies in setting up and administering pensions, smaller firms should be more likely than larger firms to report set-up and administrative costs as a greater impediment to pension offerings. However, the EBRI (2001) survey data do not support this hypothesis. Comparing firms with five to twenty employees with those that have twenty-one to one hundred employees, the survey found that the smallest firms were only one-half as likely to cite set-up and administration costs as the most important reason for not offering a pension plan (11 percent versus 22 percent). The very smallest firms were more likely to cite employee preferences for wages and/or other fringe benefits (20 versus 11 percent) and revenue uncertainty (19 versus 6 percent) as the most important reasons for not offering a pension.

The EBRI data also reveal that while the SEP and SIMPLE are common choices for small firms, the most popular plan is the 401(k). Among companies with one hundred or fewer employees that offer a DC plan, 58 percent offer a 401(k), 22 percent offer a SIMPLE, 22 percent offer a deferred profit sharing plan, and 13 percent offer a SEP. The SEP and SIMPLE combined represent about one-third of pension offerings for small firms with DC plans. This fact may lead one to the conclusion that the SEP and SIMPLE played an important role in improving coverage at small firms. However, it is possible that the firms that adopted SEP or SIMPLE plans would have adopted an alternative type of pension anyway.[7] Hence, it is difficult to estimate the effect of the SEP and SIMPLE on coverage at small firms. The approach we take is to estimate the effect of other variables on coverage at small firms, and to treat any "residual" effect as possibly reflecting the effects of legislative initiatives such as the SEP or SIMPLE.

TRENDS IN PENSION COVERAGE AT SMALL AND LARGE FIRMS

The March Current Population Survey (CPS) provides information on whether a worker is employed by a firm offering any of its workers a pension and, if so, whether the worker is covered by the plan. Our analysis draws on data from 1989 to 2005 and focuses on differences by firm size in the percentage of workers included in a pension plan (henceforth, the "coverage rate").[8] The March CPS data place firms into one of five size categories based on the number of employees: 1–24, 25–99, 100–499, 500–999, and 1000+. For the analysis below, the sample is restricted to individuals aged twenty-two to fifty-five who worked at least one week in the prior year and whose longest job in the prior year was in the private sector.

Figure 6.1 illustrates the trend in the pension coverage rate from 1979 through 2004 for private-sector workers aged twenty-two through fifty-five as well as those sixteen and over.[9] It is useful to compare the pension coverage rate for prime age workers to the overall coverage rate since school enrollment and early retirement decisions may affect the coverage rate of workers outside the prime age range. A comparison of the two age groups reveals that, while the level of pension coverage is higher in the twenty-two- to fifty-five-year-old population than in the sixteen and over population, the trends in the two groups are quite similar. During the 1980s, coverage rates fell by approximately five percentage points for both age groups. Even and Macpherson (1994) find that much of the decline in coverage for men in the 1980s was caused by employee participation rates dropping as firms switched to 401(k) plans and gave workers a choice of whether to join the pension plan. The trend reversed in the 1990s, and by the year 2000 coverage rates had returned to the 1980 levels. The coverage rate rose in the 1990s due to a rise in coverage at small firms. Since 2000, coverage rates have begun to decline again.[10] (Because the March CPS provides information on firm size beginning in 1989, this study focuses on size-related differences in pension coverage since 1988. It is worth noting that this ignores the 1980s, when pension coverage fell fairly substantially. We are unable to determine whether the decline in coverage during this period differed by firm size.)

Figure 6.2 presents pension offer, coverage, and participation rates for the five firm size categories available in the March CPS. The offer rate is the percentage of workers employed at a firm that offers at least some of its workers a pension plan. The participation rate is the percentage of workers who are offered a pension who are enrolled. The coverage rate is the percentage of workers who are enrolled in an employer-sponsored pension.

The data shown in figure 6.2 support several conclusions. First, pension coverage rises with firm size. Most of the reason for this is that small firms are less likely to offer pension plans, although a small part of the explanation is that workers at small firms are slightly less likely to participate in the pension plans offered. Second, since 1988, pension coverage rose most among the smaller firms. Over the 1988–2004 period, the percentage point increase in pension coverage was seven among firms with 1–24 employees, eleven among firms with 25–99 employees, seven among firms with 100–499 employees, and three among those with 500–999 employees. Coverage fell two percentage points among firms with one thousand or more employees. Third, the growth in coverage among the smallest firms occurred primarily since the mid-1990s, whereas coverage fell since 2000 in the larger size categories. Finally, while much of the decline in coverage rates in the 1980s was due to a decline in participation rates, participation rates were quite stable during the 1990s. Most of the increase in coverage during the 1990s was the result of an increase in the percentage of firms offering pension plans.

While it is clear that workers at small firms are much less likely to have pension coverage, the importance of this fact depends on how many workers are employed at such firms. Figure 6.3 illustrates that a substantial share of workers is employed at small firms, and that the share of employment at small firms has been quite stable over time. In 2004, 41 percent of private-sector workers aged twenty-two to fifty-five were employed at firms with less than one hundred employees (27 percent at firms with one to twenty-four employees and another 15 percent at firms with twenty-five to ninety-nine employees).

An important question raised by this study is why pension coverage has risen more among small than among large firms in recent decades. To investigate the source of this decline in the gap in pension coverage, we estimate how much of the gap is accounted for by the fact that small and large firms employ different kinds of workers. We do this by estimating a probit model of pension coverage for each worker in the CPS sample with controls for worker and firm characteristics. The size of the firm is not included as one of the control variables. Then, based on the probit model of pension coverage, we impute a probability of pension coverage for each worker in the sample. The predicted probabilities are averaged across workers within a given firm size category to generate a coverage rate for each firm size category. With this approach, differences in the predicted coverage rate across firm size categories result solely from differences in the type of workers employed by firms of different size. This portion of size-related differences in coverage is explained by differences in worker characteristics. The remainder is considered unexplained. The unexplained portion reflects differences in the costs or benefits of administering pensions that are not accounted for by differences in worker characteristics.

The probit model of pension coverage includes controls for worker and firm characteristics that are likely to affect pension coverage. The worker characteristics include income, age, education, race, weeks worked, part-time employment, region, occupation, and marital status. All of these characteristics are expected to affect pension coverage.

While the characteristics of the individual worker are an important determinant of whether the worker is employed by a firm offering a pension plan, the characteristics of coworkers at the firms are important as well. One reason for this is that nondiscrimination rules require that pension plans cannot be skewed toward high-income employees. Consequently, a low-wage worker is more likely to be covered by a pension plan if the majority of her coworkers have high incomes.[11] In the CPS data, we know relatively little about the firm beyond its industry and the number of employees. To proxy workforce characteristics for a firm, firms within a given firm size and three-digit industry code are combined to estimate the distribution of earnings and educational attainment.

For the decomposition of size-related differences, the coverage rates of the four smallest firm size categories are subtracted from the coverage rate of the largest firms (over one thousand employees) to generate four different "size gaps" in coverage. Each of these size gaps is then decomposed into an explained and unexplained portion according to the process described above. Separate analyses are performed for 1988 and 2004 with results summarized in table 6.1.

The decompositions provide insight into why pension coverage is lower among smaller firms. First, in both 1988 and 2004, the shortfall in coverage among smaller firms that can be attributed to workforce characteristics is substantial. In 1988, for example, as table 6.1 shows, the size gap in pension coverage for firms with less than twenty-five employees was 49.5 percentage points, with 33.5 points accounted for by differences in workforce characteristics. Moving into larger firm size categories reduces the size gap and the amount explained by differences in workforce characteristics. The overall pattern in both 1988 and 2004 suggests that much of the reason that smaller firms have lower pension coverage is that they employ different types of workers.

The unexplained portion of the size gap in coverage represents differences in coverage that are not accounted for by workforce characteristics. In 1988, the unexplained portion of the size gap ranged from 15.9 percentage points among the very smallest firms (less than twenty-five employees) to 4.4 percentage points among the largest (500–999 employees). Holding workforce characteristics constant, then, we find that smaller firms are less likely to provide pension coverage. Higher per capita administrative costs are one plausible explanation for this difference. Alternatively, it could be that smaller firms find that pensions are less valuable as a means to retain workers or enhance productivity.

Comparing the decompositions for 1988 and 2004 yields some important clues as to why the size gap in coverage is diminishing. One reason is that the explained gap in coverage between small and large firms fell over the period. Hence, either workers at small and large firms became more similar over time, or the effect of worker characteristics on pension coverage diminished. We return to this distinction later.

The unexplained portion of the size gap, as table 6.1 shows, fell over time in three of the four size categories, but it rose slightly for firms in the smallest category. Consequently, it appears that smaller firms continue to be less likely to provide coverage for a given type of worker. Moreover, if workforce characteristics are held constant, the size gap between the very smallest and largest firms grew over time. This is despite numerous legislative attempts to reduce the administrative and regulatory burdens of pensions for small firms.

Since workforce characteristics explain a large share of the size gap, it is useful to examine which differences account for the largest share. Table 6.2 reports a breakdown of the explained portion of the size gap according to groups of workforce characteristics.[12] For the four size gaps examined, the combination of worker- and industry-level earnings accounts for virtually the entire explained gap in coverage. In 1988, lower worker earnings account for 11.4 percentage points of the gap in coverage between firms in the smallest and largest firm size categories. Measures of the workforce earnings distribution play an even larger role in accounting for fifteen percentage points of the gap;[13] the other characteristics included in the model explain relatively little of the gap. Inspection of the decompositions for the other firm size categories (25–99, 100–499, and 500–999) yields a similar conclusion. Earnings differentials are the most important source of explained differentials in pension coverage across firm size.

Comparing the decompositions for 1988 and 2004 reveals that the most important reason the explained gap in coverage diminished over time is that earnings differentials across firm size categories diminished in importance. Either earnings have converged across firm size categories, or earnings differences have become less important determinants of coverage.

Additional evidence on the role of the differential earnings trend in explaining the narrowing of the size gap in coverage is presented in table 6.3, which shows a decomposition of the change in pension coverage for each firm size category. The decomposition is performed by estimating a separate model of pension coverage for each firm size category with the 1988 data. Using this model, a predicted change in pension coverage is generated for each firm size category based upon observed changes in worker and industry characteristics between 1988 and 2004. The results suggest that earnings growth (individual earnings and the workforce distribution of earnings combined) among the smallest firms contributed to a modest increase (1.6 percentage points) in predicted coverage over the period. In contrast, a decline in earnings among the largest firms contributed to a modest decrease (2.2 percentage points) in predicted coverage. In total, differential trends in earnings explain 3.8 percentage points of the 9.2 percentage point decline in the coverage gap between the smallest and largest firms. Another 1.4 percentage points of the decline in the gap are explained by differential trends in individual and industry education levels across firm size. The results for the other firm size categories support a similar conclusion. A narrowing of earnings and education differentials across firm size categories contributed to a more equal distribution of coverage across firm size categories.

Evidence that earnings differentials narrowed across firm size categories is found in table 6.4. Between 1988 and 2004, the total growth in average real annual earnings (1993 dollars) ranged from a low of 6.5 percent among the largest firms to a high of 25.2 percent among the smallest firms. The distribution of real earnings within a given firm size/industry category also changed between 1988 and 2004. Among the smallest firms, the fraction of the workforce with earnings under $15,000 fell by 12.5 percentage points, whereas it fell by 0.5 percentage points among the largest firms. Also, the fraction of workers in the middle-income groups ($35,000–$49,999, $50,000–$64,244) rose 1.8 and 0.9 percentage points among the smallest firms but fell by 4.3 and 1.3 percentage points among the largest firms. Over time, the distribution of earnings at large and small firms has become more equal, and this has contributed to a convergence in pension coverage rates.

We provide additional evidence on trends in the size gap in pension coverage using data from the Survey of Consumer Finances (SCF) administered between 1983 and 2001.[14] To provide time-consistent firm size categories, firms are divided into those with more or less than one hundred employees.[15] We restrict the sample to private-sector wage and salary workers aged twenty-one to fifty-four.[16] Consistent with the trends discovered in the March CPS series, the SCF coverage rates presented in figure 6.4 illustrate a decline in the size gap in pension coverage. The coverage rates of firms with less than one hundred employees rose from 21.3 percent in 1983 to 30.6 percent in 2001. In contrast, the coverage rate at firms with one hundred or more employees fell from 68.0 percent in 1983 to 64.4 percent in 2001.[17]

Compared to the rates calculated with the CPS data, the SCF coverage rates are generally higher. Part of the explanation for the different coverage rates in the SCF and CPS is that the sampling of workers is necessarily different. The SCF includes people who were working at the time of the survey. The CPS includes anyone who was working at any time in the prior year. This difference causes the CPS to include more transient workers and generates lower pension coverage rates.[18] Also, unlike the SCF, the CPS does not explicitly ask about coverage by a 401(k) plan. Consequently, some workers with 401(k) plans in the CPS might not be counted as covered by a pension in the CPS.

Another difference between the CPS and SCF data is that the former show pension coverage rising over time at firms with more than one hundred workers, and the latter show it falling over time. The best explanation we can find for this difference is that the SCF coverage rate in 1989 is substantially higher than that in the CPS. Moreover, the workers sampled at large firms differed systematically between the two surveys during that year, and this generated a higher coverage rate in the SCF.[19] Using methods identical to those employed with the CPS data, the explained portion of the gap in pension coverage between small (less than one hundred employees) and large firms is estimated with the SCF data for the years 1983, 1989, and 2001. The probit model of pension coverage includes many of the same controls as were employed for the CPS data. The major differences are that, unlike the CPS, the SCF provides information on employee tenure with the firm and on union membership. The SCF has less detailed information on industry (six categories) than the CPS, however.

Table 6.5 shows that both the explained and unexplained portion of the size gap in coverage declined over time, just as we found with the CPS data. Whereas differences in workforce characteristics contributed to a 40.4 percentage point difference in pension between small and large firms in 1983, they contributed to a 29.9 percentage point gap in coverage in 2001. The unexplained gap in coverage between small and large firms fell from 6.3 percentage points in 1983 to 3.9 percentage points in 2001.

A breakdown of the explained portion of the size gap is presented in the bottom of table 6.5. In the SCF, the combination of individual and workforce earnings accounts for the largest share of the size gap in coverage. Size-related differences in earnings accounted for 23.2, 27.2, and 12.7 percentage points of the size gap in 1983, 1989, and 2001, respectively. Consistent with the CPS results, the effect of earnings differences on the coverage gap diminished in the 1990s.

Changes in characteristics other than earnings had modest impacts on the size gap in coverage. For the 1983 to 2001 period, no single worker or firm characteristic accounted for more than a two percentage point decline in the coverage gap.

Taken together, the March CPS and SCF data lend support to several conclusions. First, the gap in coverage between small and large firms diminished in the 1990s. Second, the majority of the size gap in pension coverage is accounted for by differences in worker and firm characteristics. Third, the most important explanation for the convergence in coverage is that the level and distribution of earnings at small and large firms became more similar over time. Finally, despite the fact that a wide array of worker and firm characteristics are observed, our statistical models are unable to account for the entire decline in the coverage gap. Both the CPS and SCF data indicate that changes in unobservable worker or firm characteristics contributed to the declining gap, except for the very smallest firms (less than twenty-five employees) in the CPS. This might reflect a decrease in the administrative costs of pensions at small relative to large firms. It is important to reiterate, however, that the majority of the decline in the coverage gap is due to a convergence in the earnings of workers employed at small and large firms.

PENSION TYPE AND FIRM SIZE

Over the past twenty years, firms offering a pension have shifted away from defined benefit and toward defined contribution plans. From the employer perspective, the DC plans may be preferred for several reasons. First, they allow employers to shift rate of return risk and plan contributions to their employees. Second, they allow firms to directly pass the administrative expenses to employees by charging these expenses to the plan. Alternative explanations for the shift from DB to DC plans include a shift of employment away from the types of firms that were most likely to offer DB plans (e.g., large unionized firms); regulatory changes driving up the administrative cost of DB plans relative to DC plans; and the introduction of the 401(k) plan, which made DC plans more attractive by allowing for greater flexibility in their design.[20]

The shift from DB to DC plans has several potential consequences. First, the shift will affect retirement incentives. DB plans encourage retirements within a certain range of service and/or age, whereas DC plans are essentially neutral with respect to retirement. Second, the shift from DB to DC plans could raise the level and inequality of pension wealth at retirement.[21] Given that DC plans are more portable than DB plans, a third potential effect of the shift from DB to DC plans is that worker turnover may increase. This has both positive and negative effects on labor market efficiency. On the positive side, if DC plans allow workers to switch to jobs where they are more productive, labor market efficiency is increased. On the negative side, if firms are less confident in their ability to retain workers, they may be less inclined to invest in job-specific training.

The shift from DB to DC plans has not been uniform across plan size categories. Purcell and Graney (2001) summarize data from Internal Revenue Service Form 5500 on the number of active participants in DB and DC plans for the period 1990 through 1997. Among pension plans with one hundred or more participants, DB enrollments dropped from 25.2 million to 22.1 million over the period, while DC enrollments rose from 28.7 million to 38.8 million. This represents a 12.3 percentage point drop in DB enrollments and a 35.2 percentage point increase in DC enrollments among large plans. Among small plans (under one hundred participants), DB enrollments dropped from 1.2 million to 660,000, and DC enrollments rose from 6.8 million to 9.2 million. This represents a drop in DB enrollments of 45 percentage points and an increase in DC enrollments of 35.2 percentage points. Overall, the data point to similar rates of growth in DC enrollments in small and large plans, but greater percentage point declines in DB enrollments among small plans.

SCF data on plan type by firm size, shown in figure 6.5, also reflect the trend away from DB and toward DC plans. Between 1989 and 2001, the percentage of workers with only a DB plan fell from 8.7 to 4.2 percent at small firms and from 25.9 to 10.6 percent at large firms. At the same time, the percentage of workers with only a DC plan rose from 11.0 to 23.7 percent at small firms and from 22.6 to 41.0 percent at large firms. The fraction of workers with both a DB and DC plan was fairly stable at small firms over the period (in the range of 2.6 to 2.9 percent), whereas it fell from 19.6 to 12.8 percent among large firms.

Turning now to workers with pension coverage, we see notable differences by employer size in the types of pension plan offered. While the fraction of covered workers with only a DB plan is quite similar for large and small firms, small firms are much more likely to have only a DC plan, and large firms are much more likely to have both a DB and DC plan. For example, in 2001, 13.7 and 16.5 percent of covered workers at small and large firms had only a DB plan; 77.4 and 63.7 percent had only a DC plan; and 9.0 and 19.8 had both a DB and DC plan. Comparing these statistics to those in earlier years reveals, for both large and small firms, a substantial decrease in the percentage of workers with only a DB plan and an increase in the percentage of workers with only a DC plan. The fraction of covered workers with both a DB and DC plan was fairly stable for small firms but fell sharply for large firms.

In deciding whether to offer a DB or DC plan, employers must consider the advantages and disadvantages of each. Dorsey (1987) outlines several important advantages of the DB plan. First, whereas DC plans are viewed as portable, the DB plan has the ability to defer pay and penalize workers who leave prior to retirement. The deferred pay aspect of DB plans would be particularly valuable to employers for whom hiring or training investments are large. Second, rate of return risk is absorbed by employers in DB plans, but by employees in DC plans. If employers are less risk-averse than employees, DB plans may be preferred. Third, DB plans give employers a means to encourage retirement within a given age range, whereas DC plans are virtually neutral with respect to retirement age. Fourth, the ability to underfund a DB plan affords employers the opportunity to improve employee interest in firm survival. This feature can be particularly important in a collective bargaining environment (Ippolito, 1985).

The DB plan has some disadvantages relative to the DC, notably from the point of view of employees, who, concerned with the potential for job lock[22] or firm failure,[23] may not like the deferred pay aspect of the plan. Even from the employer's point of view, there remains the fact that, except in very large plans, DC plans have lower administrative costs than DB plans.[24]

In sum, both worker and firm characteristics affect the choice of plan type. Since the cost disadvantage of DB plans generally declines with plan size, it is not surprising that DB plans are less common among small firms. However, the cost disadvantage of DB plans is not overwhelming. Hay-Huggins (1990) estimates that in 1991, the per capita administrative cost of a DB plan was only $224 higher than a 401(k) plan in a plan with fifteen participants. In a plan with one hundred participants, the cost disadvantage shrinks to $70 per capita. While the greater administrative cost of DB plans is undoubtedly an important factor in the greater tendency of small firms to offer DC plans, an alternative explanation for this tendency is that small firms employ workers who have a greater preference for portable pensions.

To determine whether differences in worker characteristics can account for the fact that small firms are less likely to choose DB plans, we first estimate a bivariate probit model of DB and DC plan coverage. The model can be described as follows:

$$DB_i = 1 \text{ if } DB_i^* = X_i\beta_1 + e_{1i} > 0$$
$$= 0 \text{ otherwise}$$
$$DC_i = 1 \text{ if } DC_i^* = X_i\beta_2 + e_{2i} > 0$$
$$= 0 \text{ otherwise}$$

where DB_i and DC_i are dummy variables indicating whether person i has DB or DC coverage, X_i is a vector of characteristics influencing the net benefit of either a DB or DC plan, β_1 and β_2 are vectors of coefficients, and e_{1i} and e_{2i} are random errors with standard normal distributions which may be correlated with each other.

Estimates of the bivariate probit model are summarized separately for the 1989 and 2001 data in table 6.6. For each year, separate vectors of coefficients are presented for the DB and DC probit equations. The sign of a coefficient in the DB or DC equation indicates whether the variable has a positive or negative effect on that coverage. If the size of a coefficient is larger in the DB than the DC equation, the variable has a larger effect on the probability that a DB plan will be offered than on the probability that a DC plan will.

Several variables are particularly important determinants of the probability that either a DB or DC plan is offered. For example, the probability of either DB or DC coverage rises as a person's income rises. However, the probability of DC coverage rises more rapidly with income than the probability of DB coverage. Consistent with earlier findings on the effect of unions, unionism increases the probability of DB coverage in both years, but it has a statistically insignificant negative effect on the probability of DC coverage.

After estimating the bivariate probit equation for a pooled sample of small and large firms, the parameter estimates are employed to generate a predicted fraction of workers, by firm size, who will have only a DB plan, have only a DC plan, have both a DB and DC plan (henceforth DBDC), and have no pension. To the extent that differences in worker characteristics alone can account for the differences in the frequency of plan types, size-related differences in the type of plan are explained by differences in worker characteristics.

The portion of the gap in coverage between large and small firms that can be accounted for by differences in worker and employer characteristics is summarized in table 6.7 for the 1989 and 2001 samples. Differences in the frequency of plan offerings between small and large firms are explained predominantly by differences in workforce characteristics. For each of the four types of coverage (DB-only, DC-only, DBDC, and no pension), more than two-thirds of the difference between small and large firms can be accounted for by differences in worker and employer characteristics.

Comparing the 1989 and 2001 data reveals a dramatic shift away from DB plans, particularly for large firms. DC-only coverage rose, while DB-only and DBDC coverage dropped. Workers at small and large firms became more similar in terms of the probability of DB-only and DBDC coverage. At the same time, however, the gap between workers at small and large firms with DC-only coverage rose over time.

The growth in DC-only coverage is due to entirely different phenomena at small and large firms. At small firms, the growth is due primarily to a rising share of workers with some type of pension coverage and to a lesser extent to a decline in the fraction with DB coverage. At large firms, the growth is due primarily to a switch away from DB or DBDC plans to DC-only coverage.

Table 6.8 presents a breakdown of the importance of each worker and employer characteristic in accounting for size-related differences in pension types. The most important explanations for the size gap in plan choices are size differences in the level and distribution of earnings. Over time, diminution of size differences in worker earnings made small and large firms more alike in their propensity to have DB-only or DBDC coverage. On the other hand, size differences in worker earnings have become a more important source of size differences in DC-only coverage. The fact that earnings differentials are leading to a convergence in DB-only coverage but a divergence in DC-only coverage may seem contradictory. However, the seeming contradiction can be explained by the fact that the influence of worker earnings on the probability of DC coverage rose over time.

An alternative means to examine differences in plan choices is to estimate, by firm size, the determinants of plan choice, and then to estimate for a given firm size how much of the change in plan type choices can be explained by changes in worker and employer characteristics. This approach, presented in table 6.9, reveals that changes in the level and distribution of earnings are the most salient explanation for changes in coverage and the type of plan chosen. Examination of the results reveals that changes in the earnings distribution contributed to a shift from DB to DC plans, but the effects were greater at large firms.

While changes in worker and employer characteristics account for the majority of the change in plan choices, the growth in DC coverage is greater than predicted for both small and large firms. At small firms, the percentage of workers with DC coverage rose by 12.6 percentage points, yet only a 6.8 percentage point hike can be accounted for by changes in worker and employer characteristics. At large firms, there was an 18.4 percentage point increase in workers with only a DC plan, and 13.5 percentage points are accounted for by changing characteristics.

In summary, several conclusions can be drawn regarding firm size differentials in the frequency of pension plan offerings. Differences between small and large firms in terms of the level and distribution of earnings explain a large share of the difference in plan offerings. Changes in earnings across time led to a shift away from DB plans and toward DC plans—particularly at large firms. While changing worker and employer characteristics account for the majority of the change in plan choices, these characteristics alone do not account for the entire shift. Other factors that are not controlled for in our statistical models appear to be amplifying the shift away from DB and toward DC plans at both small and large firms.

PENSION GENEROSITY AT SMALL AND LARGE FIRMS

Pension generosity varies widely across employers. Using data from the Health and Retirement Study (HRS), Even and Macpherson (1998) simulate the benefits that a worker with average earnings would receive after thirty years of inclusion in the various pension plans found in HRS. Among the universe of DB plans ranked according to generosity, the plan at the 75th percentile is estimated to be 3.7 times more generous than the plan at the 25th percentile. This 75–25 ratio is 2.7 for non-401(k) DC plans and 3.4 for 401(k) plans.

Although pension generosity varies considerably among firms with pension plans, the determinants of generosity levels are not well understood. The existing evidence suggests that unionized firms provide more generous pensions and that pensions are more generous in the public sector.[25] Presumably, the factors that influence whether a pension is offered also influence the generosity level. For example, given the tax advantages of pensions, employees in higher tax brackets may want to devote a larger share of pay to their pension. The fact that Social Security replaces a smaller fraction of income for high-income workers could amplify this effect.

Administrative costs are likely to have differential effects on pension coverage and generosity. Clearly, higher administrative costs could reduce the likelihood that a firm offers a pension. However, when a company provides a pension, administrative costs are not likely to affect the level of generosity, since such costs are not likely to vary with the level of generosity.

Evidence on the generosity of pensions from the SCF and HRS is provided in table 6.10. Separate tabulations are provided for DB and DC plans. For DC plans, the percentage of pay contributed to the plan by the employer and employee combined is listed. For DB plans, the percentage of final pay replaced per year of service (the "generosity rate") is listed.[26]

Both the 1989 and 2001 SCF data show that DC plans were slightly more generous at large firms. At firms with one hundred or more employees, the percentage of pay contributed to the plan was 10.03 percent in 1989 and 11.04 percent in 2001. At small firms, the contribution rates were 9.36 percent in 1989 and 10.27 percent in 2001. In both 1989 and 2001, the hypothesis that contribution rates are identical for small and large firms is rejected at the .05 significance level. While the differences are statistically significant, they are relatively modest in size. That is, workers included in DC plans at small firms accumulate on average at least 90 percent of what is accumulated by workers at large firms.

Evidence from the 1992 HRS, however, runs contrary to the pattern in the SCF. In the HRS, contribution rates are higher at the small firms, but the difference is not statistically significant at conventional levels. The conflicting findings between the HRS and SCF may reflect the fact that the HRS focuses only on older workers, whereas workers from a wide range of ages are in the SCF.

Comparing the DB generosity rates at small and large firms reveals significantly more generous plans for small firms in the 1989 and 2001 SCF. Large plans have an average generosity rate that is between 76 percent (2001) and 83 percent (1989) of that at small firms. Results from the 1992 HRS, however, are opposite to the pattern in the SCF. In the HRS, generosity rates are insignificantly higher at the large firms.

Overall, it appears that if a pension plan is offered, the average generosity of both DB and DC pensions is quite similar at small and large firms. While there are some statistically significant differences, the pattern is not consistent across data sets. When the differences are statistically significant, they are relatively modest in size. Consequently, if the shortfall in pension coverage for workers at small firms can be eliminated, most of the gap in pension accumulation will disappear as well.

CONCLUSION

Workers at small firms are much less likely to have pension coverage than those at large firms. Explanations for this fact can be broken into two broad categories. First, it is more expensive on a per capita basis for small firms to administer pension plans. Second, employees at small firms systematically differ from those at large firms and are less willing to sacrifice earnings for pension saving.

Data from the Current Population Survey and Survey of Consumer Finances reveal that the gap between coverage rates at large and small firms diminished in the 1990s. The empirical analysis reveals that approximately two-thirds of the size gap in coverage in 1988 and 2001 is due to differences in the type of workers employed by small and large firms. Specifically, differences in the level and distribution of earnings of workers at small and large firms are important explanations for the size gap in coverage. Moreover, between 1988 and 2001, a convergence in the level and distribution of earnings at small and large firms reduced the size gap in coverage.

Using data from the Survey of Consumer Finances and the Health and Retirement Survey, we examined size differences in the type and generosity of plan. We found that among firms offering a pension, small firms are more likely than large firms to offer only a DC plan. Large firms are more likely than small firms to offer either only a DB plan or both a DB and DC plan. During the 1990s, the percentage of workers offered only a DC plan grew at both large and small firms, but the source of the change differed at small and large firms. At small firms, the growth in coverage by only a DC plan was primarily the result of increases in pension coverage and, to a lesser extent, a decrease in the percentage of workers with only a DB plan. At large firms, it was primarily the result of workers losing coverage by only a DB or by both a DB and DC plan.

Empirical analysis of pension choices reveals that over two-thirds of the size difference in choices of plan type is due to size differences in the type of workers. As with the coverage decision, differences in the level and distribution of earnings are especially important reasons for the greater propensity among small firms to offer only a DC plan. Firms with a relatively large fraction of workers in middle- to high-income categories are the most likely to choose a DC plan, and this effect became more pronounced in the 1990s. Moreover, changes in the distribution of workforce earnings and education contributed to almost two-thirds of the shift away from DB and toward DC plans, at both large and small firms.

Among firms offering a pension, there are only modest differences between small and large firms in terms of the level of plan generosity. The main conclusion drawn from the analysis of generosity rates is that the most important concern for pension saving among workers at small firms is coverage, not pension generosity for those with coverage.

Overall, there are several major conclusions we draw from this study. While scale economies in the administration of pension plans may contribute to small firms' lower pension coverage rates and greater propensity to choose DC plans, the majority of the differences between small and large firms can be explained by differences in the characteristics of the workforces that they employ. During the 1990s, a convergence in the level and distribution of earnings at small and large firms contributed to a substantial closure in the gap in coverage and differences in the type of plan offered. Based on these results, we conclude that legislative attempts to improve pension coverage at small firms by reducing administrative costs (e.g., through the SEP and SIMPLE) address only one aspect of the problem with low coverage rates at small firms. A potentially fruitful approach would focus on improving the coverage rates of workers with low-income levels, possibly by providing greater tax incentives for pension saving among low-income workers.

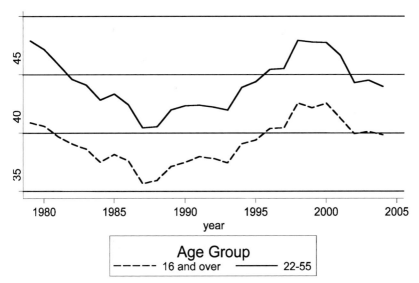

Note: Coverage rates calculated from March Current Population Surveys for private-sector workers.

FIGURE 6.1.
Pension Coverage Rates: 1979–2000

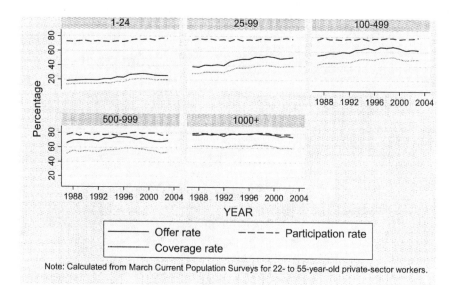

FIGURE 6.2.
Offer, Coverage, and Participation Rates by Number of Employees

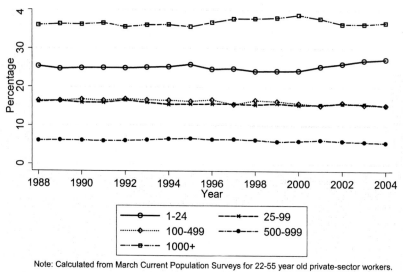

Note: Calculated from March Current Population Surveys for 22-55 year old private-sector workers.

FIGURE 6.3.
Employment Share by Firm Size

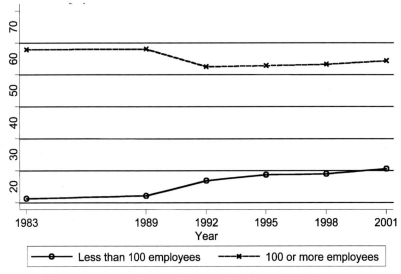

Note: Estimates from Survey of Consumer Finances for 21- to 54-year-old private-sector workers.

FIGURE 6.4.
Pension Coverage by Firm Size: 1983–2001

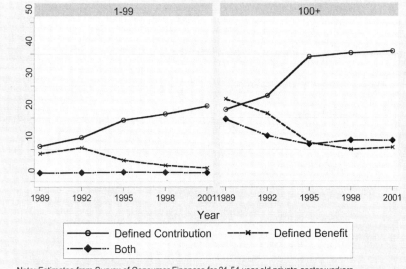

Note: Estimates from Survey of Consumer Finances for 21-54 year old private-sector workers.

FIGURE 6.5.
Type of Pension Coverage by Firm Size

Table 6.1. Decomposition of Pension Coverage Differentials by Firm Size

Firm Size by Number of Employees	Gap in Coverage Relative to Firms with 1,000 or More Employees	Explained Portion of Gap (Differences in Workforce Characteristics)	Unexplained Portion of Gap	Portion Explained
1988				
<25	49.5%	33.5%	15.9%	67.8%
25–99	33.5%	20.4%	13.1%	61.0%
100–499	19.2%	12.4%	6.9%	64.2%
500–999	10.4%	6.0%	4.4%	57.4%
2004				
<25	40.2%	24.0%	16.2%	59.7%
25–99	20.0%	11.9%	8.2%	59.3%
100–499	9.8%	5.4%	4.4%	54.6%
500–999	4.7%	1.6%	3.1%	34.2%

Note: Decompositions are based on probit model of coverage using data from the 1989 and 2005 March Current Population Survey data. Sample sizes for 1989 and 2004 are 41,182 and 60,953, respectively.

Table 6.2. Factors Accounting for Pension Coverage Differentials by Firm Size in March CPS

Variable	Firm Size (No. of Employees)			
	1–24	25–99	100–499	500–999
1988				
Individual Earnings	11.4%	6.6%	4.4%	2.5%
Distribution of Workforce earnings	15.0%	9.4%	6.2%	3.3%
Weeks Worked	1.2%	0.7%	0.4%	0.0%
Individual Education	0.2%	0.2%	0.1%	0.0%
Distribution of Workforce Education	1.3%	0.9%	0.5%	0.0%
Part-time	0.9%	0.1%	−0.1%	0.0%
Industry	1.6%	1.7%	0.8%	0.2%
Age	0.6%	0.5%	0.2%	0.2%
Occupation	0.4%	0.3%	0.0%	−0.2%
Other Demographics[a]	0.9%	0.0%	−0.2%	−0.1%
Total Explained	33.5%	20.4%	12.4%	6.0%
2004				
Individual Earnings	17.0%	3.3%	1.7%	0.7%
Distribution of Workforce Earnings	9.9%	4.6%	1.4%	0.2%
Weeks Worked	0.6%	0.3%	0.2%	0.0%
Individual Education	0.9%	0.6%	0.4%	0.2%
Distribution of Workforce Education	1.9%	1.1%	0.8%	0.3%
Part-time	0.7%	0.0%	−0.2%	−0.1%
Industry	1.5%	1.4%	0.9%	0.7%
Age	0.2%	0.1%	0.0%	−0.1%
Occupation	0.7%	0.5%	0.1%	−0.1%
Other Demographics	0.6%	0.2%	0.0%	−0.1%
Total Explained	24.0%	11.9%	5.4%	1.6%

[a] Other demographics includes race, Hispanic or not, gender, and region.

Table 6.3.   Factors Contributing to the Change in Pension Coverage between 1988 and 2004 by Firm Size

Variable	Firm Size (No. of Employees)				
	1–24	25–99	100–499	500–999	1,000+
Individual Earnings	1.8%	2.3%	2.1%	4.8%	−0.1%
Industry Earnings	−0.2%	1.3%	0.5%	−6.6%	−2.1%
Weeks Worked	0.3%	0.6%	0.6%	1.6%	0.3%
Individual Education	0.1%	0.2%	−0.1%	−1.8%	−0.1%
Industry Education	0.8%	0.7%	2.1%	5.3%	−0.4%
Part-time	0.2%	0.0%	0.0%	0.0%	−0.1%
Industry	0.1%	0.1%	−0.5%	−2.9%	−0.3%
Age	0.3%	1.3%	0.8%	2.8%	0.7%
Other Demographics[a]	0.1%	−0.6%	−0.4%	−2.3%	−0.3%
Occupation	−0.1%	−1.0%	−0.3%	−1.4%	−0.8%
Total Predicted Change	3.5%	4.8%	4.7%	−0.5%	−3.2%
Total Change	7.8%	12.1%	8.0%	4.2%	−1.4%

Note: The decomposition is based upon the probit coefficients for the 1988 model of pension coverage.
[a] Other demographics includes race, Hispanic or not, gender, and region.

Table 6.4.   Change in Level and Distribution of Real Earnings by Firm Size between 1988 and 2004

Variable	Firm Size (No. of Employees)				
	1–24	25–99	100–499	500–999	1,000+
Percentage Change in Average Earnings	25.2%	17.5%	14.6%	12.6%	6.5%
Percentage Change in Share of Workers in Earnings Categories					
< $15,000	−12.5%	−18.3%	−7.5%	−4.2%	−0.5%
$15,000–$24,999	5.3%	3.4%	0.9%	−0.5%	1.6%
$25,000–$34,999	2.6%	1.6%	2.4%	1.2%	0.2%
$35,000–$49,999	1.8%	1.6%	0.5%	−1.0%	−4.3%
$50,000–$64,245	0.9%	0.1%	0.4%	0.9%	−1.3%
>$64,245	1.9%	2.9%	3.2%	3.6%	4.3%

Note: Earnings estimates are based on data from the 1989 and 2005 March CPS. Real earnings are measured in 1993 dollars.

**Table 6.5. Factors Contributing to Size Gap in Pension Coverage:
Survey of Consumer Finances**

	Year		
Variable	1983	1989	2001
Total Gap	46.7%	45.9%	33.8%
Unexplained Gap	6.3%	4.6%	3.9%
Explained Gap	40.4%	41.3%	29.9%
Portion of explained gap due to:			
Union	4.0%	2.1%	1.8%
Individual Earnings	4.9%	2.7%	1.8%
Industry Earnings	18.3%	24.5%	10.9%
Tenure	5.7%	4.5%	3.8%
Individual Education	0.3%	0.4%	1.5%
Industry Education	5.5%	1.3%	7.6%
Part-time	0.6%	1.8%	1.3%
Industry	0.9%	2.4%	0.0%
Other	0.3%	1.4%	1.2%
Sample Size[a]	1,932	7,861	12,124

Note: Size gap in coverage refers to difference between coverage rate at firms with one hundred or more
employees and those with less than one hundred employees.
[a] For 1989 and later, the SCF replicates each observation five times to allow for sampling variation in imputed variables. Consequently, sample sizes for these years are overstated by a factor of approximately
five.

Table 6.6. Bivariate Probit Model of DB and DC Plan Choice

Variable	1989 DB coeff.	DB t-stat	1989 DC coeff.	DC t-stat	2001 DB coeff.	DB t-stat	2001 DC coeff.	DC t-stat
Individual Earnings:								
$15,000–24,999	-0.03	-0.41	0.64	9.30	0.24	3.85	0.42	9.38
$25,000–34,999	0.09	1.25	0.68	9.24	0.22	3.31	0.68	13.74
$34,000–49,999	-0.02	-0.20	0.90	10.54	0.27	3.66	0.78	13.90
$50,000–64,244	0.29	2.66	1.50	13.65	0.27	3.21	1.10	15.30
$64,245+	0.08	0.68	1.17	10.59	0.35	4.18	1.02	14.22
Industry Earnings:								
$15,000–24,999	0.00	0.51	-0.01	-2.34	-0.01	-2.35	0.02	6.54
$25,000–34,999	0.02	4.22	0.03	4.89	0.03	3.39	0.01	1.87
$35,000–49,999	0.02	5.58	0.01	2.17	0.01	2.36	0.00	0.44
$50,000–64,244	0.07	6.56	0.02	2.55	0.03	2.74	0.03	4.53
$64,245+	-0.01	-0.52	-0.01	-0.90	0.03	3.10	0.02	2.65
Years of Schooling:								
9–11	-0.14	-1.11	-0.35	-2.54	0.22	1.75	0.40	3.89
12	-0.20	-1.91	-0.10	-0.78	0.37	3.25	0.43	4.56
13–15	-0.20	-1.73	0.10	0.82	0.27	2.29	0.43	4.46
16	-0.21	-1.72	-0.03	-0.22	0.56	4.62	0.67	6.70
17+	-0.24	-1.86	0.24	1.71	0.54	4.35	0.74	6.90
Industry Schooling:								
12	0.01	2.42	0.00	-0.68	-0.01	-0.92	0.00	-0.01
13–15	0.02	2.90	-0.02	-3.29	-0.03	-3.72	0.01	1.93
16+	0.02	2.67	0.01	1.79	0.03	2.46	0.03	3.37
Female	-0.06	-1.23	0.18	3.73	0.05	1.40	-0.03	-0.81
Nonwhite	-0.20	-3.58	-0.12	-2.29	-0.02	-0.51	0.00	0.05
Part-time	-0.44	-5.44	-0.39	-4.95	-0.21	-2.99	-0.20	-4.13
Tenure	0.11	13.33	0.09	10.60	0.05	8.50	0.11	20.58
Tenure Squared	0.00	-7.57	0.00	-9.31	0.00	-2.95	0.00	-17.29
Union Coverage	0.63	10.37	-0.10	-1.71	0.70	15.83	-0.03	-0.60
Marital Status:								
Married	-0.18	-2.76	0.15	2.32	0.11	2.58	-0.03	-0.95
Spouse Absent	-0.03	-0.36	0.03	0.37	-0.01	-0.17	0.02	0.42
Industry[a]:								
Mining, Construction	-1.09	-5.73	-0.01	-0.03	1.11	3.46	-0.59	-3.78
Manufacturing	-0.31	-1.69	0.53	2.76	0.62	2.14	-0.39	-2.77
Trade	0.15	0.78	0.76	3.67	1.19	3.66	-0.42	-3.47
FIRE, Business/Repair Service	0.27	1.14	0.53	2.15	-0.02	-0.07	-1.20	-7.91
TCU, Other Services	0.12	0.48	0.13	0.50	0.66	2.11	-1.00	-5.72
Occupation:								
Tech, Sales, Clerical	0.02	0.26	0.06	1.11	-0.11	-2.39	0.13	3.38
Service and Farm	-0.10	-1.10	0.01	0.14	-0.24	-3.24	-0.13	-2.26
Precision Production, Craft, Repair	0.02	0.19	-0.16	-2.05	-0.02	-0.34	-0.16	-2.80
Operators, Laborer	-0.04	-0.52	-0.22	-2.85	-0.15	-2.31	0.03	0.49
Age:								
26–30	0.47	4.68	0.33	3.57	0.10	1.22	-0.06	-1.07
31–35	0.54	5.44	0.41	4.57	0.17	2.13	0.05	0.79
36–40	0.77	7.74	0.26	2.82	0.24	2.98	0.12	2.05
41–45	0.68	6.55	0.26	2.81	0.20	2.51	-0.01	-0.19
46–50	0.54	5.05	0.42	4.39	0.22	2.65	0.05	0.75
51–54	0.80	7.08	0.48	4.52	0.46	5.40	-0.09	-1.35
Constant	-3.82	-10.01	-2.57	-7.60	-3.67	-7.29	-3.11	-9.04
Rho[b]	-0.14	-5.00			-0.08	-3.75		

Note: Bivariate probit model is estimated using the 1989 and 2001 SCF data.
[a] FIRE denotes Finance, Insurance, and Real Estate. TCU denotes Transportation, Communications, and Utilities.
[b] Rho is the correlation coefficient for the error terms in the DB and DC equations.

Table 6.7.   Decomposition of Size Differences in Type of Pension Coverage between 1989 and 2001

Firm Size:	DB Only 1989	DB Only 2001	DC Only 1989	DC Only 2001	DB and DC 1989	DB and DC 2001	No Pension 1989	No Pension 2001
<100	8.7%	4.2%	11.0%	23.7%	2.6%	2.7%	77.8%	69.4%
100+	25.9%	10.6%	22.6%	41.0%	19.6%	12.8%	31.9%	35.6%
Total Gap	17.3%	6.4%	11.6%	17.4%	17.0%	10.0%	−45.9%	−33.8%
Explained Gap	13.1%	4.8%	8.3%	13.8%	20.0%	10.9%	−41.4%	−29.5%
Portion Explained	75.9%	74.9%	71.3%	79.4%	117.2%	108.6%	90.1%	87.2%

Note: Size differences in coverage are based on comparison of firms with more or less than one hundred employees in the 1989 and 2001 SCF.

Table 6.8. Factors Contributing to Size Differences in Plan Choice between 1989 and 2001

Variable	DB only	DC Only	DB and DC	No Pension
		1989		
Individual Income	0.1%	1.8%	1.4%	−4.4%
Distribution of Workforce Earnings	8.0%	3.9%	10.7%	−22.3%
Individual Education	−0.1%	0.2%	0.1%	−0.3%
Distribution of Workforce Education	0.9%	1.0%	1.5%	−3.8%
Tenure	2.5%	0.8%	4.8%	−6.4%
Female	0.1%	−0.1%	0.0%	0.2%
Marital Status	−0.0%	0.0%	0.0%	0.0%
Nonwhite	−0.1%	0.0%	−0.1%	0.1%
Union Coverage	0.8%	−0.1%	0.4%	−0.9%
Industry	0.0%	0.5%	0.3%	−1.1%
Occupation	0.1%	−0.1%	0.0%	0.0%
Age	0.4%	0.1%	0.3%	−0.8%
Part-time	0.5%	0.3%	0.6%	−1.6%
Total	13.1%	8.3%	20.0%	−41.4%
		2001		
Individual Income	0.2%	3.0%	1.1%	−5.0%
Distribution of Workforce Earnings	2.4%	4.1%	4.2%	−10.2%
Individual Education	0.2%	0.6%	0.4%	−1.2%
Distribution of Workforce Education	1.1%	4.1%	3.1%	−8.3%
Tenure	0.5%	1.7%	1.6%	−3.5%
Female	−0.0%	0.0%	0.0%	0.0%
Marital Status	0.0%	0.0%	0.0%	0.0%
Nonwhite	0.0%	0.0%	0.0%	0.0%
Union Coverage	0.5%	−0.1%	0.5%	−0.5%
Industry	−0.2%	−0.1%	−0.4%	0.5%
Occupation	0.1%	0.3%	0.2%	−0.6%
Age	0.1%	−0.1%	0.1%	0.0%
Part-time	0.1%	0.3%	0.2%	−0.6%
Total	4.8%	13.8%	10.9%	−29.5%

Note: Size differences in plan choice are measured as difference in frequency of a particular plan choice between firms with one hundred or more employees and firms with less than one hundred employees.

Table 6.9. Factors Contributing to Change in Plan Choice by Firm Size between 1989 and 2001

Variable	DB only	DC Only	DB and DC	No Pension
	Firms With Less Than 100 Employees			
Individual Income	−0.2%	0.7%	0.0%	−0.5%
Distribution of Workforce Earnings	−3.5%	5.1%	0.0%	−2.1%
Individual Education	−0.0%	0.3%	0.0%	−0.2%
Distribution of Workforce Education	0.8%	1.5%	−0.1%	−1.7%
Tenure	−0.3%	−0.5%	0.0%	0.5%
Female	−0.0%	0.0%	0.0%	0.0%
Marital Status	0.1%	0.2%	0.0%	−0.3%
Nonwhite	−0.1%	−0.2%	0.0%	0.2%
Union Coverage	−0.3%	−0.1%	0.0%	0.2%
Industry	0.8%	−0.4%	0.0%	−0.2%
Occupation	−0.3%	−0.2%	0.0%	0.4%
Age	0.1%	0.0%	0.0%	0.0%
Part-time	0.2%	0.2%	0.0%	−0.3%
Explained Change	−2.6%	6.8%	−0.1%	−4.1%
Total Change	*−4.5%*	*12.6%*	*0.2%*	*−8.3%*
	Firms With 100 or More Employees			
Individual Income	−0.2%	0.2%	0.2%	−0.2%
Distribution of Workforce Earnings	−7.2%	8.8%	−3.8%	2.6%
Individual Education	−0.0%	0.1%	0.4%	−0.3%
Distribution of Workforce Education	−4.1%	5.3%	−1.7%	1.0%
Tenure	−0.3%	−0.4%	−1.8%	1.7%
Female	−0.0%	0.0%	0.0%	0.0%
Marital Status	−0.0%	0.0%	−0.1%	0.1%
Nonwhite	−0.0%	0.0%	0.0%	0.0%
Union Coverage	−0.4%	0.5%	−0.2%	0.1%
Industry	1.3%	−1.5%	−0.1%	0.1%
Occupation	−0.1%	0.1%	0.0%	0.0%
Age	−0.3%	0.3%	−0.4%	0.4%
Part-time	0.0%	0.0%	0.1%	−0.1%
Explained Change	−11.4%	13.5%	−7.5%	5.4%
Total Change	−15.3%	18.4%	−6.9%	3.8%

Table 6.10.   DC Contribution and DB Generosity Rates

	Firms with Less Than 100 Employees	Firms with 100 or More Employees	P-value for Equality[a]
DC Contribution Rates			
1989 SCF	9.36%	10.03%	0.05
2001 SCF	10.27%	11.04%	0.00
1992 HRS	10.08%	9.75%	0.62
DB Generosity Rates			
1989 SCF	1.53%	1.27%	0.00
2001 SCF	1.84%	1.39%	0.00
1992 HRS	1.09%	1.30%	0.17

Note: The DC contribution rate is the percentage of pay contributed by both the employer and employee for the average worker with a DC plan. The DB generosity rate is the percentage of final pay replaced per year of service for the average worker with a DB plan.
[a] The p-value for equality is the lowest significance level at which the null hypothesis that contribution rates in DC plans (or generosity rates in DB plans) are equal for small and large firms can be rejected.

NOTES

1. See, for example, Poterba, Venti, and Wise (1996), Engen, Gale, and Scholz (1996), and Gale (2005).

2. Calculations are from the March 2005 Current Population Survey.

3. See Even and Macpherson (2003) for a review of the productivity effects of pensions.

4. Information on the extent of scale economies in pension plan administration is found in Andrews and Mitchell (1981); Andrews (1989); Hay-Huggins (1990); and Ghilarducci and Terry (1999).

5. Employee Benefit Research Institute, "The 2001 small employer retirement survey: Summary of findings" (Washington, D.C.: Employee Benefit Research Institute, 2002).

6. Employee Benefit Research Institute, "The 2003 small employer retirement survey: Summary of findings" (Washington, D.C.: Employee Benefit Research Institute, 2003).

7. A similar controversy surrounds the 401(k) plan: some have argued that the 401(k) plan represents "new" pension coverage, whereas others argue that it is simply a replacement of older plans. See, for example, Papke (1999) and Ippolito (2000).

8. We do not examine size differences in the fraction of workers employed at firms that sponsor a pension plan (i.e., the "offer rate"). With the growing popularity of

voluntary participation features inherent in 401(k) plans, the difference between the offer rate and participation rate has grown over time.

9. While the CPS data range from 1980 through 2005, the survey asks about pension coverage in the year prior to the survey.

10. Munnell, Lee, and Meme (2004) report a very similar pattern of declining coverage in the 1980s, followed by increases in the 1990s, followed by a post-2000 decline.

11. Evidence that coworkers affect the probability that an individual worker is covered is found in Carrington, McCue, and Pierce (2002) and Scott, Berger, and Black (1989).

12. The decomposition of the explained portion into the part explained by each characteristic is accomplished using the approach in Even and Macpherson (1990).

13. The portion of the size gap attributed to individual earnings or workforce earnings distribution is quite robust to the number of variables used to characterize them. For example, doubling the number of earnings categories used to characterize the workforce earnings distribution changed the portion of the size gap explained by that factor by at most 0.4 percentage points. Adding a cubic and quartic term to reflect individual earnings changed the size gap explained by earnings differences by at most 0.8 percentage points. In most cases, the portion explained by either the workforce earnings distribution or individual earnings changed by less than 0.2 percentage points.

14. The 1986 SCF was not used because firm size information was not available in the survey.

15. The March CPS data reveal that the size distribution of firms within the <100 and 100+ categories was remarkably stable over time. Between 1988 and 2004, there was less than a two percentage point change in the percentage of workers in the five different size categories (1–24, 25–99, 100–499, 500–999, 1,000+). Consequently, there is no evidence that the growth in coverage at small firms is due to the small firms becoming larger, or that the decline in coverage at the large firms is because the big firms are becoming smaller.

16. The SCF does not include a public-sector worker status variable. To delete those employed in the public sector, we excluded individuals employed in the public administration industry as well as imputed public-sector workers employed outside the public administration industry. We imputed public-sector status in the following manner. First, a model of public-sector status was estimated among a sample of

private-sector workers and public-sector workers employed outside the public administration industry in the April 1993 CPS. Second, the coefficients from the model were applied to nonpublic administration workers in the SCF to generate a predicted probability of public-sector status (with a randomization term) for each worker. Third, a sufficient number of workers were deleted from the SCF on the basis of their predicted probability of being public-sector workers in order to match the percentage of nonpublic administration industry workers employed in the public sector according to each year's Outgoing Rotation Group (ORG) CPS.

17. The 1983 firm size categories are <100 and 100+. The firm size categories for 1989 and later are <10, 10–19, 20–99, 100–499, and 500+.

18. In a separate analysis, we restricted the CPS sample to workers who were employed at least thirty-nine weeks in the prior year. This increases the CPS coverage rates by two to six percentage points depending on the year and firm size category.

19. This conclusion was made by pooling the CPS and SCF data for large firms and performing a regression analysis of pension coverage. While coverage rates are higher in the SCF for large firms in 1989, approximately one-half of the difference can be explained by differences in the characteristics of the workers in the SCF and CPS.

20. Studies exploring the source of the shift from DB to DC plans include Kruse (1995), Gustman, Mitchell, and Steinmeier (1992), Ippolito (1995), Aaronson and Coronado (2005), and Friedberg and Owyang (2004).

21. See Samwick and Skinner (2004) and Even and Macpherson, forthcoming.

22. Richard Ippolito, "Pensions and indenture premia," *Journal of Human Resources* 29 (Summer 1994): 795–812.

23. Michael Curme and Lawrence Kahn, "The impact of the threat of bankruptcy on the structure of compensation," *Journal of Labor Economics* 8 (October 1990): 419–47.

24. Hay-Huggins, "Pension plan expense study for the pension benefit guaranty corporation," Philadelphia: Hay-Huggins, September 1990.

25. Freeman (1985) and Allen and Clark (1986) find that unionism is associated with a more generous pension plan. Evidence that pensions are more generous in the public than private sector is found in Ippolito (1987), Lovejoy (1998), and Wiatrowski (1994).

26. The generosity rate is computed differently for two groups of employees, depending on whether their expected retirement benefits were reported as a percentage of final pay or as a dollar amount. For the first group, the generosity rate is computed as the percentage of pay received at retirement divided by years of service at retirement. For the second group, the generosity rate is computed as annual benefits expected divided by the product of years of service and projected pay at retirement. To project pay at retirement, we assume a 1.1 percent growth in real wages and a 2.84 percent inflation rate. Additional details on the methods employed are described in Even and Macpherson (1998).

Success Stories from the Telecom Industry

How to Become an Entrepreneur

Eric Meltzer

What is it that makes entrepreneurs take risks? My own experience suggests that they take risks because they are oblivious to risk.

When I founded a company called Oneida Communications, an experience I describe in more detail below, it is not merely that I did not think very much about the risks involved. I truly did not think of the undertaking as especially risky. To be sure, it was necessary to find an acquisition opportunity, to form a management team, to raise capital to fund the acquisition, and to work out all the details involved in closing a series of related agreements. And it was necessary to do so in spite of the fact that the seller of the acquisition opportunity also had a completely acceptable offer from Sprint Nextel—a far better buyer than our new company. From an outsider's perspective, the undertaking clearly did involve risk. But for reasons that will become clear, I saw only one possible outcome: success.

I am convinced that, whether we are aware of them or not, risk-taking opportunities are available to most everyone at some point in life. Risk-taking is not simply a function of our genetic endowment; there is no "risky" gene that determines who will and will not become a risk-taker. And although it may be that some people are born with a predisposition toward taking risks, it does not seem that genetics determines entrepreneurship, or that one is simply born (or not born) an entrepreneur.

Neither is risk-taking necessarily a function of upbringing. My own case is instructive. My father, a tenured professor who has worked hard his entire life and for whom I have great love and respect, has certainly been a role model for me, but I cannot say that he modeled risk-taking behavior. He has been at the same university for almost fifty years. He has achieved a great many things, but teaching me how and when to take risks is not one of them.

I graduated from the University of Rochester, where I was a very good student but not an exceptional one. What did characterize my approach to school was my desire always to seek the core of any subject I studied; I wanted to probe a subject to its elemental roots. This tendency influences my behavior even today, and it certainly influenced my path after college. Working as I did in the administrative side of a nonprofit, I felt myself at the periphery of the organization, not part of its central function. It was then I decided to pursue an M.B.A. from the University of Chicago; in business school, I felt, I could get back to the core of something. I graduated from business school at the age of twenty-eight and have been working in investment banking since that time.

My own experience leads me to believe that sensible risk-taking opportunities in business become available at some point to most people. I will draw on my experiences in the telecommunications industry as I explore some of the elements that go into a decision to engage in entrepreneurial activity. Perhaps my story—supplemented by the stories of a few other entrepreneurs—can provide a yardstick of sorts by which others may evaluate their own risk-taking opportunities.

Since I became an investment banker twenty years ago, I have focused on telecommunications. In 1991, I completed the first institutional financing of a small communications tower company. Tower companies rent space to wireless communications companies that use the towers to elevate their transmit and receive antennas. Towers are used by, among others, paging companies, cell phone companies, and specialized mobile radio (SMR), which is a type of two-way radio. SMR was later to become the foundation upon which Nextel Communications was built. Coincidentally, two years after the tower financing, my firm raised $13 million for a small two-way radio company—that is, an SMR company—based in Lexington, Kentucky.

What distinguishes that first SMR transaction in my mind is that I spent my entire company visit with the chief technology officer, probing in excruciating detail how the technology worked. I was plumbing the elemental roots—that is, not behaving like a typical banker. I think it irked the company's president that I spent almost no time with him, but by the end of the day, I had a very good basic understanding of how SMR worked—from the software to the networks, and to the spectrum.

A saying on Wall Street is that once you've closed a deal in an industry, you're an expert. This is obviously a low standard for expertise, since it requires nothing other than money changing hands. My understanding of this very specific, narrow business was unusually deep for an investment banker's. In three short years, I had in truth become one of a handful of SMR experts on Wall Street. This was not based on a lifetime of learning; it was only three years earlier that I had heard the acronym for two-way radio—SMR—for the first time.

Some background on the SMR industry is necessary for assessing the risk involved in my next transaction. Nextel Communications was founded by Morgan O'Brien, a Federal Communications Commission (FCC) attorney at Jones Day, and by Brian McCauley, a cellular executive. Beginning in 1987, Nextel raised venture capital to buy up SMR two-way radio licenses in many of the biggest cities, including New York, Los Angeles, and Chicago. Nextel's success in raising venture capital immediately begat numerous regional mini-Nextels: DialCall in Atlanta and the Southeast, OneComm in Denver and the West, and Dispatch Communications in Boston and New England, as well as several others.

Because of its first-mover status, as well as its substantial financial backing and its control of licenses in the major U.S. cities, Nextel was always perceived as the industry leader. Nextel became a publicly traded company in November 1992. By the next summer, most of the other regional operators had also gone public or had raised venture capital. Less than a year after Nextel's initial public offering, most of these companies had been acquired and consolidated by Nextel. As a result of this near-overnight wave of consolidation, Nextel had become virtually the entire SMR industry by the end of 1993.

In February 1993, six months after closing my first SMR capital raise for the company in Lexington, Kentucky, I attended the SMR industry trade show in

Washington, D.C. As an investment banker, I try to meet people who might have an interest in raising capital, selling their company, or completing some other type of financial transaction, and I found myself talking with Ed Blocker, an operator from Mobile, Alabama, who was desperately trying to find $300,000 to buy a competitor in his local market. The competitor owned a two-way radio system operating on twenty channels. Given that there are about 280 SMR channels in every market, the strategic benefit of acquiring a twenty-channel system is practically zero. Real strategic benefit would require owning at least 220 of the 280 channels, and the cost of buying so many channels could be justified only in a major city. In any event, an investment banker trying to live off the fees from raising $300,000 would starve.

I asked Ed one of the classic investment banking questions: What would you do if money were not an issue? By the end of the day, we had mapped out a plan to raise $10 million to consolidate the markets in Louisiana, Alabama, Mississippi, and the Florida panhandle. As it happened, Merrill Lynch had just put out a report indicating that New Orleans was the only top-thirty market that had not yet been consolidated either by Nextel or one of the larger already-funded regional operators.

Ed Blocker turned out to be the right person in the right place at the right time. Between us, we had the necessary mix of specific human capital—he was an operator and I was a capital raiser—in an environment where a disruptive transformation was occurring. In simpler times we used plainer language: we said that luck is what happens when preparation meets opportunity.

The only thing missing in that adage is an appreciation of the element of risk. Luck—good or bad—may just randomly shine (or rain) down upon us, but far more often we have to make our own luck. And that means taking risks. Preparation may indeed meet opportunity, but if you do not take advantage of the opportunity, it will pass you by. That is, a willingness to take risks is necessary, but preparation makes it possible to engage in sensible risk-taking.

The story of Ed Blocker, a classic entrepreneur, is in a different way as instructive as my own. Born the youngest of six children in rural Georgia, he was one of only two in his family to go to college. Ed says that when he was three years old, his father died of lead poisoning. The simple truth is that Ed's mother shot and killed his father. (I find it telling that, so far as I know, Ed's mother did not go to jail.) Ed's older siblings say he was lucky not to have known his father.

Ed left home at fifteen and supported himself through his junior and senior years of high school. He put himself through college in Atlanta and immediately went to work for Motorola, selling two-way radios. Ten years later, he became one of the youngest regional managers Motorola had ever promoted. For six quarters in a row, he put his region (tiny Mobile, Alabama) into the top ten for Motorola's two-way radio sales in the United States—beating out Motorola managers in huge markets like New York.

Ed had the vision to see what was coming in the industry; he recognized that Nextel was going to change everything. It would consolidate the spectrum, and the profit involved in selling analog two-way radios would dry up. Indeed, analog radios would soon be buggy whips. So despite his tremendous success and high-paying position within that prestigious company, he left Motorola to start his own radio sales and service company. He was hoping to own spectrum and build his own company—which is what was eating away at him when I introduced myself.

Ed and I spent a year building Saber Communications. First, we raised $4 million to pay out as options to buy twenty-eight companies. With the options in place, we at one point found ourselves with 120 days in which to raise an additional $35 million to complete those twenty-eight purchases or lose the initial $4 million. The situation was extremely risky. Yet when an investor asked me at that time what I thought could go wrong, incredibly, I answered that I did not see how anything could go wrong. It was simply a matter of raising the money to close the acquisitions, which is in fact what happened. There are many, many acceptable answers to the question, "What could go wrong?" But "Nothing" is not among them. There is always risk.

Yet I answered as I did, I think, because I felt that I understood the industry so completely, that I had done so much research, and that I had such a clear grasp of the opportunity before us that what we were attempting made complete sense. Anyone who really understood what was going on would see what we were doing as the only rational step to take in those circumstances; it was merely a matter of seizing the opportunity before it slipped away. If we raised the money our deal would get done, and that would be the end of it. There were no other risks.

It is probably more precise to say that superior information made it possible to envision how a desired outcome might occur and, perhaps, encouraged me to assign an unduly high probability to that outcome. Many other inferior outcomes were certainly possible, but a knowledgeable and skillful person could avoid them, so they were assigned negligible probabilities. A fundamental element of risk-taking behavior, then, is to perceive as highly unlikely all outcomes but the one desired.

Someone who is not deeply familiar with a subject has no ability to distinguish among potential risks, that is, to put them in perspective. For that matter, someone new to a problem is often restrained from acting by an inability to gauge the magnitude of possible risks or to identify what constitutes a risk. Indeed, such persons likely cannot even see the opportunity. I am a little older now, so I am better at seeing risk. I take risks in very narrow sectors where I believe I have enormous relevant human capital and where I have concluded that failure is not an option. There are situations in which success is inevitable; most people just lack the necessary experience to recognize the opportunity.

Without question, random luck—the kind you can't make yourself—plays a role in success. At a point in time when the industry was rapidly consolidating, Ed and I happened to meet. That was luck. New Orleans was the only major market not yet consolidated. That was complete luck. Nextel, which went public at $15 per share in February 1992, initially stumbled, dropping to $9 as it faced challenges with technology and raising capital. As those issues were resolved, Nextel's stock soared, peaking at $54—just when Ed and I were raising capital. That was astonishing luck. A year later, after we had finished raising $38 million for Saber Communications, Nextel traded as low as $13. We had just happened to time things right. That was luck.

But it is impossible to overestimate the importance of fundamentally understanding the relevant subject matter as a means of eliminating risk. My experience in telecommunications makes this point. It is a story that has been repeated countless times in probably every business endeavor imaginable. One example I like is the story of Olin Stephens, who devoted his life to designing sailboats. Having studied and been fascinated with sailboats since his youngest days, Stephens dropped out of MIT to apprentice with yacht designers and then set up his own shop. In 1932 he built his first boat, Dorade. Fifty-three feet long and a mere ten feet wide, it was unlike any ship ever built before: for thousands of years, ballast had been loaded within the frame of a sailboat, but the Dorade had a lengthy lead keel that put the ballast far below the waterline, where it would be much more effective in counterbalancing the force of the wind.

Olin Stephens sold Dorade to his father since, I suspect, no one else would invest in such an untested design. If all you knew was the world of internal ballast—which at the time meant everyone except Olin Stephens—capsizing and drowning seemed a certain thing. Stephens, his father, and his younger brother led the crew that raced Dorade to England from Newport, Rhode Island. I expect many assumed it was the last that would be seen of the Stephens family. As it happened, Dorade finished the race an incredible two days ahead of any other boat—almost all of which were far bigger and therefore presumably had an advantage over the Dorade.

A November 2006 *Wall Street Journal* profile of Stephens reported: "Yacht design would never be the same. The assumptions that had limited naval architects to incremental advances were abandoned and the modern age of racing design, defined by an endless quest to produce lighter but more powerful yachts, commenced. No one benefited from this more than Mr. Stephens, who became the most successful designer of the 20th century."[1]

Seventy-four years after the race, at age ninety-eight, Olin Stephens commented on the Dorade and that race: "I knew that a lighter boat with outside ballast was the way to go, and that a deep and narrow hull would go through the sea nicely. It was obvious. It was like taking candy from a baby. It just had to win." To an expert, in other words, success appears obvious and inevitable.

And what of Ed Blocker? He made a small fortune from Saber Communications, which, like all consolidators in the industry, was sold to Nextel Communications. After working for a year at Nextel, Ed left and bought a homebuilding company. It was a business he had always loved but knew nothing about. Ed personally guaranteed the debt of the company and, largely because of fraud on the part of the seller, he lost most of the fortune he made with Saber. Another company he started was forced into bankruptcy when his partner was paralyzed in a car crash.

Three years ago, Ed got into the tanning salon business by buying out a salon owner on terms. His back was to the wall, and he had little money for a down payment. He agreed to an absurdly high purchase price but with modestly favorable terms. Today Ed has over fifty salons (on a franchise basis) in nine states and continues to grow rapidly. Having received the ultimate on-the-job training, Ed is an expert in an industry he knew nothing about three years ago. His story helps explain the roller coaster existence of so many entrepreneurs who make and lose multiple fortunes.

True entrepreneurs like Ed seem to share a number of traits. I told you about Ed because I think his story most starkly conveys these traits. Here are some of the traits that come to mind:

They are unstoppable. Like Rasputin, who was shot, stabbed, and drowned, but refused to die, entrepreneurs are unrelenting, determined survivors who fight to the bitter end.

They are creative and flexible. When confronted with an obstacle, entrepreneurs can divine a novel solution. They win negotiations through cleverness and problem solving, only rarely through brute force.

They know how to learn on the job. Entrepreneurs seem to start off in the trenches after obtaining a degree from some unremarkable educational institution. When they tell you the name of the college they attended, you have to ask where it is located. This education lands them an entry-level position. Because of their determination and flexibility they tend not to stay at the bottom very long, but as a result of starting out there, they learn a business from the bottom up. It is this training that they can later exploit when they open their own business. (As an aside, I would point out how few entrepreneurs went to Ivy League schools. Perhaps because their impressive credentials secure them a position high in the corporate structure, Ivy League graduates never learn the fundamentals that someone starting out at the bottom is exposed to. Furthermore, with their relatively high salaries, they find the opportunity cost of becoming an entrepreneur too high: their secure positions pay too much to justify risking it all for some uncertain bonanza.)

They are people with a certain magnetism whom others want to follow. This was certainly true of Ed Blocker. Even before I met him, when he had a struggling two-way radio sales and service shop, Ed had a following—about twenty people on his payroll crammed into a one-story brick office on the side of a highway outside of Mobile. Clearly, people want to be part of a team that is winning.

What lessons about risk can be learned from my experiences creating Oneida Communications? Although I completed my first transaction in that spectrum band in the mid-1990s, I waited ten years to form the company, which is an aggregator of licenses in the 2.5 gigahertz (GHz) band. Why the wait? And what's 2.5 GHz anyway?

To answer these questions, we need to consider the development of broadband mobile wireless services taking place today. Handheld wireless devices now have the capability to deliver Internet access, though handheld service is both more expensive and much slower than that provided by a cable modem or DSL. In addition to Internet service, most cellular providers now also offer packages of perhaps fifteen or twenty pre-selected television channels that can be watched on a cell phone. At this point, though, the pictures are small and the service is more hype than reality.

But broadband mobile wireless is clearly going to improve and change. Within a decade, perhaps even within five years, wireless networks will enable truly mobile, truly broadband wireless services. This will mean gaming, video, music, and Internet access at speeds similar to those now available at home or the office. User devices will be customized to meet the different requirements of gamers, businessmen, music or movie lovers, and others.

The biggest impediment to the deployment of these networks is a lack of spectrum. Today, almost all the spectrum dedicated to mobile applications is consumed by voice services, so that the capacity for broadband services over the existing networks is severely constrained.

When cellular service started in the early 1980s, the FCC granted two licenses of 20 MHz each, so that there was initially a total of 40 MHz of spectrum available nationwide for all cellular phone services. Usage grew, and the FCC auctioned off more phone spectrum in 1995, 1996, and 1997. The 1995 auction added 60 MHz of spectrum nationwide in two licenses; the 1996 auction added another 30 MHz license; and the 1997 auction added three more licenses of 10 MHz each, for a total of 30 MHz more.

Currently only 160 MHz of spectrum—the original 40 and the 120 auctioned by the FCC over three years—is available for cellular use. This is the spectrum that Verizon, AT&T Wireless, T-Mobile, and all other providers must rely on to supply wireless mobile service. If we add the 20 MHz of spectrum owned by Nextel (which was licensed differently), the total amount of wireless mobile spectrum in use today is approximately 180 MHz, which is mostly used for voice services. The 2.5 GHz band of spectrum, which Oneida is aggregating, was not originally used for mobile services, and it is not included in the aggregate180 MHz of mobile spectrum.

The licenses held by cellular operators were granted in significant blocks— 10 MHz or even 30 MHz. These dense blocks of spectrum covered significant geographic regions. In most instances, the cellular spectrum allocated by the FCC was licensed in fifty-one geographic regions. In other cellular license bands, the United States was cut up into 493 puzzle pieces. Depending upon the band, then, as few as fifty-one licenses could serve the entire United States. These regions do not overlap, and each region within a given band has the same amount of bandwidth (from 10 MHz up to 30 MHz depending on band).

The spectrum that Nextel started with was different. By the count of Tom Hazlett, an expert in telecommunications policy who teaches at George Mason University Law School, Nextel succeeded in consolidating an incredible forty-two thousand separate licenses.[2] Ed Blocker and I helped pull together 3 percent of that total. Each Nextel-type SMR license was only 25 kHz wide—or 1/40 of an MHz. Thus, at any location Nextel needed 400 SMR licenses to have as much spectrum as the thinnest cellular license with 10 MHz of spectrum. It took many SMR licenses to actually amount to very much spectrum.

Furthermore, Nextel's 800 MHz SMR licenses were for circular license areas seventy miles across. What Nextel had to buy was not like cellular spectrum, which consisted of perfectly interlocking puzzle pieces of spectrum, but rather like layers of raindrops, with each layer four hundred drops thick and no conformity among the different layers. This licensing scheme made consolidation extremely difficult. In Tom Hazlett's formulation, it was left to man to put together what the FCC had torn asunder. Despite significant regulatory and technical challenges, however, Nextel did stitch all these licenses together and in the end created billions of dollars in value.

The licensing of 2.5 GHz has been similarly messy. Like the 800 MHz channels, the 2.5 GHz channels are licensed in circles seventy miles across. Unlike SMR channels, however, the 2.5 GHz channels are each 6 MHz wide and the total amount of spectrum in the 2.5 GHz band is a staggering 194 MHz, or more than the combined total of 180 MHz that now constitutes all mobile spectrum.

The FCC started licensing channels in the 2.5 GHz band during the Kennedy administration. Until the mid-1990s the spectrum was used for "wireless cable" television service (which is what the FCC allowed it to be used for). The strategy was to offer "poor man's cable"—a pay-TV service that made available fewer channels than traditional cable television but at a lower price. This business plan proved to be a near universal failure, although before it became entirely clear that Americans wanted more channels, not fewer, Wall Street had managed to raise a few billion dollars for a half dozen or so operators that went public. By this time, there was a new business plan: fixed wireless Internet access. Except this wireless downstream Internet delivery service required a telephone line for the upstream return, and the cost of the customer equipment was $700, rendering the plan not yet ready for prime time.

When the high-yield bonds issued by these companies began to mature, the wireless cable companies faced certain bankruptcy. At that point, in 1998, all but one of the public companies disappeared, their debt having been purchased either by MCI or by Sprint. Through restructurings, MCI and Sprint quickly came to control 2.5 GHz licenses covering about 75 percent of the United States. The only other significant licensee was BellSouth; the remaining licenses were held by a wide scattering of small owners.

It was fairly clear that MCI and Sprint would use the 2.5 GHz band to provide Internet access and that they would consolidate the remaining license holders. Investing in 2.5 GHz looked like a good idea, until MCI filed for bankruptcy and everything came to a dead halt. Then, in 2003, Nextel acquired the 2.5 GHz holdings of MCI. Now it was Nextel and Sprint that held licenses covering about 75 percent of the United States. A year later, Sprint and Nextel merged.

By combining, Sprint Nextel created a near nationwide footprint in the enormous 2.5 GHz band. I believe that the sole reason for the Sprint Nextel merger was to bring together their respective holdings in the 2.5 GHz band. I avoid saying this to potential investors in Oneida because doing so would make me appear irresponsible or worse. This was a $35 billion merger, and the spectrum in the 2.5 GHz band has almost always traded at trivial values. But if we are indeed moving toward a world in which substantial spectrum is needed to deliver not only voice but video, Internet access, gaming, and just about every other type of communication and entertainment service, then it is not messianic to believe that 2.5 GHz spectrum is of paramount strategic value. On the contrary, it is all but obvious to those who understand what they are looking at.

It was about the time that Sprint and Nextel closed their merger that Oneida was formed. Consider some of the uncertainties that still existed:

- The band had not been reorganized, although reorganization was necessary and now permitted by the FCC.
- Sprint Nextel had not announced a strategy for the band.

- No equipment existed that would allow the band to be used for broadband mobile.
- We did not know what services would be offered on any Sprint system.
- We did not know what a system would cost to build or operate.
- We did not even know whether Sprint would choose simply to warehouse the spectrum, meaning that years might go by before the spectrum was used at all.

For most investors, the decision whether to invest in 2.5 GHz spectrum was simple—the answer was no. But from another perspective, the answer was clearly now or never. If we waited any longer, the opportunity for Oneida to consolidate markets not yet owned by Sprint Nextel would evaporate. Sprint would buy them. The final stages of consolidation would occur without our playing any part.

Clearly, the formation of Oneida was a risky undertaking. I think the most important thing I did to reduce the risk was to build a powerful team that made the company more attractive to funders, who play a significant role in facilitating or inhibiting risk-taking.

Embarking upon an endeavor that requires venture capital funding means that the risk being taken is subjected to the market—and that is a pretty severe test. The vast majority of private risk capital is private equity, not venture capital. Of the estimated $1.5 trillion of private equity commitments raised since the early 1980s, easily $1.2 trillion has been committed to the leveraged buyout sector, not venture capital. As one of my clients used to say, the two things in short supply among venture capitalists are venture and capital. It can be hard to find investors who understand your hopes and dreams well enough to actually risk an investment.

One positive trend for entrepreneurs is the declining cost of computers and software, which in turn lessens a start-up's expenses and the need to rely on expensive venture capital. The reduced cost of information technology increases the opportunities for individual innovators, since difficulty procuring venture capital can be a very significant inhibitor of risk-taking. Start-ups today may be closer than in the recent past to the classic American model of entrepreneurship: businesses begun by taking a risk and made successful through determination and hard work.

It is worth pointing out that even risk-averse people can find themselves becoming entrepreneurs. I know a lawyer in Washington, D.C., who advises congressmen regarding Federal Election Commission (FEC) compliance. A leading figure in her narrow specialty, she is the breadwinner in a family that includes three young children. Understandably, her family situation forces her to be cautious. But after years of being passed over for a partnership—largely, I believe, because she is devoted to her family—she finally went into practice on her own. Before she did, she made sure all of her clients would stick with her, ensuring herself of an immediate revenue stream and minimizing the risk to her family. Hers was a case of being so taken advantage of by employers that going it alone—taking that risk—became almost a necessity. She absolutely had the necessary specific human capital needed to thrive.

Compare this scenario with that of my neighbor, who wanted to quit his job in software sales and to go out on his own. His new company would be a sales-oriented company, he said; it would sell—anything. The lack of a specific goal, the lack of near-term revenue visibility, and the lack of relevant experience and contacts were a recipe for certain disaster. But he hated his job and he took the plunge. He has unsuccessfully chased one will-o-the-wisp after another.

To explore the impulse that is necessary for entrepreneurial risk-taking, I conclude with a look at the card game Hearts. In Hearts, the highest card in the lead suit wins the hand and leads the next trick. If players cannot follow suit, they may play any card, including a heart. Players want to avoid getting hearts because each one counts as a point, and the first player to reach one hundred points loses.

Most players quickly learn to get rid of their high cards to avoid being stuck with any hearts. They try to win as few tricks as possible. But there is another strategy that can be employed—to win all the heart cards and reduce your score by twenty-five points, a strategy called "shooting the moon." It is a risky strategy, since you must win all the hearts to enjoy the payoff; there is no greater disaster in the game than attempting to shoot the moon and winding up with some but not all the hearts.

With most hands, shooting the moon is impossible, and I have no choice but to simply play the hand out. But every time the cards are dealt, I see what I can do to try to shoot the moon. Shooting the moon is an exhilarating experience; when the cards are right, your opponents are helpless to stop you. But many players never try—ever. My sense is that someone who is willing to shoot the moon in Hearts is willing to follow the same risk-taking impulse that is required of an entrepreneur.

There is one other element of the game Hearts that bears mentioning. With each trick and each card, more information is revealed. This enables a risk-taker to constantly re-evaluate the wisdom of trying to shoot the moon. It is possible to go far down the path of this risky play and still be able to back out. In business as in Hearts, taking risks is not all black and white, not an all-or-nothing proposition.

Although I love Hearts, I am indifferent to most other card games and to casino gambling. Games involving random luck hold little appeal. I have taken some huge risks in my life, but I am not a gambler.

NOTES

1. Bruce G. Knecht, "Olin Stephens's radical yacht," *Wall Street Journal*, November 4, 2003, 14(P).

2. Thomas W. Hazlett, "Is federal preemption efficient in cellular phone regulation?" *Federal Communications Law Journal* 56, vol. 1 (December 2003): 157–237.

Bibliography

CHAPTER 2

Banatao, Dado P., and Kevin A. Fong. "The valley of deals: How venture capital helped shape the region." 295–313 in *The Silicon Valley Edge: A Habitat for Innovation and Entrepreneurship*, ed. Chong-Moon Lee, William F. Miller, Marguerite Gong Hancock, and Henry S. Rowen. Stanford, CA: Stanford University Press, 2000.

Barkley, David, Deborah Markley, and Julie Rubin. "Public investment in venture capital funds: Lessons from three program alternatives." Columbia, MO: Rural Policy Research Institute, 1999.

Biotechnology Industry Organization. "Laboratories of innovation: State bioscience initiatives 2004." Washington, D.C., 2004.

Bresnahan, Timothy, and Alfonso Gambardella, eds. *Building High-Tech Clusters: Silicon Valley and Beyond*. Cambridge: Cambridge University Press, 2004.

Bygrave, William D., and Jeffry A. Timmons. *Venture Capital at the Crossroads*. Boston: Harvard Business School Press, 1992.

Castilla, Emilio J. "Networks of venture capital firms in Silicon Valley." *International Journal of Technology Management* 25 (2003): 113–35.

Cochrane, John H. "The risk and return of venture capital." *Journal of Financial Economics* 75 (2005): 3–52.

Cohen, Stephen S., and Gary Fields. "Social capital and capital gains: An examination of social capital in Silicon Valley." 190–217 in *Understanding Silicon Valley: The Anatomy of an Entrepreneurial Region*, ed. Martin Kenney. Stanford, CA: Stanford University Press, 2000.

Florida, Richard, and Donald Smith. "Venture capital's role in economic development: An empirical analysis." 183–209 in *Sources of Metropolitan Growth*, ed. Edwin Mills and John McDonald. New Brunswick, NJ: Center for Urban Policy Research, 1992.

Gompers, Paul, and Josh Lerner. *The Venture Capital Cycle.* Cambridge, MA: MIT Press, 1999.

———. "Money chasing deals? The impact of fund inflows on private equity valuations." *Journal of Financial Economics* 55 (2000): 281–325.

Gompers, Paul, Josh Lerner, and David Scharfstein. "Entrepreneurial spawning: Public corporations and the genesis of new ventures, 1986–1999." *Journal of Finance* 60 (2005): 577–614.

Hellmann, Thomas F. "Venture capitalists: The coaches of Silicon Valley." 276–94 in *The Silicon Valley Edge: A Habitat for Innovation and Entrepreneurship*, ed. Chong-Moon Lee, William F. Miller, Marguerite Gong Hancock, and Henry S. Rowen. Stanford, CA: Stanford University Press, 2000.

Hellmann, Thomas, and Manju Puri. "Venture capital and the professionalization of start-up firms: Empirical evidence." *Journal of Finance* 57 (2002): 169–97.

Henton, Doug. "A profile of the Valley's evolving structure." 46–58 in *The Silicon Valley Edge: A Habitat for Innovation and Entrepreneurship*, ed. Chong-Moon Lee, William F. Miller, Marguerite Gong Hancock, and Henry S. Rowen. Stanford, CA: Stanford University Press, 2000.

Horvath, Michael. "Imitating Silicon Valley: Regional comparisons of innovation activity based on venture capital flows." 280–330 in *Building High-Tech Clusters: Silicon Valley and Beyond*, ed. Timothy Bresnahan and Alfonso Gambardella. Cambridge: Cambridge University Press, 2004.

Hsu, David H. "What do entrepreneurs pay for venture capital affiliation?" *Journal of Finance* 59 (2004): 1805–44.

Kenney, Martin, ed. *Understanding Silicon Valley: The Anatomy of an Entrepreneurial Region.* Stanford, CA: Stanford University Press, 2000.

Kenney, Martin, and Richard Florida. "Venture capital in Silicon Valley: Fueling new firms' formation." 98–123 in *Understanding Silicon Valley: The Anatomy of an Entrepreneurial Region*, ed. Martin Kenney. Stanford, CA: Stanford University Press, 2000.

Koepp, Rob. *Clusters of Creativity: Enduring Lessons on Innovation and Entrepreneurship from Silicon Valley and Europe's Silicon Fen.* Hoboken, NJ: John Wiley & Sons, 2003.

Kosseff, Jeffery. "House OKs venture capital bill." *Oregonian,* business section, B01. July 11, 2003.

Lecuyer, Christophe. "Fairchild Semiconductor and its influence." 158–83 in *The Silicon Valley Edge: A Habitat for Innovation and Entrepreneurship*, ed. Chong-Moon Lee, William F. Miller, Marguerite Gong Hancock, and Henry S. Rowen. Stanford, CA: Stanford University Press, 2000.

Lee, Chong-Moon, William F. Miller, Marguerite Gong Hancock, and Henry S. Rowen, eds. *The Silicon Valley Edge: A Habitat for Innovation and Entrepreneurship*, Stanford, CA: Stanford University Press, 2000.

Leslie, Stuart W. "The biggest 'angel' of them all: The military and the making of Silicon Valley." 48–67 in *Understanding Silicon Valley: The Anatomy of an Entrepreneurial Region*, ed. Martin Kenney. Stanford, CA: Stanford University Press, 2000.

Metcalfe, Bob. "Asian tour provides useful insight on Silicon Valley's worldwide Internet edge." *Infoworld Electric* (March 2, 1998) <http://www.infoworld.com/cgi-bin/displayNew.pl?/metcalfe/980302bm.htm> (accessed January 4, 2006).

Pounds, Stephen. "Venture investors keep eye on Scripps." *Palm Beach Post,* business section, 1F. May 2, 2004.

Rosenberg, David. *Cloning Silicon Valley.* New York: Pearson Education, 2002.

Saxenian, Anna Lee. *Regional Advantage: Culture and Competition in Silicon Valley and Route 128.* Cambridge, MA: Harvard University Press, 1994.

Schumpeter, Joseph A. *The theory of Economic Development.* Cambridge, MA: Harvard University Press, 1934.

Sorenson, Olav, and Toby E. Stuart. "Syndication networks and the spatial distribution of venture capital investments." *American Journal of Sociology* 106 (2001): 1546–88.

Stuart, Toby, and Olav Sorenson. "Social networks and entrepreneurship." 211–28 in *Handbook of Entrepreneurship Research: Disciplinary Perspectives*, ed. Rajshree Agrawal, Sharon Alvarez, and Olav Sorenson. Berlin: Springer-Verlag, 2005.

VentureOne Corporation. *The VentureOne Venture Capital Sourcebook.* San Francisco, 2000.

———. *Venture Capital Industry Report.* San Francisco, 2001.

Von Burg, Urs, and Martin Kenney. "Venture capital and the birth of the local area networking industry." *Research Policy* 29 (2000): 1135–55.

Wallsten, Scott. "The role of government in regional technology development: The effects of public venture capital and science parks." 229–79 in *Building High-Tech Clusters: Silicon Valley and Beyond*, ed. Timothy Bresnahan and Alfonso Gambardella. Cambridge: Cambridge University Press, 2004.

Webb, Andrew. "Venture group to promote startups." *Albuquerque Journal*, October 9, 2004.

Zhang, Junfu. *High-Tech Start-Ups and Industry Dynamics in Silicon Valley.* San Francisco: Public Policy Institute of California, 2003a.

———. "Growing Silicon Valley on a landscape: An agent-based approach to high-tech industrial clusters." *Journal of Evolutionary Economics* 13 (2003b): 529–48.

———. "A study of academic entrepreneurs using venture capital data." Working Paper No. 2006.01, Public Policy Institute of California, San Francisco, 2006.

———. "Access to venture capital and the performance of high-tech start-ups in Silicon Valley." *Economic Development Quarterly*, Vol. 21, 124–47, May 2007.

Zook, Mathew A. *The Geography of the Internet Industry.* Malden, MA: Blackwell Publishing, 2005.

CHAPTER 3

Bhidé, Amar V. *The Origin and Evolution of New Businesses.* New York: Oxford University Press, 2000.

Blanchflower, David G., and Andrew J. Oswald. "What makes an entrepreneur?" *Journal of Labor Economics* 16 (January 1998): 26–60.

Cagetti, Marco, and Mariacristina DeNardi. "Entrepreneurship, default risk, bequests and wealth inequality." Manuscript, Department of Economics, University of Virginia, Charlottesville, 2004.

Charles, Kerwin Kofi, and Erik Hurst. "The correlation of wealth across generations." *Journal of Political Economy* 111 (December 2003): 1155–82.

Coleman, Susan. "Constraints faced by women small business owners: Evidence from the data." *Journal of Developmental Entrepreneurship* 7 (2004): 151–74.

Dunn, Thomas, and Douglas Holtz-Eakin. "Capital market constraints, parental wealth and the transition to self-employment among men and women." Discussion paper, Bureau of Labor Statistics, Washington, D.C., 1995.

Evans, David S., and Boyan Jovanovic. "An estimated model of entrepreneurial choice under liquidity constraints." *Journal of Political Economy* 97 (August 1989): 808–27.

Evans, David S., and Linda S. Leighton. "Some empirical aspects of entrepreneurship." *American Economic Review* 79 (June 1989): 519–35.

Fairlie, Robert W. "The absence of the African-American owned business: An analysis of the dynamics of self-employment." *Journal of Labor Economics* 17 (January 1999): 80–108.

———. "Entrepreneurship among disadvantaged groups: An analysis of the dynamics of self-employment by gender, race and education." In *Handbook of entrepreneurship*, ed. Simon C. Parker, Zoltan J. Acs, and David R. Audretsch. Boston: Kluwer Academic Publishers, 2005.

Gentry, William M., and Glenn R. Hubbard. "Entrepreneurship and household saving." *Advances in Economics Analysis and Policy* 4 (1): article 8, 2004 <http://www.bepress.com/bejeap/advances/vol4/iss1art8>.

Holtz-Eakin, Douglas, David Joulfaian, and Harvey S. Rosen. "Sticking it out: Entrepreneurial survival and liquidity constraints." *Journal of Political Economy* 102 (February 1994a): 53–75.

———. "Entrepreneurial decisions and liquidity constraints." *Rand Journal of Economics* 25 (Summer 1994b): 334–47.

Hurst, Erik, and Annamaria Lusardi. "Liquidity constraints, household wealth and entrepreneurship." *Journal of Political Economy* 112 (April 2004): 319–47.

Hurst, Erik, and Frank P. Stafford. "Home is where the equity is: Liquidity constraints, mortgage refinancing and consumption." *Journal of Money, Credit, and Banking* 36, no. 6 (2004): 985–1014.

Meyer, Bruce D. "Why are there so few black entrepreneurs?" Working Paper no. 3537, National Bureau of Economic Research, 1990.

Quadrini, Vincenzo. "The Importance of Entrepreneurship for Wealth Concentration and Mobility." *Review of Income and Wealth* 45 (March 1999): 1–19.

U.S. Bureau of the Census, 2003, 2004.

CHAPTER 4

Blanchflower, David G., and Andrew J. Oswald. "What makes an entrepreneur?" *Journal of Labor Economics* 16, no. 1 (1998): 26–60.

Blau, David M. "A time-series analysis of self-employment in the United States." *Journal of Political Economy* 95, no. 3 (1987): 445–67.

Briscoe, Geoff, Andrew Dainty, and Sarah Millett. "The impact of the tax system on self-employment in the British construction industry." *International Journal of Manpower* 21, no. 8 (2000): 596–613.

Bruce, Donald. "Effects of the United States tax system on transitions into self-employment." *Labour Economics* 7, no. 5 (2000): 545–74.

———. "Taxes and entrepreneurial endurance: Evidence from the self-employed." *National Tax Journal* 55, no. 1 (2002): 5–24.

Bruce, Donald, and Tami Gurley. *Taxes and Entrepreneurial Activity: An Empirical Investigation Using Longitudinal Tax Return Data*. A Report to the U.S. Small Business Administration under Contract No. SBAHQ-04-M-0521, 2005.

Bruce, Donald, and Douglas Holtz-Eakin. "Who are the entrepreneurs? Evidence from taxpayer data." *Journal of Entrepreneurial Finance and Business Ventures* 1, no.1 (2001): 1–10.

Bruce, Donald, Douglas Holtz-Eakin, and Joseph Quinn. "Self-employment and labor market transitions at older ages." Mimeo, Department of Economics, Syracuse University, 2000.

Bruce, Donald, and Mohammed Mohsin. "Tax policy and entrepreneurship: new time series evidence." *Small Business Economics* 26, no. 5 (2006): 409–25.

Carroll, Robert, Douglas Holtz-Eakin, Mark Rider, and Harvey S. Rosen. "Entrepreneurs, income taxes, and investment." 427–55 in *Does Atlas Shrug? The Economic Consequences of Taxing the Rich*, ed. Joel B. Slemrod. New York: Russell Sage Foundation, 2000a.

———. "Income taxes and entrepreneurs' use of labor." *Journal of Labor Economics* 18, no. 2 (2000b): 324–51.

———. "Personal income taxes and the growth of small firms." 121–147 in *Tax Policy and the Economy, Vol. 15*, ed. James Poterba. Cambridge, MA: MIT Press, 2001.

Cline, Robert, Tom Neubig, and Andrew Phillips. "Total State and Local Business Taxes: Nationally 1980–2005, by State 2002–2005." *State Tax Notes* 40, no. 5 (May 1, 2006).

Crain, W. Mark, and Thomas D. Hopkins. *The Impact of Regulatory Costs on Small Firms: A Report for the Office of Advocacy, U.S. Small Business Administration.* Washington, D.C.: Small Business Administration, RFP no. SBAHQ-00-R-0027, 2001.

Domar, Evsey D., and Richard A. Musgrave. "Proportional income taxation and risk-taking." *Quarterly Journal of Economics* 58 (1944): 388–422.

Dunn, Thomas, and Douglas Holtz-Eakin. "Financial capital, human capital, and the transition to self-employment: Evidence from intergenerational links." *Journal of Labor Economics* 18, no. 2 (2000): 282–305.

Evans, David S., and Boyan Jovanovic. "An estimated model of entrepreneurial choice under liquidity constraints." *Journal of Political Economy* 97, no. 4 (1989): 808–27.

Evans, David S., and Linda S. Leighton. "Some empirical aspects of entrepreneurship." *American Economic Review* 79, no. 3 (1989): 519–35.

Fairlie, Robert W., and Bruce D. Meyer. "Trends in self-employment among white and black men during the twentieth century." *Journal of Human Resources* 35, no. 4 (2000): 643–69.

Feenberg, Daniel R., and Elizabeth Coutts. "An introduction to the TAXSIM model." *Journal of Policy Analysis and Management* 12 (Winter 1993): 189–94.

Gentry, William M., and R. Glenn Hubbard. "Tax policy and entrepreneurial entry." *American Economic Review* 90 (May 2000): 283–87.

Headd, Brian. "Redefining business success: Distinguishing between closure and failure." *Small Business Economics* 21, no. 1 (2003): 51–61.

Holtz-Eakin, Douglas. "Should small businesses be tax-favored?" *National Tax Journal* 48, no. 3 (1995): 387–95.

Holtz-Eakin, Douglas, David Joulfaian, and Harvey S. Rosen. "Sticking it out: Entrepreneurial survival and liquidity constraints." *Journal of Political Economy* 102, no. 1 (1994a): 53–75.

———. "Entrepreneurial decisions and liquidity constraints." *Rand Journal of Economics* 25, no. 3 (1994b): 334–47.

Joulfaian, David, and Mark Rider. "Differential taxation and tax evasion by small business." *National Tax Journal* 51, no. 4 (1998): 675–87.

Long, James E. "Income taxation and the allocation of market labor." *Journal of Labor Research* 3, no. 3 (1982a): 259–76.

———. "The income tax and self-employment." *National Tax Journal* 35 (1982b): 31–42.

Moore, Robert L. "Self-employment and the incidence of the payroll tax." *National Tax Journal* 36 (1983): 491–501.

Parker, Simon C. "A time series model of self-employment under uncertainty." *Economica* 63 (1996): 459–75.

———. "Does tax evasion affect occupational choice?" *Oxford Bulletin of Economics and Statistics* 65, no. 3 (2003): 379–94.

Robson, Martin T. "The rise in self-employment amongst UK males." *Small Business Economics* 10 (1998): 99–212.

Robson, Martin T., and Colin Wren. "Marginal and average tax rates and the incentive for self-employment." *Southern Economic Journal* 65, no. 4 (1999): 757–73.

Schuetze, Herbert J., and Donald Bruce. "Tax policy and entrepreneurship." *Swedish Economic Policy Review* 11, no. 2 (2004): 235–65.

Slemrod, Joel, Marsha Blumenthal, and Charles Christian. "Taxpayer response to an increased probability of audit: Evidence from a controlled experiment in Minnesota." *Journal of Public Economics* 79 (2001): 455–83.

CHAPTER 5

Andersson, Pernilla, and Eskil Wadensjö. "Self-employed immigrants in Denmark and Sweden—A way to economic self-reliance?" Swedish Institute for Social Research, Stockholm University, 2003.

Baron, Salo W., Arcadius Kahan, and others. *Economic History of the Jews*, ed. Nachum Gross. New York: Schocken Books, 1975.

Bates, Timothy. *Assessment of State and Local Government Minority Business Development Programs*. Report to the U.S. Department of Commerce Minority Business Development Agency. Washington, D.C.: U.S. Department of Commerce, 1993.

———. "Race, self-employment and upward mobility: An illusive American dream." Washington, D.C./Baltimore: Woodrow Wilson Center Press and John Hopkins University Press, 1997.

Blanchflower, David G., Phillip B. Levine, and David J. Zimmerman. "Discrimination in the small business credit market." *Review of Economics and Statistics* 85 (November 2003): 930–43.

Blanchflower, David G., and Andrew J. Oswald. "What makes an entrepreneur?" *Journal of Labor Economics* 16 (1998): 26–60.

Blau, Francine, and Lawrence Kahn. "Gender and assimilation among Mexican-Americans." In *Mexican Immigration to the United States*, ed. George Borjas. Chicago: University of Chicago Press, forthcoming spring 2007.

Bleakley, Hoyt, and Aimee Chin. "Language skills and earnings: Evidence from childhood immigrants." Working Paper, Economics Department, University of California, San Diego, 2003.

Bonacich, Edna, and John Modell. "The economic basis of ethnic solidarity in the Japanese American community." Berkeley: University of California Press, 1980.

Borjas, George. "The self-employment experience of immigrants." *Journal of Human Resources* 21, no. 4 (1986): 487–506.

Borjas, George, and Stephen Bronars. "Consumer discrimination and self-employment." *Journal of Political Economy* 97 (1989): 581–605.

Bradford, William D. "The wealth dynamics of entrepreneurship for black and white families in the U.S." *Review of Income and Wealth* 49, no. 1 (2003): 89–116.

Brown, Charles, James Hamilton, and James Medoff. *Employers Large and Small*. Cambridge, MA: Harvard University Press, 1990.

Cavalluzzo, Ken, Linda Cavalluzzo, and John Wolken. "Competition, small business financing, and discrimination: Evidence from a new survey." *Journal of Business* 75, no. 4 (2002): 641–79.

Clark, Kenneth, and Stephen Drinkwater. "Pushed out or pulled in? Self-employment among ethnic minorities in England and Wales." *Labour Economics* 7 (2000): 603–28.

Cobb-Clark, Deborah A., and Vincent Hildebrand. "The wealth of Mexican Americans." Discussion Paper No. 1150, Institute for the Study of Labor (IZA), Bonn, 2004.

Dustmann, Christian, and Arthur van Soest. "Language and the earnings of immigrants." *Industrial and Labor Relations Review* 55, no. 3 (2002): 473–92.

Evans, David, and Boyan Jovanovic. "An estimated model of entrepreneurial choice under liquidity constraints." *Journal of Political Economy* 97 (August 1989): 808–27.

Fairlie, Robert W. "The absence of the African-American owned business: An analysis of the dynamics of self-employment." *Journal of Labor Economics* 17, no. 1 (1999): 80–108.

———. "Does business ownership provide a source of upward mobility for blacks and Hispanics?" 153–79 in *Public Policy and the Economics of Entrepreneurship*, ed. Doug Holtz-Eakin and Havey S. Rosen. Cambridge, MA: MIT Press, 2004.

Fairlie, Robert W., and Harry Krashinsky. "Liquidity constraints, household wealth, and entrepreneurship revisited," working paper, UC Santa Cruz, 2005.

Fairlie, Robert W., and Bruce D. Meyer. "Ethnic and racial self-employment differences and possible explanations." *Journal of Human Resources* 31 (Fall 1996): 757–93.

———. "Trends in self-employment among black and white men: 1910–1990." *Journal of Human Resources* 35, no. 4 (2000): 643–69.

Fairlie, Robert W., and Christopher Woodruff. "Mexican entrepreneurship: A comparison of self-employment in Mexico and the United States." In *Mexican Immigration to the United States*, ed. George Borjas. Chicago: University of Chicago Press, forthcoming spring 2007.

Flota, Chrystell, and Marie T. Mora. "The earnings of self-employed Mexican Americans along the U.S.-Mexico border." *The Annals of Regional Science* 35 (2001): 483–99.

Hout, Michael, and Harvey S. Rosen. "Self-employment, family background, and race." *Journal of Human Resources* 35, no. 4(2000): 670–92.

Hurst, Erik, and Annamaria Lusardi. "Liquidity constraints, household wealth, and entrepreneurship." *Journal of Political Economy* 112, no. 2 (2004): 319–47.

Kidd, Michael P. "Immigrant wage differentials and the role of self-employment in Australia." *Australian Economic Papers* 32 (June 1993): 92–115.

Kossoudji, Sherrie A., and Deborah A. Cobb-Clark. 2002. "Coming out of the shadows: Learning about legal status and wages from the legalized population." *Journal of Labor Economics* 20, no. 3 (2002): 598–628.

Light, Ivan. *Ethnic Enterprise in America.* Berkeley: University of California Press, 1972.

Loewen, James W. *The Mississippi Chinese: Between Black and White.* Cambridge, MA: Harvard University Press, 1971.

Lofstrom, Magnus. "Labor market assimilation and the self-employment decision of immigrant entrepreneurs." *Journal of Population Economics* 15, no. 1 (2002): 83–114.

Lucas, Robert E. "On the size distribution of firms." *Bell Journal of Economics* 9, no. 2 (1978): 508–23.

McManus, Walter, William Gould, and Finish Welch. "Earnings of Hispanic men: The role of English language proficiency." *Journal of Labor Economics* 1, no. 2 (1983): 101–30.

Meyer, Bruce. "Why are there so few black entrepreneurs?" Working Paper No. 3537, National Bureau of Economic Research, 1990.

Min, Pyong Gap. "Some positive functions of ethnic business for an immigrant community: Koreans in Los Angeles." Final Report submitted to the National Science Foundation, Washington, D.C., 1989.

———. "Korean immigrants in Los Angeles." 185–204 in *Immigration and Entrepreneurship: Culture, Capital, and Ethnic Networks,* ed. Ivan Light and Parminder Bhachu. New Brunswick, NJ: Transaction Publishers, 1993.

Passel, Jeffrey, Randy Capps, and Michael Fix. "Undocumented immigrants: Facts and figures." Working paper, Urban Institute, 2004.

Trejo, Stephen J. "Why do Mexican Americans earn low wages?" *Journal of Political Economy* 105, no. 6 (1997): 1235–68.

———. "Intergenerational progress of Mexican-origin workers in the U.S. labor market." *Journal of Human Resources* 38, no. 3 (2003): 467–89.

U.S. Census Bureau. *1992 Economic Census: Characteristics of Business Owners.* Washington, D.C.: U.S. Government Printing Office (1997).

U.S. Immigration and Naturalization Service. *Statistical Yearbook of the Immigration and Naturalization Service, 1995.* Washington, D.C.: U.S. Government Printing Office, 1997.

———. *Estimates of Unauthorized Immigrant Population Residing in the United States: 1990 to 2000.* Washington, D.C.: Office of Policy Planning, 2003.

Yuengert, Andrew M. "Testing hypotheses of immigrant self-employment." *Journal of Human Resources* 30, no. 1 (1995): 194–204.

CHAPTER 6

Aaronson, Stephanie, and Julia Coronado. "Are firms or workers behind the shift away from DB pension plan?" *Board of Governors of the Federal Reserve System (U.S.),* Finance and Economics Discussion Series No. 2005-17, 2005.

Allen, Steven G., and Robert Clark. "Unions, pension wealth, and age-compensation profiles." *Industrial and Labor Relations Review* 39 (July 1986): 502–18.

Andrews, Emily. "Pension policy and small employers: At what cost coverage?" Washington, D.C.: Employee Benefit Research Institute, 1989.

Andrews, Emily, and Olivia Mitchell. "Scale economies in private multi-employer pension systems." *Industrial and Labor Relations Review* 34 (July 1981): 522–30.

Carrington, William J., Kristin McCue, and Brooks Pierce. "Nondiscrimination rules and the distribution of fringe benefits." *Journal of Labor Economics* 20 (April 2002): S5-S33.

Curme, Michael, and Lawrence Kahn. "The impact of the threat of bankruptcy on the structure of compensation." *Journal of Labor Economics* 8 (October 1990): 419–47.

Dorsey, Stuart. "The economic functions of private pensions: An empirical analysis." *Journal of Labor Economics* 5 (October 1987): S171–S189.

Employee Benefit Research Institute. "The 2001 small employer retirement survey: Summary of findings." Washington, D.C.: Employee Benefit Research Institute, 2002.

———. "The 2003 small employer retirement survey: Summary of findings." Washington, D.C.: Employee Benefit Research Institute, 2003.

Engen, Eric, William Gale, and John Karl Scholz. "The illusory effects of saving incentives on saving." *Journal of Economic Perspectives* 10 (Fall 1996): 113–38.

Even, William E., and David A. Macpherson. "Plant size and the decline of unionism." *Economics Letters* 32 (March 1990): 393–98.

———. "Why did male pension coverage decline in the 1980s?" *Industrial and Labor Relations Review* 47 (April 1994): 439–53.

———. "The impact of rising 401(k) pension coverage on future retirement income." Final Report to U.S. Department of Labor Pension and Welfare Benefits Administration, 1998.

———. "Benefits and productivity." 43–57 in *Benefits for the Workplace of the Future*, ed. Olivia S. Mitchell, David S. Blitzstein, Michael S. Gordon, and Judith F. Mazo. Philadelphia: University of Pennsylvania Press, 2003.

———. Forthcoming. "Defined contribution plans and the distribution of pension wealth." *Industrial Relations*.

Freeman, Richard. "Unions, pensions, and pension funds." 89–118 in *Pensions, Labor, and Individual Choice*, ed. David A. Wise. Chicago: University of Chicago Press, 1985.

Friedberg, Leora, and Michael Owyang. "Explaining the evolution of pension structure and job tenure." Working Paper 10714, National Bureau of Economic Research, 2004.

Gale, William. "The impact of pensions and 401(k) plans on household saving and wealth." 103–21 in *The Evolving Pension System: Trends, Effects, and Proposals for Reform*, ed. William G. Gale, John B. Shoven, and Mark J. Warshawsky. Washington, D.C.: Brookings Institution Press, 2005.

Ghilarducci, Teresa, and Kevin Terry. "Scale economies in union pension plan administration: 1981–1993." *Industrial Relations* 38 (January 1999): 11–17.

Gustman, Alan, Olivia Mitchell, and Thomas Steinmeier. "The stampede towards defined contribution plans." *Industrial Relations* 31 (Spring 1992): 361–69.

Hay-Huggins Company. "Pension Plan Expense Study." Final report submitted to the Pension Benefit Guaranty Corporation. Philadelphia: Hay-Huggins, September 1990.

Ippolito, Richard. "The economic function of underfunded pension plans." *Journal of Law and Economics* 28 (October 1985): 611–52.

———. "Why federal workers don't quit." *Journal of Human Resources* 22 (Spring 1987): 281–99.

———. "Pensions and indenture premia." *Journal of Human Resources* 29 (Summer 1994): 795–812.

———. "Toward explaining the growth of defined contribution plans." *Industrial Relations* 34 (January 1995): 1–20.

———. "The survival rate of defined-benefit plans, 1987–1995." *Industrial Relations* 39 (April 2000): 228–45.

Kruse, Douglas. "Pension substitution in the 1980s: Why the shift toward defined contribution?" *Industrial Relations* 34 (April 1995): 218–41.

Lovejoy, Lora Mills. "The comparative value of pensions in the public and private sectors." *Monthly Labor Review* 111 (December 1998): 18–26.

Munnell, Alicia, James Lee, and Kevin Meme. "An update on pension data." *Center for Retirement Research*, Issue Brief 20, July 2004.

Papke, Leslie. "Are 401(k) plans replacing other employer-provided pensions? Evidence from panel data." *Journal of Human Resources* 34 (Spring 1999): 346–68.

Poterba, James M., Steven F. Venti, and David A. Wise. "How retirement saving programs increase saving." *Journal of Economic Perspectives* 10 (Fall 1996): 91–112.

Purcell, Patrick, and Paul Graney. "Pension issues: Small employer plans." *Congressional Research Service Report*, August 2001.

Samwick, Andrew A., and Jonathan Skinner. "How will 401(k) pension plans affect retirement income?" *American Economic Review* 94 (March 2004): 329–43.

Scott, Frank, Mark Berger, and Dan Black. "Effects of the tax treatment of fringe benefits on labor market segmentation." *Industrial and Labor Relations Review* 42 (January 1989): 216–29.

Wiatrowski, William J. "On the disparity between private and public pensions." *Monthly Labor Review* 117 (April 1994): 3–9.

CHAPTER 7

Hazlett, Thomas W. "Is federal preemption efficient in cellular phone regulation?" *Federal Communications Law Journal* 56 (December 2003): 157–237.

Knecht, Bruce G. 2006. "Olin Stephens's radical yacht." *Wall Street Journal* (November 2006): 14(P).

Index

401(k) plans, 126, 127, 128, 135, 153n7

African Americans: liquidity constraints and transition into entrepreneurship, 57–58; self-employment, 100

AMD, 16

American Research and Development (ARD), 19

angel investors, 18, 20

area codes, 44n37

Asian immigrants: sectoral composition, 103–4, *115–16*; self-employment rates, 102, *114*

BellSouth, 167

bivariate probit model, 137–38, *150*

Blocker, Ed, 160–61, 162, 163–64, 166

Boston: access to venture capital and, 25, 26, 28, 29, 30, 31; area codes, 44n37; performance of start-ups, 30–31; Route 128 area, 21

broadband mobile wireless services, 164–65

business entry: business type as a factor in, 56–57; cuts in marginal tax rates and, 85, 86; household wealth and, 48, 54–55, 60, *65*; housing capital gains and, 59; inheritance and, 58–59; liquidity constraints and, 57–58, 60; parental wealth and, 6–7, 55–56, *65*; rates of, *80–81*; tax rates and, 83–84. *See also* start-ups

business equity, 51–52

business owners. *See* entrepreneurs

business ownership, liquidity constraints and, 47–48

business plans, Silicon Valley start-ups and, 33

wealth: business entry and, 5–7, 48,
54–55, 60, *61*; entrepreneurship and,
50–53; immigrant self-employment
and, 10, 99–100, 112, 113; nonlinear
affect on self-employment, 121n26.
See also household savings and
wealth; parental wealth
wealth distribution, 6
West Virginia, state venture capital
policies, 18
wireless cable industry, 166–67

wireless services, 164–65
women: liquidity constraints and
transition into entrepreneurship, 57,
58. *See also* immigrant women;
Mexican-American women
immigrants

yacht designing, 162–63
young households, liquidity constraints
and transition into entrepreneurship,
57, 58

About the Contributors

Donald J. Bruce is an associate professor in the Center for Business and Economic Research (CBER) and the Department of Economics at the University of Tennessee, Knoxville. He holds a B.A. with honors in economics from Drew University and M.A. and Ph.D. degrees in economics from Syracuse University. Dr. Bruce specializes in empirical policy research, particularly on behavioral responses to tax policies. Since earning his Ph.D. in 1999, he has published numerous articles in academic journals and presented his work at several professional meetings. Much of his research has examined the effects of taxes on small business activity. His paper on tax policy and entrepreneurial endurance was awarded the National Tax Association's Richard Musgrave Prize for the most outstanding article published in the *National Tax Journal* in 2002. His recent SBA-funded research has considered the impacts of a diverse array of federal and state taxes on entrepreneurial start-up and survival rates. In early 2005, he was invited to present findings from some of this work to the President's Advisory Panel on Federal Tax Reform.

William E. Even is a professor of economics at Miami University. He is also a research fellow at the Institute for the Study of Labor (IZA) and the Employee

Benefits Research Institute. He is an applied-labor economist whose research has focused on pension economics, the effects of minimum wage laws, gender differences in the labor market, and labor unions. Professor Even has authored articles appearing in leading national economic journals, including the *American Economic Review, Journal of Labor Economics, Journal of Human Resources,* and the *Review of Economics and Statistics.* He received his Ph.D. in economics from the University of Iowa.

Robert W. Fairlie is an associate professor of economics and the director of the Masters Program in Applied Economics and Finance at the University of California, Santa Cruz. He was a visiting fellow at Yale University and is a research affiliate of the National Poverty Center at the University of Michigan and the Institute for the Study of Labor (IZA). His research interests include ethnic and racial patterns of self-employment, entrepreneurship, access to technology and the "Digital Divide," the effects of immigration on U.S. labor markets, racial patterns in unemployment and job displacement, welfare reform, education, and health insurance. Dr. Fairlie's research has been published in leading economics, public policy, and management journals. He has received grants from the National Science Foundation, the William T. Grant Foundation, U.S. Small Business Administration, U.S. Department of Labor, Kauffman Foundation, Russell Sage Foundation, Spencer Foundation, and Public Policy Institute of California. He has testified to the U.S. Congress, U.S. Department of Treasury and the California State Assembly, Committee on Utilities and Commerce, regarding the findings from his research. Dr. Fairlie holds a Ph.D. and M.A. in economics from Northwestern University and a B.A. with honors from Stanford University.

Diana Furchtgott-Roth is a senior fellow at Hudson Institute and directs the Center for Employment Policy. From February 2003 to April 2005 Ms. Furchtgott-Roth was chief economist of the U.S. Department of Labor. Previously she served as chief of staff at the President's Council of Economic Advisers. Ms. Furchtgott-Roth is coauthor of *Women's Figures: An Illustrated Guide to the Economics of Women in America* and *The Feminist Dilemma: When Success Is Not Enough.* She is a weekly economics columnist for *The New York Sun.* Her articles have been published in *The Washington Post, The Financial Times, The Wall Street Journal, Investor's Business Daily, The Los Ange-*

les Times, and *Le Figaro*, among others. Ms. Furchtgott-Roth was also assistant to the president and resident fellow at the American Enterprise Institute from 1993 to 2001. Prior to that, she served as deputy executive director of the Domestic Policy Council and associate director of the Office of Policy Planning in the White House under President George H. W. Bush. From 1987 to 1991 she was an economist at the American Petroleum Institute, where she authored papers on energy and taxation. Ms. Furchtgott-Roth was also an economist on the staff of President Reagan's Council of Economic Advisers from 1986 to 1987. She received her B.A. in economics from Swarthmore College and her M.Phil. in economics from Oxford University.

Tami Gurley-Calvez is an economist at the U.S. Government Accountability Office. She received a B.A. in political science and economics from the University of Colorado, Boulder, and M.A. and Ph.D. degrees in economics from the University of Tennessee, Knoxville. Dr. Gurley-Calvez has broad research interests in public policy and a particular interest in behavioral responses to tax policy. Much of her work has focused on the effects of taxes on entrepreneurs and she has presented this work at various professional meetings. Her dissertation on the effects of tax policy on entrepreneurs received a fellowship from the Ewing Marion Kauffman Foundation and she has recently conducted SBA-funded research on the effects of tax rates and health insurance deductibility on current and potential entrepreneurs.

Erik Hurst is a professor of economics and the John Huizinga Faculty Fellow at the University of Chicago's Graduate School of Business and research fellow at the National Bureau of Economic Research. Professor Hurst received his Ph.D. in economics from the University of Michigan in 1999. His research focuses on many aspects of household financial behavior, including work on black/white saving differentials, bankruptcy reform, the correlation in saving propensities between parents and their children, the effects of recent welfare reform on the savings of low-educated single mothers, the adequacy of retirement savings, the effects of household mortgage refinancing on consumption spending, the effect of social security laws on household's credit card borrowing, how households allocate time towards shopping and home production to reduce their consumption expenditures, racial discrimination in vehicle lending, and the effects of borrowing constraints on household small business formation. His research has been published in top academic journals, including *The Journal of Political Economy*, *The American Economic Review*, *The Review of Economics and Statistics*, and *The Brookings Papers on Economic Activity*. Currently, Professor Hurst is working on documenting the extent to which household leisure time has evolved over the last five decades and the importance of signaling status in household consumption and portfolio decisions.

Annamaria Lusardi is a professor of economics at Dartmouth College. She is also a research associate at the National Bureau of Economic Research, a member of the Technical Review Committee for the Bureau of Labor Statistics' National Longitudinal Surveys Program, and a member of the Academic Advisory Board of the Center for Private Equity and Entrepreneurship at the Tuck School of Business. Professor Lusardi's main areas of research are savings, Social Security and pensions, entrepreneurship, and macroeconomics. She has worked with both U.S. and international data. She is the author of numerous articles analyzing the impact of risk on wealth accumulation, the effects of liquidity constraints on occupational choice, the importance of planning costs, the effects of financial literacy and financial education, and the behavior of saving across countries. Dr. Lusardi received her Ph.D. degree in economics from Princeton University. Previously, she won a research fellowship from the Irving B. Harris Graduate School of Public Policy Studies at the University of Chicago and a junior faculty fellowship from the John M. Olin Foundation. Her research has been supported by several institutions, such as the National Institute on Aging, the National Science Foundation, the U.S. Department of Labor, TIAA-CREF, and the Social Security Administration via the University of Michigan Retirement Research Center and the Center for Retirement Research at Boston College.

David A. Macpherson is the Rod and Hope Brim Eminent Scholar of Economics at Florida State University. He is also director of the Pepper Institute on Aging and Public Policy and a research fellow at the Institute for the Study of Labor (IZA). Earlier, he was an associate professor of economics at Miami University. He is an applied-labor economist whose research has focused on pensions, minimum wage laws, discrimination, and labor unions. Professor Macpherson has authored articles appearing in respected economic journals, including the *Journal of Human Resources, Journal of Labor Economics,* and the *Review of Economics and Statistics.* He also coauthors the textbooks *Contemporary Labor Economics* and *Economics: Private and Public Choice.* He received his Ph.D. in economics from the Pennsylvania State University.

Eric Meltzer is a managing director of Curtis Financial Group, Inc., an investment bank based in Philadelphia. He has twenty years of investment banking experience with Drexel Burnham Lambert, Chemical Bank Investment Bank Group, and Brenner Securities Corporation. Mr. Meltzer has specialized in telecommunications transactions involving capital raising, mergers and acquisitions and exclusive sales assignments in the paging, specialized mobile radio (SMR), communications towers, and wireless cable television businesses. His current responsibilities include business development and transaction execution. Mr. Meltzer has also served as the chief financial officer of two start-up companies in the telecommunications industry, Decathlon Communications and Wireless Telecommunications, Inc. Mr. Meltzer has also been a founder of several telecommunications companies, including Saber Communications, Centrolinc Communications, and, most recently, Oneida Communications. He has been a frequent speaker at communication industry trade shows and on panels sponsored by industry research groups. Mr. Meltzer has a B.A. in political science and Russian language from the University of Rochester (1980) and an M.B.A. in finance from the University of Chicago (1988).

Christopher M. Woodruff is an associate professor of economics at the Graduate School of International Relations and Pacific Studies and director of the Center for U.S.-Mexican Studies at UCSD. His research focuses on the challenges faced by small- and medium-sized firms in developing and transition economies. Dr. Woodruff studies how firms respond when dysfunctional legal systems make formal contracting impossible, how inadequate financial systems limit access to financial capital, and how corruption makes retention of profits difficult. Geographically, his research spans a broad area of the developing world: Mexico, Vietnam, and Eastern Europe. His research has been published in the *American Economic Review,* the *Quarterly Journal of Economics,* the *Journal of Law, Economics and Organizations,* the *Journal of Public Economics,* and other scholarly journals.

Junfu Zhang is an assistant professor of economics at Clark University. He specializes in applied microeconomics. His research interests include racial housing segregation, entrepreneurship and innovations in the high-tech industry, and the employment effect of business relocation. He has held the graduate fellowship at Johns Hopkins University and the Leo Model Research Fellowship at The Brookings Institution. He received a B.A. from Renmin University of China and an M.A. and Ph.D. in economics from Johns Hopkins University. Before joining Clark University, he worked as a research fellow at the Public Policy Institute of California.